IN SEARCH OF
A NEW IMAGE
OF THOUGHT

IN SEARCH OF
A NEW IMAGE
OF THOUGHT

Gilles Deleuze and
Philosophical Expressionism

GREGG LAMBERT

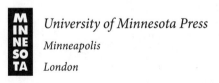

University of Minnesota Press
Minneapolis
London

Chapter 4 previously appeared as Gregg Lambert, "The Bachelor-Machine: Kafka and the Question of Minority Literature," in *Franz Kafka: A Minority Report,* ed. Petr Kouba et al., Literaria Pragensia, 7–31 (Prague: Charles University, 2011).

Earlier versions of chapter 5 appeared in Gregg Lambert, "The Subject of Literature between Derrida and Deleuze—Law or Life?" *Angelaki* 5, no. 2 (2001): 177–90, reprinted by permission of Taylor & Francis (http://www.tandfonline.com); and Gregg Lambert, "The Philosopher *and* the Writer: A Question of Style," in *Between Deleuze and Derrida,* ed. Paul Patton and John Protevi, 120–34 (London: Continuum International Publishing Group, 2003).

Sections of chapter 6 appeared in Gregg Lambert, "Cinema and the Outside," in *The Brain Is the Screen: Gilles Deleuze and the Philosophy of Cinema,* ed. Gregory Flaxman, 235–92 (Minneapolis: University of Minnesota Press, 1999).

Portions of the Conclusion appeared in Gregg Lambert, "The Unconscious Leap in Thought," *Theory@Buffalo* (Spring 2009): 21–44.

Published by the University of Minnesota Press
111 Third Avenue South, Suite 290
Minneapolis, MN 55401-2520
http://www.upress.umn.edu

Library of Congress Cataloging-in-Publication Data

Lambert, Gregg, 1961–
     In search of a new image of thought : Gilles Deleuze and philosophical
  expressionism / Gregg Lambert.
        Includes bibliographical references and index.
     ISBN 978-0-8166-7802-0 (hc : alk. paper)
     ISBN 978-0-8166-7803-7 (pb : alk. paper)
     1. Deleuze, Gilles, 1925–1995.   I. Title.
  B2430.D454L34   2012
  194—dc23   2012019265

Printed in the United States of America on acid-free paper

The University of Minnesota is an equal-opportunity educator and employer.

19 18 17 16 15 14 13 12   10 9 8 7 6 5 4 3 2 1

깃털. 당신은 내 인생에 떠내려

CONTENTS

PREFACE AND ACKNOWLEDGMENTS

It is well known that, as early as *Différence et répétition* (1968), Gilles Deleuze argued that "a search for a new means of philosophical expression . . . must be pursued today in relation to the renovation of certain other art forms, such as theatre or modern cinema."[1] What is less well known, or often ignored, is to what degree this search was singularly pursued throughout his entire philosophical project, and even constitutes fundamental and genetic principle of his style of "doing philosophy." Beginning from the period of Deleuze's *Proust and Signs* (1964), this study demonstrates how the search for a new means of philosophical expression became a central concern of all his works that followed, including the works written with psychoanalyst Félix Guattari and concluding with their last work conceived (if not actually written) together, *What Is Philosophy?* (1991).

In highlighting this fundamental concern, I have chosen a central theme that has appeared in all of Deleuze's works from the early book on Proust to the last work supposedly written by Deleuze shortly before his death. This is the theme of "the image of thought," which Deleuze describes in the 1994 preface to the English translation of *Difference and Repetition* as "the most necessary and concrete [problematic]" that serves as an introduction to subsequent works written after 1968.[2] The fact that Deleuze chooses to highlight this aspect of his work for an English-speaking audience, and in light of the reception history of his translated works to date, makes this statement an important cue, I would argue, for reorienting the understanding of his entire philosophical project both before and afterward. As Raymond Bellour recently wrote: "There would be a history to write, spanning the twenty-six books written by Deleuze alone and in collaboration [with Guattari]: a precise, tangled history of this term and idea of the Image of Thought."[3] Taking both statements to heart, this book is intended to provide a brief and accessible, yet nevertheless systematic, overview of this search for a new image of thought (or what I also refer to as a new style of philosophical expressionism), with special emphasis on the role played by modern literature (or what Deleuze and Guattari call "literary machines") and by certain modern writers in particular (namely, Proust, Kafka, Kleist, and Melville) in forging a new means of philosophical expression in their own writings, especially in Deleuze and Guattari's monumental work *A Thousand Plateaus*.

My study begins with Deleuze's earliest exposition of the Proustian image of thought, which is one of the first instances of the problem in relation to what Deleuze and Guattari later define as "the literary machine," and then follows the "tangled history" of the idea of the image of thought that runs through the subsequent works that follow, including *Kafka: Toward a Minor Literature*, *The Rhizome* (which serves as the introduction to *A Thousand Plateaus*), and several of the later works from the late 1980s gathered in *Essays Critical and Clinical*. It concludes by showing how this concern underlies Deleuze's studies of modern cinema in the early 1980s, where the image of thought is a predominant theme in the analysis of the cinematic image, especially in *Cinema 2: The Time-Image*. It also returns around the central concern of the brain that is proposed in the conclusion of *What Is Philosophy?*, where the brain is defined as "the nexus where the planes composed by modern philosophy, science, and art meet," even though this conjunction will not take the form of a philosophical system, in the usual sense, because it is still guided by the major terms outlined under the style of expression that Deleuze and Guattari, beginning in the early 1970s, call "anti-philosophy."

By connecting together the various episodes of the major problem of the image of thought that runs throughout Deleuze's entire corpus, I hope to reorient the question of how thinking first assumes an image, and how, early on in Deleuze's philosophy, the different images of thought become identified with the problem of expression, which later becomes a primary motive for the more experimental works of philosophy written together with Guattari. Moreover, this problem, as they argue in their last work, belongs as much to the history of philosophy as to its supposed future, and thus it is not reserved either for specialists of Deleuze's philosophy or for what is often called philosophy in the academic context today, which for the most part continues to ignore the question of expression altogether.

This study concerns a distinctly modern relationship between the regions of philosophy and nonphilosophy (and literature and cinema, especially) that have become the hallmark of the term "Deleuzian," even though I will argue that this aspect of the philosopher's vision, when it has not been reduced to the question of "a certain style" (of modernism, or the postmodern, for example), has not been fully appreciated in terms of its significance for philosophy—meaning not only "for today" but, to quote Nietzsche, also "for tomorrow, and for the day after tomorrow." One of my intentions is to focus on, or to burrow into, some of the earlier observations I made concerning this relationship in *The Non-Philosophy of Gilles Deleuze*;[4] another is to perform what Deleuze defined as the "pedagogy of the concept." However, this should be defined more as a process of learning than of knowledge (much less of expertise, or mastery), because I had to become both student and teacher in writing this book. As the student I had to realize that I had "learned more" than I knew before; as the teacher, I had to learn how "to say things more clearly." Clarity, in this sense, does not define knowledge of the subject that is "clear and distinct," but instead refers to certain stylistic and expository choices in the art of pedagogy, as well as in certain kinds of commentary, whose goal would be to guide or "to orient thinking and reflection" toward a particular region of expression in which the commentary functions as the double (or "mirror image") of the author's own expression, allowing the thought that remains virtual to become actualized through a process that Deleuze describes as a "highly specific and remarkable singularization."[5]

Therefore, if my earlier work took up the relationship between philosophy and nonphilosophy more generally, the overall goal of this study is certainly much more modest: to provide a more genealogical narrative of the development of the image of thought in Deleuze's philosophy to show the very pattern of a search that first becomes perceptible around the period of *Proust and Signs* (1964). In the Conclusion, moreover, I will argue that in the last work this search for a new image of thought did not actually conclude as much as it was proposed again as the only true object of philosophical understanding, which is still incapable of grasping this object in the very attempt to consider it as immanent to the movement of thought itself, if not with the very form of immanence as such. For if the history of philosophy is a movement of thinking that is bound up with the series of images, then the future of this movement would necessarily remain without an image and arrives from outside this history. This study will not attempt to describe, but will simply orient itself to, the passage from thinking to an image of thought, and from each image to what necessarily exceeds or surpasses it, namely, to the nature of immanence itself.

The Introduction and chapters 1–4 were originally written as a series of seminars I delivered in Seoul, Korea, in 2010–11 at Sungkyunkwan University (January 2010), Seoul National University (July 2010), and Ehwa Women's University (January 2011). I wish to acknowledge and thank the students and faculty who honored me with an expression of intense interest and intellectual curiosity concerning a subject that might have seemed, at first, somewhat remote from their studies in literature and theory. In particular, I would like to thank all my faculty hosts: Won-Jung Kim at Sungkyunkwan University, Eun Kyung Min at Seoul National University, and Sooyoung Chon at Ehwa University; and especially my friends and most esteemed colleagues Taek-Gwang Lee and the late Gwanghyun Shin (who first introduced me to a *vision* of the image of thought in the moon jar at Leeam Museum in 2009, and whose art of hospitality and thoughtful companionship will remain forever part of my own conceptual persona of "the friend").

The remaining chapters and the Conclusion are partially drawn from various published writings on the image of thought, and I would like to acknowledge the following editors: Frida Beckman, Ian Buchanan, David Collins, Gerald Greenway, Gregory Flaxman, Petr Kouba, Jim Kurt, Patricia MacCormick, Paul Patton, and John Protevi. I wish to thank my editor, Douglas M. Armato, whose support and encouragement I had felt for many years before I actually sent him this manuscript; and to the prescient insights of Ronald Bogue, Gregory Flaxman, and Jeffrey T. Nealon on earlier drafts. I wish to thank John Donohue and Wendy Nelson for the careful preparation of the manuscript for publication.

Of course, there are many others, around the world, who may or may not profess to be "Deleuzian" but nevertheless constitute this work's collective assemblage of enunciation. Most of all, I would like to pay homage to Jacques Derrida, "my only teacher," who first encouraged me as a graduate student to pursue my interests in the philosophy of Deleuze, because, as he said, there were already "too many Derrideans." This book is owed, in many ways, to this early remark.

INTRODUCTION
WHAT IS AN IMAGE OF THOUGHT?

- Two Images of Thought (ca. 1968 and 1991)
- "Difference" as a New Dogmatic Image of Thought
- Archaic Philosophy and Its Modern Machines

So what is an "image of thought"? Simply put, it is what philosophy has always presupposed at the beginning of the act of thinking. More precisely, the image of thought concerns the problem of presupposition in philosophy—that is, the presupposition of an image that serves as a fundamental ground for what is called thinking to appear. What kind of image is to be deduced from thought? How can thinking be determined by the image, and where does image first acquire its power over thought—that is, to induce what is called "thinking" to actually happen? Taken together, these questions pose a dilemma that philosophy, even up to its contemporary moment, has been unable to resolve: at the very moment that we begin to think, we must have already presupposed an idea of what is called thinking. From the Greek etymology, an idea *(eidos)* is first of all an image *(eidelon)*. In other words, I must already have an idea of what thinking looks like in order to recognize my own subjective process, as distinct from the processes of memory and perception, and then to be able to communicate a sign of this process to others in a form that corresponds to their own image as well. Intrinsically, therefore, thinking is already bound up with an image that, in turn, provides the conditions for producing the signs of recognition and the expression of thinking.

Deleuze describes this problem in the following way: "We live with a particular image of thought, that is to say, before we begin to think, we have a vague idea of what it means to think, its means and its ends."[1] If this statement appears tautological or circular, this is because it is the circle that modern philosophy has been trying to escape from since Descartes, who first posed this circular nature of the image of thought as a fundamental problem for philosophy to resolve. In other words, with Descartes, thinking begins with the *consciousness* of this problem and, at the same time, with a *desire* to rectify this indeterminate and circular relationship by inventing a method for selecting its own pre-philosophical image in place of a "vague idea of what it means to think." Summarizing Deleuze's early argument from *Difference and Repetition* (1968), although classical philosophy resolved this problem by presupposing an image of thought that is identified with common sense ("what everyone knows"), or by proposing a natural representation of what it means to think *(cogitatio natura universalis),* both of these solutions exposed the philosopher's activity as being grounded on nothing more than opinion *(doxa),* and more generally on a certain order of representation that formally qualified as thinking without predetermining its ends or its contents (i.e., the problem of rationalism). Eventually this led to the realization that, following Descartes, philosophy could not justify its image as being sufficiently grounded, or that, following Hume, thinking itself could be identified only as a higher form of Habit and therefore could not be grounded in Reason. Both insights, however, will turn out to provide the necessary conditions for modern philosophy, following Kant, to become truly "critical" of its own image of thought or, following Hegel, to arrange all the previous images of thought in a dialectical progression that leads up to the contemporary moment where the circular nature of the relationship between idea and image is grounded in the movement of Ideology. In this sense, we might understand Deleuze's own formulation of the problem of the image of thought to belong to this same tradition of modern philosophy; consequently, in his search for a new image of thought, one whose genesis is grasped in the act of thinking itself, Deleuze is not that different from other contemporary philosophers (especially Heidegger). In fact, almost all can be united around the same refrain: "Yes, what we are looking for these days is a new image of the act of thought, its functioning, its genesis in thought itself."[2]

But how does one approach the question of thinking without already giving it an image? In other words, how does one conceptualize thought without providing it with an image that already determines it in advance, even without determining its ends? Here one might immediately notice the recourse to temporal reference to the future, or to a spatial reference to a notion of exteriority, to an image of thought that is in both senses "outside" the present of consciousness, as a means of solving this problem by establishing a new ground upon which the image appears in relation to the "unthought," the "yet to be thought," or in relation to those inert forms of being "that do not think." For example, this is the solution offered by Heidegger, and in a different sense by Foucault in *The Order of Things* (1966), as the image of thought that determines the conditions of a distinctly "modern *cogito*."

> In this form, the *cogito* will not therefore be the sudden illuminating discovery that all thought is thought, but the constantly renewed interrogation as to how thought can reside elsewhere than here and yet be very close to itself; how it can *be* in the forms of non-thinking.[3]

But, then, this manner of solving the problem of image and tradition introduces a new problem, which of course is the problem of repetition itself, or as Deleuze says, "Repetition In-Itself." For even the invocation of the "unthought" does not cause philosophy to suddenly leap outside the closed circle of thinking, but merely restates the same problem, this time replacing the image of common sense, or the "vague idea of what it means to think," with "a dimension where thought addresses the unthought and articulates itself upon it."[4] Consequently, if all thinking is already repetition and is helpless to step outside this vicious circle of virtual image and actual expression of thinking, then how does one begin to think without a predetermined image, or rather, how does one truly *begin* to think at all? The answer to this question is both too simple and too tortuous, at the same time, which is why it still remains unresolved by contemporary philosophy today. In the very opening of his reflections on this problem, in 1968, Deleuze comes to the conclusion "[that] there is no true beginning in philosophy, or rather that the true philosophical beginning, Difference, is in-itself already Repetition."

For if it is a question of rediscovering at the end what was there in the beginning, if it is a question of recognizing, bringing to light or making explicit what is at first merely conceptual and abstract, what was already known implicitly without concepts—whatever the complexity of this process, whatever the apparent differences in the procedure or method—the fact remains that all this is still too simple, and that this circle is truly not yet tortuous enough. Instead, the circular image of the image of thought would reveal that philosophy is truly powerless to begin, or authentically to repeat.[5]

In the same year as the publication of *Difference and Repetition,* Deleuze already comments on a change that is taking place in the world that directly corresponds to the change of the image of thought in modern philosophy. In an interview for *Lettres françaises,* later titled "On Nietzsche and the Image of Thought," Deleuze exclaims: "Obviously, no-one really believes any more in the I, the Self, in individual characters or persons. . . . Individuation is no longer enclosed in a word. Singularity is no longer enclosed in an individual."[6] In place of these forms, Deleuze remarks, "what we're uncovering right now, in my opinion, is a world packed with *impersonal individuations,* or even *pre-individual singularities.*"[7] In other words, the traditional notion of the subject is no longer seen as a vessel or an envelope that can contain these two events: individuation takes place below or before the consciousness of a subject who thinks, feels, perceives, wills, or desires; the world is no longer bounded by a horizon, but rather is constituted by events and singularities that unfold to infinity, bordering chaos. Deleuze frequently employs the poetic formula from Rimbaud to underline the above situation and its significance for both modern literature and philosophy: "I is an Other" *(Je est un Autre).*

But where is Deleuze's evidence for the statement "Obviously, no-one believes any more in the I, the Self . . ."? This is not, I would argue, some joyful refrain of Nietzschean exuberance, but rather is simply based on an empirical observation of what artists and writers, for the most part, were already doing in their own domains. In other words, Deleuze is simply observing things and states of affairs that are already happening on the ground, so to speak, in order to draw the conclusion that "no one really believes." What was happening? In the domain of literary works, writers and poets were already breaking with earlier forms and genres in an intensive period of experimentation to discover new possibilities of expression that were both highly artificial and yet more approximate to "real experience." Here we might think of the later works of Beckett, or the writers of the *Nouveau Roman* to whom Deleuze is referring at this moment: "The new novelists talk of nothing else: they give voice to these non-personal individuations, these non-individual singularities."[8] In Beckett's novels, for example, the representation of character *(Molloy)* is gradually dissolved until it assumes the form of a mouth speaking inside a barrel *(The Unnamable)*; throughout the course of this dissolution, moreover, we witness fragments flying off that become individuals, characters that reproduce other characters that they mistake either for their own children or for themselves at a moment that they cannot remember; characters that have only a vague recollection that they are the same person who has been speaking all along. The form and content of the narrative are overcome by an interminable repetition until we witness only a voice that speaks incessantly, but in this way Beckett makes heard an "I" reduced to an automaton, to purely the habit of saying "I," with no need for eyes or ears, or even a body, to persist in its strangely impersonal life.

Finally, the gesture of "painting a canvas" in the modern period has given way to "tearing or ripping," "pasting," "spraying"—activities that belong to a different theory of perception and that can take place only in a violence performed upon the perceived or "the consciousness of the given." The form of sensibility that the modern artwork embodies presupposes certain violence, and the perception of the artwork cannot exist alongside the common and quotidian perceptions that constitute the everyday; instead it enters into battle with the latter in order to destroy or to "work over" (similar to the function of the dream work) the stock and clichéd sensibility. In other words, all perception must be "cut up," "ripped open," "destroyed and then reconstructed." The difference between this determination of the artwork and the classical one is that the material of perception is no longer offered a "natural" or independent perspective that the artist simply amplifies and resonates with in order to transform it into a style of a personality or genius. Rather, the material of perception is already an interpretation of a dominant perspective that organizes and directs the senses and assembles the range of materials for expression. The formal procedures available to the artist at this stage are as infinite as the materials themselves; each material component has a certain range of formal properties (density, color, texture, pliability, etc.) that determine its possibilities for expression. For example, paper has certain possibilities that are absent in plaster but present in cloth; ink expresses certain attributes (the line, for instance) that metamorphose in pastel or watercolors, and even more in collage, mixed media, or metal. This heteronomy with which art is said to occupy itself—in order to draw from it its materials, its textures, its color, its figures—bears the conditions of the production of the modern artwork.

At the time when Deleuze was referring to these formal discoveries that were happening in the fields of modern literature, theatre, and painting (and, by extension, in the other modern art forms as well, such as in modern cinema, which Deleuze will make central to the philosophical search for a new image of thought in the 1980s), there was also a generally held belief that the innovation of these forms would have a transformative effect in other cultural domains, particularly in the region of philosophy, where the image of thought no longer resembles its natural presupposition by the empirical ego. However, at precisely this very same moment Deleuze also observes that philosophy still lags behind these other domains, which have undergone progressive technical and formal transformations, if not continual revolution, and express a greater openness to experimentation in the modern period. Although there may have been similar innovations taking place in the philosophy of this same period, they had little effect in revolutionizing the greater part of the Western philosophical tradition, in part because these innovations were mostly relegated to minor considerations of "style" and thus did not fundamentally transform the dominant image of thought presupposed by traditional notions of thinking and ideas of "common sense." In this context we might understand the special importance that Deleuze at this point ascribes to the new relationship with nonphilosophy, one in which philosophy still lags behind and now attempts to infuse itself with new technical methods and, most importantly, new experimental procedures of expression.

"What are we doing in philosophy today?" Deleuze asks the same question in the preface to *Difference and Repetition* in 1968 and then again (with Guattari) more than twenty years later in 1991 in the opening to *What Is Philosophy?* On both occasions, the answer is remarkably similar. In 1968 Deleuze responds: "We're looking for 'vitality.' Even psychoanalysis needs to address certain 'vitality' in the patient, which the patient has lost, but which the analyst has lost, too. Philosophical vitality is not much different, nor is political vitality."[9] This term has led to many mistaken assumptions that Deleuze was addressing here a traditional notion of philosophical vitalism *(Lebensphilosophie),* but Deleuze was referring to something else when he speaks about "vitality" in relation to the "uncovering of a world of pre-individual, impersonal singularities" in place of a world that was occupied by Individuals and Persons.

One explanation would pertain to a generalized revolt on the part of a younger generation of philosophers against the classical forms of academic philosophy, especially in France and Germany, which has often gone under the tricolored banners of Marxism, psychoanalysis, and semiotics. As a result of these "new sciences of Man," the world that was formerly occupied by individuals and persons was being determined from elsewhere, either from below in the cellar of Structure (whether the idea of structure is represented by Language, the unconscious, or the division of labor in capitalist societies) or in "things themselves." In the phenomenology of Merleau-Ponty, for example, consciousness is reduced to a luminescent flesh that spreads over objects and subjects to the degree that the distinction between subject and object is no longer perceptible and constitutes the infinitesimal point of a Fold, or of multiple folds that do not line up on a single surface or volume (a world). The previous relationship in which the subject stood apart and over against a world of objects, which the subject represented to itself in conscious thought, is gradually replaced by a world that emerges only in a mottled patchwork and by a subject that was incapable of assembling this patchwork into a totality—in other words, by the presence of a reality that was immanent to experience, but yet that thought was not capable of attaining in the form of conscious representation. In place of presupposing a thought that was capable of representing the empirical I, or the

Self, philosophy began to *presuppose* a plane of immanence that the subject could not occupy. In short, philosophy changed concepts many times in order to designate this plane, or according to Deleuze's phrase, it changed "plans of immanence." Nevertheless, as a result the image of thought presupposed by contemporary philosophy becomes differentiated to a degree that it can no longer be called thinking in the traditional sense, which will have profound implications for recognizing the genre of philosophy itself in the postmodern period, which gets mixed up and begins looking more like literature or conceptual art. Eventually this discovery leads to a period of intense experimentation lasting through the end of the 1970s, and certainly Deleuze and Guattari's works from this period can be seen to belong to this moment. As Deleuze remarks, "it's a confused and rich period."[10]

Perhaps another way of addressing this confusion is to say that the contemporary philosophy could no longer identify the act of thinking with its own previous images of thought. On the one hand, as I have recounted above, this led to the most intensive phase of historicism whereby philosophy sought either to organize all these images in a systematic science of Ideology, as in the case of Hegel, or, following Heidegger, to lay bare what remains "unthought" in each epochal image and thereby to bring this history to a close with the pronouncement that "the most thought provoking thing is that we are still not yet thinking."[11] On the other hand, this also led to a period that was characterized by subjectivism and even extreme solipsism, as Deleuze often remarks, as if at the close of its modern period philosophy could not remain content with only placing in doubt all of its external presuppositions, following Descartes, but in its contemporary moment entered into the most dangerous game where it was forced to call into question—or, at least, suspend under a form of radical *skepsis*—most of its subjective presuppositions as well, including the "will to truth" and the innate goodwill of the thinker, exposing thought to an experience that was often compared to madness, as exemplified by Artaud and Blanchot, or to limit-experiences of amnesia and aphasia as Deleuze and Guattari themselves recall in the beginning of *What Is Philosophy?*[12]

As an example of the latter, I will briefly refer again to Heidegger as a philosopher at the close of this tradition of post-Kantian critical philosophy who brought the problem of the "image of thought," or generally the problem of presupposition, from a vague idea of what it means to think, to its most extreme formulation. According to Heidegger's earlier formula, in fact, "the image of thought" was actually forgotten long ago, since the early Greeks, and by every philosopher since Descartes who mistook this image for a subject of representation. Heidegger's late philosophy further dramatizes the cause of this confusion, defined poetically as a fundamental forgetting of an original image of thought and of the autochthonous subjective identity of the thinker who as a foreigner and an emigrant has lost his language and discovers himself far from his native land. Consequently, he sets out in his own philosophy to reorient the highest task of the philosopher as the remembering and recollection of this original image, and in the late meditations on poetry, in particular, to search for "hints and clues" of this original image in the *saying (Sagen)* of certain poets. Of course, Heidegger turned to only a small number of German poets (especially Hölderlin), as if to relocate the original wellspring of philosophy, that is, to institute a new image of thought and to carve out a plan of immanence, on his native German soil.[13]

The example of Heidegger offers us only one expression of the confusion and disorientation that leads directly to a new relationship between philosophy and nonphilosophy. There are many other examples, including Wittgenstein, that do not necessarily lead through poetry, literature, or the creative arts but could be said to participate in the same task of discovering a renewed or more essential image of thought through the analysis of ordinary language. In contrast to Heidegger, who constitutes an important predecessor for other contemporaries such as Derrida, Deleuze does not define the cause of confusion as the forgetting of a more original and authentic image of thought. Although it is useful fiction to propose that the modern philosopher would wake up one day to discover that he or she no longer knows what it means to think and could no longer simply presuppose an earlier image of thought, the cause for Deleuze will be neither the forgetting of an autochthonous image nor the long history of "Error" in which thinking goes astray. Instead, Deleuze often refers to "a violent encounter" that strikes against both the objective and the subjective conditions of thought itself, and that, according to another frequent refrain, represents the force of a shock that causes the former faculties to undergo a violent rearrangement: "Discord of the faculties, chain of force and function along which each confronts its limit, receiving from (or communicating to) the other only a violence which brings it face to face with its own element, as though with its disappearance or its perfection."[14] Here we find a completely different account of "what we are doing today" than we find in the post-Heideggerian tradition of phenomenological deconstruction of the History of Metaphysics, one that finds the true source of the confusion not in the long history of an Error, nor in the infinite deferral or delay of an original source, but rather in a change in the very nature of immanence itself. In Deleuze's philosophy, this confusion is affirmed as a rich source of possibilities for a new image of thought and, thus, as the condition of a search for a new manner of "doing philosophy" in a contemporary sense.

To summarize our brief survey of the problem of the image of thought, although contemporary philosophy continues to presuppose an image of thought, this image has threatened to become formless and chaotic and exhibits a tendency to undo any representation in the very moment it is posited.[15] This happens because of the infinite speed at which thoughts tend to fly off and become too abstract, or fail to correspond to the interiority of the object-world, or by means of an infinitesimal difference that no longer relates the subject to an identity, a difference that was discovered to belong to the very order of Representation itself. This would be the basis for Derrida's great project of deconstruction; the concept of *différance* (the amalgamation of ontological difference and Structuralist differentiation) has become the common presupposition of a new image of thought that belongs to a certain tradition of post-Kantian critical philosophy, the recurrent features of which have been an obsessive concern over the limits of representation and the critique of subjectivity ("anti-psychologism"), an allergic reaction to modern science and technology in the Heideggerian phase, and an ethical comportment toward otherness in an anxious reflection that tears away any remaining subjective presuppositions belonging to the natural *cogito*. The main objective of this tradition has been to expose the limits of all representational systems by a regressive procedure of critical reason that leads them into a state of crisis as an anticipatory step to their radical reconstruction; the second objective is to lay bare all naive and subjectivist constructions of identity, which leads to the introduction of difference from the critical perspectives of "the inert network of what does not think" (especially language, or Structure), or from an anthropological expression of *alterity*, as exhibited in the recent critical perspectives surrounding the animal and the posthuman. As early as 1966, Foucault already saw this movement toward the periphery of being as the final exhaustion of the last vestiges of "Humanism" belonging to the previous tradition of philosophy, after Kant, but also as resulting from the "shifted function" in phenomenology of the modern *cogito,* which points no longer to an apodictic existence of the being that thinks but instead to all the manners in which thought is grounded on the primacy of the multiple forms of Error.

> This is why phenomenology has never been able to exorcise its insidious kinship, its simultaneously promising and threatening proximity, to the empirical analysis of man; this is also why, although it was inaugurated by a reduction to the *cogito,* it has always been led to questions, to *the* question of ontology. The phenomenological project continually resolves itself, before our eyes, into a description— empirical despite itself—of actual experience, and into an ontology of the unthought that automatically short-circuits the primacy of the "I think."[16]

The obvious shortcomings of this tradition of post-Kantian philosophy, particularly deconstructive phenomenology, have been found in the fact that the anticipated radical phase of construction has never become a positive event as such, and the discovery of new possibilities for subjectivity has been through a glass darkly. In other words, the philosophies of this tradition have never fully been able to depart from a critical (or deconstructive) phase of "de-centering"; as a result, the future is posited as a static and essentially "empty form of time," often accompanied by a highly speculative image of the event itself as the undetermined and the ungrounded, hence "radical," commencement of an entirely new ontological order. In short, we have merely replaced one metaphysics with another, namely, *a metaphysics of difference*. More-over, we have supplanted the universal pretensions of the Kantian Subject with an increasing number of new radical subjectivisms. What, after all, is the recent turn to the animal (or to the nakedness of *Zoē* itself) if not yet another in a series of attempts to "de-center the meta-physics of the Western [human] subject" that was already prepro-grammed by this tradition of radical critique *(epokhē)*?

Today, it is the fundamental presupposition of difference as such that unites most postmodern philosophies, all of which now stand on the precipice of this founding presupposition and new dogmatic image of thought. In other words, these days *everyone knows* that difference is a common name for that which causes us to think, that the vague idea of difference is what gives food for thought, although this presupposition does not provide any reassurance with regard to whether (or not) we are still not yet thinking. In other words, the concept of difference has grown stale and no longer even provides us with an image sufficient to shock us out of our usual furrows of thought. Deleuze cautions, "We have no reason to take pride in this [new] image of thought, which involves much suf-fering without glory and indicates the degrees to which thinking has become more difficult: immanence."[17] But what is immanence? Is this just a new, perhaps more contemporaneous, name for difference? Although my answer will be, in some sense, affirmative, we have already been misled by posing the question of immanence in the form of a new con-cept. Deleuze and Guattari write, on the contrary, "The plane of imma-nence is not a concept that is or can be thought but rather the image of thought, the image of thought that gives itself of what it means to think, to make use of thought, to find one's bearings in thought."[18]

Although Deleuze and Guattari also claim that philosophers place their signatures on the concepts they have created, it naturally follows from the above statement that, because "immanence" is not a concept, it cannot be determined as an exclusive feature of Deleuze's philosophy.[19] It stands for something else, something that preexists the particular concepts that come to occupy it but that nevertheless cannot be said to actually exist outside of these concepts that presuppose it and that are described as its "inseparable variations."[20] This would serve as a word of caution to the discussions of immanence that are taking place in many circles today: the plane of immanence is not to be confused with the concept that is often spoken about currently in academic debates where Deleuze's philosophy is contrasted with that of some other philosopher on the basis of "the concept of immanence." It is strange to think, moreover, that philosophy had to wait for Deleuze to discover the idea of immanence itself, as if it had not been there all along, simply even hiding under another term like Substance, God, World, Being, or the One. Against this view I would argue, on the contrary, that the turn to the problem of immanence in the last works is a great and unifying gesture on Deleuze's part, one that allows several modern philosophical approaches to share the same presupposition as an image of thought, the same "ground" or "pre-philosophical image" upon which contemporary philosophy depends in the creation of new concepts, as if to partition the same image of thought according to different "diagrammatic features" on a shared plane. In other words, the different philosophical approaches represented by often opposing methods can be understood as united in an attempt to discover a new image of thought. This also implies that the problem of immanence should not be seen as an exclusive feature of Deleuze's thought to be used in setting his philosophy up in opposition to other approaches, as has so often been done. Deleuze himself already forewarns us against this kind of disciplinary model of the "original thinker": "Those who do not renew the image of thought are not philosophers but functionaries who, enjoying a ready-made thought, are not even conscious of the problem and are unaware even of the efforts of those they claim to take as their models."[21]

In the secondary commentary on Deleuze, regardless, there has been a noticeable tendency to lionize Deleuze as an absolutely singular thinker among his generation, without peer or influence and with a unique choice of subjects. In many respects this is a myth fabricated by those who prefer not to see that many topics were, in fact, quite unremarkable—at least, I would argue, prior to his encounter with Guattari. For example, many French philosophers of the same generation had something to say on Proust, following the critical influences of Benjamin, Blanchot, Genette, and Ricardou; they had even more to say on Artaud, Kafka, Sade, and Beckett. Likewise, Deleuze's thesis on Hume (which became his first major book in 1953) can be partly explained by the fact that selections from Hume's *Treatise on Human Nature* appeared in the English-language oral explication of the doctoral exam seventeen times between 1937 and 1958, and thus was regularly part of the *concours* in preparation for the exam.[22] (In 1960–64, Derrida also lectured on Hume at the Sorbonne, where he taught "general philosophy and logic.")[23] Though Deleuze's *Nietzsche and Philosophy* (1962) was the first book to appear on the philosopher in postwar France, and was thought to have ignited the commentary on Nietzsche during the 1960s, Alan Schrift suggests that a knowledge of French academic practices might offer another explanation for this explosion: "*On the Genealogy of Morals* appears on the reading list of the *aggregation de philosophie*—the annual examination that must be passed by anyone hoping for an academic career in philosophy—in 1958, the first time his work appears on that examination's reading list in over 30 years."[24] Contrary to the usual portraits of Deleuze as an "untimely philosopher" (á la Nietzsche and Emerson), a portrait that he sometimes indulges in himself in interviews and video séances, the above examples might also portray a more realistic or pragmatic picture of a brilliant "professor" who chooses as his major subjects authors that are just being instituted within the educational apparatus, in part because this gives him a unique vantage from which to influence younger generations and thus direct the future of the academic discipline of philosophy in France.[25]

Even concerning the originality of *Difference and Repetition,* which Deleuze has famously described as his first "autonomous work of philosophy," in an early interview coinciding with its publication Deleuze himself confesses that the motive for writing a systematic study of the concepts of difference and repetition was not without extrinsic influence. In fact, he describes it as absolutely unoriginal: "Yes, I finished the book—on repetition and difference (they're actually the same thing) as the actual categories of our thought. . . . These themes must mean something if philosophers and novelists keep circling around them. . . . So why not join in?"[26] Of course, the themes of difference and repetition are present in most philosophies of this period, and following Deleuze and Guattari's own terms, we can say that it was the concept of difference that instituted a plan of immanence for many postmodern philosophies, all of which sought to lay claim to the concept in an intense rivalry or antagonism. For example, we also have Derrida's great works *Writing and Difference* and *Of Grammatology*, which were written during the same period as *Difference and Repetition*, even though Derrida was often viewed as a younger contemporary. In these works, the concept of difference is instituted on a plane that is defined by "the closure of Western Metaphysics," whereby the earlier image of thought that belonged generally to a logocentric tradition of philosophy since the Greeks is exhausted and opened to an infinite differentiation brought about by modern systems of representation, at which point the possibility of philosophical thinking gets either lost or, worse, trapped by its own powers of dissimulation. Of course, in contrast to Derrida, Deleuze and Guattari will not speak of History, but only of geological movements.

Everything I have said above does not detract in the least from the significance of Deleuze's own search for a new image of thought. Of course, in each of the examples above there *are* singular variations that Deleuze introduces into his reading of each of the philosophers and writers he chooses to take up—and I will not speak here of his infamous method of reproduction defined as "buggery" *(encoulage)*—and many of his choices are made to serve the goal of what he already defines in *Difference and Repetition* as "anti-philosophy."[27] But then, on its own this term explains nothing, but instead needs to be explained. In fact, it only heightens the need to determine the criteria by which one can say when a philosopher goes "against the grain," or has provided a new image that has changed what it means to think, or has merely changed direction and reoriented the possibility for the discipline of philosophy, even if only to revitalize the belief that *philosophy still has a future!*

Returning to our main theme, the problem of presupposition, in order to separate the pre-philosophical image of thought, namely, the plane of immanence, from its contingent and historical features (which function like deeply held opinions that can change over time), amounts to proposing something that belongs to thought *"by a kind of right!"*[28] According to Deleuze and Guattari, what belongs rightfully to thinking is movement, but a movement of a very particular kind—a movement toward infinity. "Thought demands only 'movement' that can be carried to infinity."[29] This movement neither presupposes spatiotemporal coordinates, nor a subject nor even a transcendental subject as in Kant.

Thus, they write, "'to orient oneself in thought' implies neither objective reference point nor moving object that experiences itself as a subject and that, as such, strives for or needs the infinite."[30] As I will return to discuss in the Conclusion, this specific movement is grasped in its purest form in the Bergsonian concept of philosophical intuition, closely approximating the immediate and mystical knowledge of the universe, but, according to its modern scientific image, is mapped onto the function of the brain. This is why philosophy needs nonphilosophy today, and particularly a contemporary scientific knowledge of the brain, even though contemporary philosophy does not merely download and install this knowledge like a program running on a computer, as if this new knowledge suddenly forfeits its right to create its own concepts—this would not be called philosophy. According to Deleuze and Guattari's last work, therefore, philosophy truly begins to become philosophy only by presupposing, and first of all as an image, a pre-philosophical or even nonphilosophical intuition of "One-All" that, nevertheless, does not exist outside of philosophy. Thus, in answer to the question "What is philosophy?" Deleuze and Guattari propose that philosophy be defined, at any given moment historically, by the specific and internal nature of this first presupposition.

> Of course, in the history of philosophy there have been many presuppositions: For Descartes, it is a matter of a subjective understanding implicitly presupposed by the "I think" as first concept; in Plato, it is a virtual image of an already-thought [or idea] that doubles every actual concept. Heidegger invokes a "pre-ontological understanding of Being," a "pre-conceptual" [existential] understanding that seems to imply the grasp of a substance of being in relationship with a predisposition of thought.[31]

As in all the above examples, however, the image of what is presupposed is not merely deduced from a preexisting plane of images that represent the infinite power of the One-All; in each case the philosopher must first create a concept that functions to orient thinking "toward" this pre-philosophical intuition that its concepts will "constantly develop through slight differences in intensity."[32] Nonetheless, following both

Leibniz and Bergson, Deleuze also points out that inevitably the power of philosophical creation has never been equal to the task of grasping the power of the original intuition in its concept. What inevitably occurs, as in all the cases above, is that the concept loses its intensity and can no longer develop or remain consistent with the original intuition. It loses touch with the plane of immanence, which begins to dissipate once more into chaos. Thus, Deleuze and Guattari write, "the problem of philosophy is to acquire a consistency without losing the infinite into which thought plunges itself (in this respect chaos has as much a mental as a physical existence)."[33] But then, this refers back to the problem concerning difference as an intensive sign. Simply put, today we have grown indifferent to its sign. It fails to shock or provoke us into the act of thinking. Merely replacing the concepts of difference and repetition with a concept of immanence will not help matters much, even though we might understand this positively in this sense as an attempt to revive and stimulate philosophy again—as Deleuze said earlier on, to "revive the patient" and make philosophy more vital again! Consequently, this is how I understand the effect of the discussions today of immanence as a first concept, which now stands for the originary intuition of the power of One-All, and most of these discussions can be viewed generously as attempts at "orienting" thinking toward a region of the problem again and, at the same time, as efforts engaged in instituting a new plan for philosophy.

But how does one begin to orient thinking today in a situation of generalized confusion and disorientation? At this point I turn to the answer given by Deleuze and Guattari to the earlier question: "What are we doing in philosophy today?" Again, the answer that they give in 1991 is the same as the one given by Deleuze in 1968—"We are looking for vitality!" Although here vitality is defined as the creative art of "forming, inventing, and fabricating concepts."[34] And yet it also appears that the situation has only grown more desperate over the past twenty years and Deleuze and Guattari must admit that philosophy today can no longer even lay "a rightful claim" to the concept of creation, which now belongs to the field of conceptual art and to the technical knowledge of marketing and modern advertising. This is not to say that philosophy is no longer creative, but instead it has been encumbered by too much history, which slows it down and defines a movement that is no longer carried to infinity. What is called "philosophy" today is more like a slow-motion shot in the golden days of cinema, an expressionist canvas hanging in the Louvre, an absolute book that has become bloated by too much interpretation. Put differently, judged as an art of creating new concepts (of perception, affection, memory, and consciousness), "modern philosophy still lags behind" and still has yet to achieve and successfully pass through a period of intensive experimentation comparable to those that have taken place in both the arts and the sciences over the last two centuries. This is especially true when we consider that all the earlier hopes of infusing philosophy with the modernist principles of creative experimentation and "revolutionary stirrings" have, more recently, been replaced by the more sober and "serious" sentiments of a class of professional philosophers, for whom drugs are only a metaphor, popular culture is a dead end, and any talk of actual revolutions is a dangerous affair. After all, no one really believes any more in revolutions—at least, that is how we are speaking these days!—even though, oddly enough, we still believe in "the I, the Self, in Individuals and Persons."

Concerning the idea of revolution, Deleuze responds, "Philosophy remains tied to a revolutionary becoming that is not to be confused with the history of revolutions."[35] In fact, in a 1974 discussion with Guattari, "On the Two Regimes of Madness," which later becomes the title of a posthumous collection of his writings between 1975 and 1995, this is expressed in the form of an *Either/Or*: either we continue to find reasons to believe in "revolutionary becoming," despite all the madness that has been associated to the idea, or we go about the business of promoting the actual madness produced by late-capitalist societies (e.g., global poverty, famine; harsh inequalities, entire populations excluded from "free markets"; new forms of slavery and human trafficking; wars, terror, and new genocides). In large part, *What Is Philosophy?* is written wholly in response to the bankruptcy of contemporary philosophy, which has completely failed to create any vital form of resistance to this worsening situation, and partly in response to how their own early attempts to infuse philosophy with "revolutionary becoming" were being received by a new generation of philosophers in France.[36] However, despite the expressions of world-weariness and pessimism that are present in this work, Deleuze and Guattari *do* offer us a very modest and practical solution: "Perhaps more attention should be given to the plane of immanence laid out as an abstract machine and to created concepts as parts of the machine."[37] Of course, anyone familiar with the work of Deleuze and Guattari will understand that there is a lot of talk about machines (technical machines, social machines, desiring machines, war machines, etc.), and as is the case with understanding any machine, as well as its function, it is always primarily a matter of knowing how these machines work.[38] Above all, they always caution that their conception of the machinic is entirely literal, and must not be understood as a metaphor. This way of understanding philosophy is already clearly apparent in *What Is Philosophy?* In responding to this question, they immediately begin describing its three component parts (concepts, a plan of immanence, conceptual personae), and a fourth component, which constitutes a surface inscription or recording (a territory and an earth) that philosophy needs in order to exist in a milieu also occupied by peoples, nations, and worlds (like the Greek or Hellenic world, the Christian world, or the Islamic world). They write, "Thinking takes place on a plane of immanence that can be populated by figures as much as by concepts . . . it is affected by what populates and reacts on it, in such a way that it becomes philosophical."[39] Secondly, Deleuze and Guattari's famous definition of philosophy is entirely machinic and focuses only on what philosophy does and what it produces: philosophy is a machine that operates on a plane of immanence to produce concepts. That is how it works. And yet Deleuze and Guattari define philosophy as a certain machine that cannot work all by itself; it needs other machines that fit into its apparatus or assemblage and provide it with contents in order to work, in order to produce concepts. The relationship that Deleuze constructs between philosophy and nonphilosophy will work no differently; it is machinic, and consequently our role will be to understand its parts, its functions, and most of all, how it works.

This is the picture that I will employ to portray the relationship between philosophy (the creation of concepts) and the domains of nonphilosophy (art, literature, and cinema) as components of a larger machine that are assembled together in order to work, occasionally to produce something called thinking. As they say, philosophy needs nonphilosophy in order to continue to function, and here is where the domains of literature and cinema—and art, to a lesser degree, but simply because I know nothing about it!—will come into play in this study, beginning with Proust, which I will define as the first "literary machine," because these are the subjacent and molecular machines that modern philosophy connects itself to in order to continue functioning. Of course, as Deleuze describes in the chapter "Image of Thought" in *Difference and Repetition,* classical philosophy had its machines too, only these machines were different: Perception, Affection, Intuition, Cognition, Imagination, Will, and so on. In reading the *Meditations* by Descartes, he shows how these machines are reduced to their most necessary component parts in order for the *cogito* to function in producing certainty and clear and distinct perception; however, it is not by accident that Descartes was also haunted by the idea that the subject of thinking was merely machinic, that the mind was only a machine for producing a perception and cognition of external reality, which threatened the existence of both the Self and God as necessary components. Deleuze shows that later, in Kant, this Cartesian machine only becomes more complicated as the faculties of perception, understanding, imagination, and desire replace perception, cognition, and will. In both cases, Representation provided the machine with its order and its determination of the function of the working parts. Representation constituted the cardinal order (the framework or the dispositive) that determined how philosophy worked and what it produced. According to its rules of how things worked, "difference becomes an object of representation always in relation to a conceived identity, a judged analogy, an imagined opposition or a perceived similitude."[40]

Today the situation of philosophy has changed in the sense that representation can no longer determine how the machine works, or that one of the component parts has broken down. Again, recalling what I already described above as a new dogmatic image of thought, namely "difference," this is the simplest thing to understand. In order to work according to the requirements of Representation, philosophy must presuppose, as its pre-philosophical image of thought that is a common source of all its representational activities, an object that is shared by all the faculties (perception, memory, imagination, understanding, etc.). This is because this common image of thought provided philosophy with a means to determine "differences in thought as an object of representation always in relation to a conceived identity, a judged analogy, an imagined opposition or a perceived similitude," which is to say, to determine them as strictly individual or personal notions.[41] But what happens, according to Deleuze, when philosophy (by some accident or catastrophe, either internal or external to itself) is no longer able to presuppose this image and this common and universal sense? Today, in other words, the only thing that the faculties can be said to share in common is a notion of difference that remains abstract, because it is now understood or presupposed in nonrepresentational terms. It no longer works, at least according to the rules previously prescribed to it by Representation: it can no longer represent the reality of the self and the world according to the differences among identity, analogy, opposition, and similitude. Very simply, does this not accurately depict the situation of contemporary philosophy I have outlined above, for which in place of presupposing the world and the self as objects of natural representation, philosophy presupposes a pure plane of immanence that it is not yet capable of thinking according to a framework of representation? Is this not, in other words, the best image of what is presupposed by contemporary philosophy today?

In my view, perhaps the most crucial passage that states this directly occurs in *Anti-Oedipus,* where this problem is restated in the most material and even historical of terms:

> We live today in an age of partial objects, bricks that have been shattered to bits, and leftovers. We no longer believe in the myth of the existence of fragments that, like pieces of an antique statue, are merely waiting for the last one to turn up so that they may all be glued back together to create a unity that is precisely the same as the original unity. We no longer believe in a primordial totality that once existed, or in a final totality that awaits us at some future date. We no longer believe in the dull grey outlines of a dreary, colorless dialectic of evolution aimed at forming a harmonious whole out of heterogeneous bits

by rounding off their edges. We believe in totalities that are peripheral. *And if we discover such a totality alongside various separate parts, it is a whole of these particular parts but does not totalize them; it is the unity of all these particular parts but does not unify them; rather it is added to them as a new part fabricated separately.*[42]

The task of philosophy today is not to reassemble these bricks and shattered bits in relation to a Whole that is either bygone or still virtual and to come—that is, to express the Whole—but rather to know how to assemble a multiplicity from all the parts that have no relation to the Whole, to create a real multiplicity out of nothing but differences.

Here we witness a constant theme of Deleuze and Guattari's collaborative project, which even constitutes the metaphysical foundation of their entire philosophy, a refrain equally found in Deleuze's solo works such as *Difference and Repetition* and in the early work on Proust: Only the category of multiplicity, without recourse to the predicative relation between One and the Many, can account for real desiring production.[43] In other words, the metaphysical pretension of a pure multiplicity is always related to a concrete problem, if not *the* problem of the social, which concerns the current theorization of the nature of desiring production: *how to think, how to produce the various parts whose sole relationship to each other is sheer difference, that is, without recourse to an expression of the whole, either as a nostalgic whole that has been lost or as a virtual whole that is still to come.* On a materialist level, the problem of the One and the Many, or the Whole and the parts, is not merely a metaphysical problem; rather, it concerns the fragments that belong to any social organization, how they fit together to form a Whole, how they function and work together in a machine that determines the total productive capacity of a society. On a subjective and psychological level, moreover, the problem of the Whole and the parts determines the entire meaning of sexuality; although in this case the parts are not individuals or sexes, but instead machines that must be fitted together according to some arrangement in order to work. Thus, we find that the two levels—the social and productive and the subjective or psychological—are implicated in one another; the relationship is disjunctive, meaning inclusive, even though the manner in which they communicate their contents is defined by Deleuze as the problem of expression in his philosophy.

Again, I think it is crucial to notice that it is Proust who first provides Deleuze with an early intuition of the method for producing the multiplicity from a Whole that is produced alongside each of the parts, even though the Whole neither totalizes nor unifies all the parts into the One. This intuition will become the method of the "rhizome" that is applied in *A Thousand Plateaus*. It is the image of thought presupposed by the concept of the rhizome they have invented or created together that will allow Deleuze and Guattari to resolve the problem first proposed earlier: how to conceive of the idea of multiplicity in which the Whole is related to its parts only through sheer differences. To quote again the passage above, the concept of the rhizome represents the actual discovery of "such a totality alongside various separate parts, it is a whole of these particular parts but does not totalize them; it is the unity of all these particular parts but does not unify them; it is added to them as a new part fabricated separately."[44]

It may appear provocative to say that philosophy does not know how to think real multiplicity, that only literature and the modern arts do. Of course, many philosophers would immediately object—"You must be kidding!" "What about Spinoza, or Duns Scotus? What about Leibniz, or Bergson?" In response I would only point out that, for the most part, in producing an idea of real multiplicity Deleuze and Guattari refer, not to these philosophers, but instead to certain writers or "literary machines" (Proust, in this instance, and later on Kafka), whom they reference when posing the problem, in the most rigorous of terms, concerning "how to produce, to think about fragments whose sole relationship is sheer difference."[45] But why is this a problem? This only implies that philosophy is not capable of thinking real multiplicity on its own, using only its own resources or those it has inherited from its previous traditions. It requires new machines, and the literary machine especially, to allow it to think about multiplicity, in order to furnish it with the raw materials for the concept, or using Deleuze and Guattari's term, "the bricks that compose the Real." The modern relationship between philosophy and non-philosophy is not that different from the relationship between science and its own technical machines, and this, I will argue, is the particular status that the literary machine has for Deleuze and Guattari's "philosophy" as well (in terms of how it functions, or how it works vis-à-vis the philosophical apparatus). In this sense, the particular status that literary machines have for modern philosophy (in terms of how it functions, or how it works vis-à-vis the philosophical apparatus) can be likened to what Deleuze and Guattari call, in the most rigorous of terms, a "desiring machine." Therefore, following Deleuze's earliest intuition (or discovery), in the first chapter I will turn to the Proustian literary machine in order to describe how it works, what image of thought it produces, what it does to reorient the entire problem of presupposition in philosophy, and finally, what is actually presupposed by a Deleuzian philosophy, strictly determined, which Deleuze himself defined from the very beginning, as an "anti-philosophy."

1

THE IMAGE OF THOUGHT IN PROUST, OR THE FIRST LITERARY MACHINE (CA. 1964)

- What Is a Machine?
- The Proustian Narrator as a "Body without Organs"
- *Logos*—Animal or Vegetable?

I began by proposing the modern relationship between philosophy and nonphilosophy as the relation between special kinds of machines that we have found to be incorporated into philosophical expression. According to Deleuze and Guattari, this machinic definition should be understood quite literally, particularly in defining the machines created by modern art and in determining how they work. In the 1970 edition of *Proust and les signes,* where he adds the chapter on *"La Machine littéraire,"* Deleuze writes that "the modern work of art is anything it may seem; it is even its very property of being whatever we like, from the moment it works: the modern work of art is a machine and functions as such."[1] What is painting, for example, but a special kind of machine for producing perception? What is called literature, but a generic term used to designate different kinds of writing machines, whether we are talking about a novel or a poem, or the specific machines invented by writers? Because of the sheer variety, "Literature" was invented only out of convenience to provide a generically definable order of machines made or invented for producing words and phrases according to a strictly determined logic, and employing a variety of forms and technical procedures. Likewise, we might say the same thing about reading, which is literally machinic: the eye follows the hand in tracing words across the page (left to right, or right to left depending on the re- cording apparatus that controls the reader's gaze), unlocking signs that are not visible at first and yet are indistinguishable from the material signs that appear on the page. This mixture of visible and invisible signs, in turn, produces compounds that, in turn, produce a variety of effects like small explosions: images (of understanding, feeling, perception, judg- ment) that occur somewhere internal to the apparatus of reading ma- chine, which are often described as taking place in the subject of the reader, even though this is a very imprecise way of describing things because the exact nature of the relationship between the subject who is reading and these little explosive events and images is unknown, particu- larly with regard to cause and effect, which is why the ultimate determi- nation of what these images actually produce is so wildly inconsistent. Sometimes, in scanning the page, in discerning the visible and invisible signs, only certain compounds detonate; others fail to combine success- fully. This produces a different outcome, a different "meaning"—again, a vague notion in determining the outcome of this process, much less in understanding what is actually produced or how this machine actually functions.

It is not by accident that cinema becomes the modern art form *par excellence,* since it externalizes a machinic relationship that remained virtual in painting and literature, making this relationship of movement internal to the apparatus of the camera-projector and incorporating the subjective form of the viewer as a purely virtual surface for recording the image. Nevertheless, I would not say, as others have, that this repre- sents a synthesis; nor would I say, as still others have often said, that there is any teleological progression, since both literature (or the history of writing machines in general) and the artificial machines of the visual and plastic arts continue to remain autonomous and will evolve techni- cally on their own—I would even say, more rapidly than before the in- vention of modern cinema, especially when one looks at how these ma- chines have evolved over the last thirty years or so with the introduction of new digital technologies. Of course, the camera-projector apparatus does take over some the functions provided by the reader described above: it develops the image, causing it to explode autonomously and without the need of a kinesthetic process attached to the apparatus. Consequently, the subjective is reduced to occupying a purely virtual point of view that is projected in front of the image, "between the actual screen and the virtual brain." This is the point where all of the images are targeted (as one also says in modern weaponry) in the process of being assembled, a machinic process that is echoed in Deleuze's own account of the passage from the movement-image to the time-image in postwar cinema. With the gradual discovery of the techniques of framing and montage, the kinesthetic and affective possibilities of subjective variation are further refined and perfected, in effect, producing more possibilities for feeling and new subjective qualities than before, as if subjecting the receptive apparatus of the viewer to an intensive sensory training, or an "education of the senses" *(Bildung)*.[2] Thus, in a certain sense the cinematic machine requires new organs to function, even though this requirement is often mistaken for the formal and technical evolution of the movement-image (for example, from celluloid to digitally based media).

This highlights the differences between painting and cinema, particularly with regard to the subjective role of the viewer. Like the reader, the viewer of the painting introduces a wildly unpredictable moment into the total workings of the painting machine, which is one reason this machine has been vulnerable to so many breakdowns precisely from this perspective, which gradually constituted the viewer in a paranoid relationship that often determines the reception of the image in modern art. Consequently, contemporary art does not take what is merely demonstrable for its limit, but constantly seeks a presentiment of other conditions and new materials, and finer sensibilities of reception in its spectators or "public"; even though this has led to an increasingly "privatized public" composed of the artists themselves, as well as other art professionals or specialists (the critic, the curator, the dealer, the corporate consumer). In cinema, on the other hand, much less is left to the spectator with regard to the evolution of the art form itself. The director has greater control over the whole range of subjective responses to the image he or she produces, first of all because the viewer in cinema is trained to sit and quietly take the image in, to internalize the train of images in a more or less passive attitude, which is why cinema and video have become the favored art form of late-capitalist commodity culture. There is little time for thinking or random and highly subjective associations to disrupt this process; the viewer is "too busy" parrying the shocks, anticipating the next explosion, anxiously following the image as it thickens or dissipates, chasing after the image like a dog chasing a fly in the garden. Thinking occurs only at the end, if ever, and even then it takes the form of judgment. It is not like a book, which the reader can put down precisely at the moment where the image begins to unfold, preferring to defer the revelation and savor the promise of intensity; or a painting, which one can walk away from suddenly, and then choose to revisit years later, as if deciding one is now ready for the experience.

The difference between these two types of audiences might be characterized as the difference between learning and education. In viewing a painting, even upon repeated viewings, the viewer either learns to see the image or completely fails in seeing it. In cinema, the viewer is educated, she is forced to see whether or not she wants to, and what she sees is determined by whether she is a good or bad student. She can easily reject the entire experience, in which case the duration of the film becomes a "whole waste of time," even though it is already too late for judgment at this point, since the experience now fatally belongs to the spectator's life. Here we might ask: How much of our lives has been wasted on bad films and media productions, and is there some essential relationship between the commodity forms of late-capitalist culture and the quantity of wasted time that seems to increase exponentially with the invention of newer technologies and digital media? Moreover, at what point can we be led to say that "a life," like a bad film, can also be subjected to this kind of judgment today—"the whole thing was simply a waste of time"? These will be questions that I will reserve for our discussion of Proust, and later on, concerning the relationship between modern cinema and the brain.

For now, let's return to the question concerning the "presupposition of an image of thought." As I said earlier, in place of presupposing the machines of natural perception and common sense (i.e., representation), modern philosophy begins to presuppose a plane of immanence that is both too near for intuition and too distant for external perception. More provocatively, in this new situation modern philosophy suddenly awakens to discover it now has "no eyes, no ears, and no mouth." Therefore, in order to orient itself on this new plane, it must acquire different machines that will replace the organs of natural perception. Thus, the painting machine gives eyes to modern philosophy to see with; literary machines give it ears and a mouth. What does the cinematic machine provide? New compounds and a new series of images that will either allow philosophy to see farther and, at the same time, to draw nearer to inner experience; or negatively, provide a whole new set of transcendental illusions with which to contend. Is this situation any different from the case of modern science, which requires more refined technical machines to grasp the reality of the universe or the molecular composition of a living cell? In other words, perhaps the plan of immanence presupposed by modern philosophy requires no less than the modern sciences require: newer and more refined machines of perception, intuition, imagination, and expression. Of course, this is not necessarily perceived as progress at first, because the newer machines are difficult to get set up and working properly. The machine that replaces the mouth often stutters (like in a poem by Cummings or Celan), or utters purely paratactic speech (as in Artaud and Carrol), and even sometimes issues the unbearable cry of animals or sounds that are like dry leaves scraping against an open doorway (as in Kafka). The artificial eye machine produces visions that are blurred and fuzzy; objects are difficult to make out, because they are "certainly not clear and distinct," and there is a zone of indetermination between background and the figure (as in a painting by Cézanne, whom Deleuze often privileges). The soft machines of cinema produce hallucinatory visions, uninhabitable and frozen landscapes, inhuman visages, new organs and images mixed with indistinguishable blocks of sensation and feeling (as in the cinema of Cronenberg), unbearable durations in which nothing happens (as in Tarkovsky). What kind of eyes and ears are these? What kind of mouth (as Artaud described it, "no teeth, no tongue, no larynx")? Nevertheless, it is apparent that philosophy for some time has preferred these to natural organs, and even the most common language does not make much sense any more—not because it lacks understanding, but simply because it no longer has any ears! Perhaps, in this manner, we can understand why modern philosophy can be defined precisely as "a body without organs." In fact, there may not even be the requirement of a subject, in the traditional sense.

How does thinking take place in this new situation? Thinking is not a machine, but rather is a subjective determination of *an event* that happens (or more often than not, actually fails to happen!) owed to the functioning of these new machines of perception, imagination, and feeling. Philosophy, on the other hand, is a machine that produces concepts from the raw materials provided by these other machines that it includes as functions of its total mechanism; if thinking is to occur at all, even if only rarely, then it occurs in the interrelationship between these different machines, something that is produced by this interrelationship, something that either works or does not work according to this interrelationship. Consequently, thinking does not always happen; the machinery breaks down and fails to produce the desired event. As Deleuze says in *Difference and Repetition,* in order to truly begin thinking, we must first learn how to forget what thinking is, and only in this way can we actually be receptive to the event of thinking within thought.[3] In other words, modern philosophy begins to think only from a situation of stupidity—this will forecast the importance of Artaud's example for Deleuze, which I will return to discuss below—a fundamental stupidity that, in turn, will strike against philosophy's great ideas (the Self, the World, God), which Kant had already revealed to be transcendental illusions of Reason.

Once more, Heidegger provides us with a good illustration of this situation of fundamental stupidity that strikes against the innermost possibility *(potentia)* of thinking. The fact that many of his later works carry as their titles questions that could just as well be asked by children or idiots (e.g., *Was ist das—die Philosophie?*) should already indicate that the philosopher does not begin from a situation of knowledge. In one of his last works written in the period of the early 1950s, *What Is Called Thinking?,* Heidegger sets off to track down the image of thought in much the same way as Proust sets off in search of lost time. What results is a hilarious method of searching for an original image of thought, which ends with the philosopher contemplating what a child means when she says "Bow Wow Bad Bite" alongside the somewhat paratactic utterances of the pre-Socratics: "Needful: the saying also thinking too: being: to be."[4] If the comedy of this moment often goes unnoticed, it is because Heidegger's philosophy continues to be read under a sanctimo-

nious light (i.e., "the piety of Thinking") in which the most childlike utterances are mistaken for sayings of an oracle, somewhat like the character of Chance Gardner from Jerzy Kosinski's *Being There*. However,
what if we considered the opposite? What if Heidegger was really attempting to learn how to speak as a child, to forget all previous language
and signification, to become an apprentice in the things and concepts?
This would not be a situation of an enforced naivete, or as in Descartes,
an initial point of certainty arrived at through a rational method of
doubt. This would be an altogether different image, which is why stupidity might be a better concept for determining what is presupposed in
Heidegger's final image of thought. Does this not illustrate a situation
where the philosopher exposes himself to becoming stupid in order to
learn again the signs that lead to thinking, almost in the sense of seeking
to become an *embryonic consciousness* in order to experience the real
sense of words?[5]

Around the question of an apprenticeship in signs to produce an
original image of thought not presupposed by philosophy, in the traditional sense, we must now turn to Deleuze's early reading of Proust, which
exemplifies what I will call "the first literary machine." The first edition of
this study appears in 1964, under the title *Marcel Proust et les signes*, and
concludes with the chapter called "The Image of Thought." In light of the
above discussion, however, it is important to note that the second part of
this study, which is entitled the "Antilogos or the Literary Machine," is not
added until the 1970 French edition, which is around the time when Deleuze is just beginning to collaborate with Guattari on *Anti-Oedipus*.[6]
Consequently, it is Guattari's concept of "machine," which Deleuze first
encounters reading Guattari's "Machine et structure" in early summer of
1969, that becomes the fulcrum of his amended study of Proust's *Recherche* that same year. [7] It is important to point out that in 1964 Deleuze
already found in Proust a means of what he called "anti-philosophy"—in
this case, a means of posing a new concept of the idea without having to
presuppose Plato. Again, this is a manner of forgetting what was already
known beforehand in order to discover what remains to be thought, which
must be achieved by a strict method of searching, and the image of reminiscence and memory offered by Proust serves as an intermediary and a
screen that "filters out" the Platonic theory of ideas. But another change

takes place in the passage from the 1964 to the 1970 editions, and this has to do with precise meaning of "the literary machine."

First, let me quote different parts of the two editions. The first part is from the concluding section, "The Image of Thought," from the 1964 edition:

> As we have seen, this distinction between Proust and Platonism involved many more differences. *There is no Logos; there are only hieroglyphs.* To think is therefore to interpret is therefore to translate. The essences are at once the thing to be translated and the translation itself, the sign and the meaning. They are involved in the sign in order to force us to think; they develop in the meaning in order to be necessarily conceived.[8]

Now the passage that takes up the same subject in the 1970 edition:

> We have now seen how Proust revived Platonic equivalence of creating/remembering. But this is because memory and creation are no more than two aspects of the same production—"interpreting," "deciphering," and "translating" being here the process of production itself. It is because the work of art is a form of production that it does not raise a special problem of meaning, but rather of use. Even the activity of thinking must be produced within thought.[9]

In the second passage, which can be understood as a gloss on the first passage, we note the appearance of the term "production," which of course becomes a key term of Deleuze and Guattari's major thesis in *Anti-Oedipus.* Thus, "all activity of thinking must be produced within thought." Moreover, the activities of "interpreting, deciphering, and translating" are no longer related to the "sign," and the term "hieroglyph" completely drops out of the second version and is replaced by the concept of the machine that produces . . . but produces what? Simply put, in this case, Deleuze is referring to a specific machine that produces memory, which is the Proustian literary machine. It is around this point that Deleuze makes a surprising discovery of what was merely intuited in his earlier work: to remember is to produce, just as to create is to produce; memory and creation are two aspects of the same process of production.[10] Therefore, the problem of memory is no longer attributed to a sign that preexists the act of creation, it is the act of creation itself, and is attributed to a machine that *produces* a "spiritual equivalent" between memory and impression that defines the work of art. As Deleuze writes:

> This is because the meaning (truth) is never in the impression nor even in memory, but is identified with the "spiritual equivalent" of the memory or of the impression produced by the involuntary machine of interpretation. It is this notion of a spiritual equivalent that establishes new link between remembering and creating and establishes it in a process of production as a work of art.[11]

In this final passage we might confirm what was only a vague and indeterminate idea earlier on: the manner in which, in Proust's work of art, "philosophy vies with nonphilosophy" (i.e., the Proustian image of memory vies with the Platonic theory of ideas), because it is only through the writing machine invented by Proust that philosophy obtains a better understanding of the function of the idea in reminiscence, that is, a better concept of how past is produced in relation to the sensible present in a manner that is essentially productive or creative. Yet, if the thinking subject must presuppose a plane of consistency in the form of a presupposed image of thought, is this plane the same for philosophy as it is for literature, or the writing machine? How does one distinguish between the ideas of memory and the ideas of thought, if it is true that in each case ideas do not preexist the impressions that are developed into signs? Is thinking just another species of remembering, like the material form of memory expressed by habit? Moreover, what does it mean to say that the idea of thinking must be produced, like memory, by something that functions as the spiritual equivalent of memory in matter? As Proust writes, "even memory, still too material, needs a spiritual equivalent," in the sense that even memory needs a kind of machine to produce it.[12] It is around this last question, in particular, that Deleuze finds in Proust, who is described as a pure subject of writing, a different presupposition operating at the basis of the work, and thus a different image of the body without organs.[13] Therefore, a "body without organs" (BWO) is an anorganic, but nevertheless living, body that is fabricated or constructed to replace the image of the body presupposed by the empirical Ego, or Self. In this sense, all literature is replete with different kinds of bodies without organs.

But what does it mean to say that the subject who appears in the position of the narrator of the *Recherche* has no eyes, no ears, no mouth? First, it means he is neither completely naive nor stupid, but instead is "innocent of all experience," or as Deleuze says, is probably quite mad. In a 1975 "Roundtable on Proust" that was later incorporated as the last chapter ("Presence and the Function of Madness") of the 1976 edition of *Proust and Signs,* Deleuze confesses to having an impression that has only "very recently occurred to him" (and here I am only speculating that he means by this that this idea has occurred to him since the 1970 edition, which the audience would no doubt have already read):

> I have the impression that there is in this book a very important,
> very troubling presence of madness. This does not mean that Proust
> was mad, of course, but that in the Search itself there is a very vivid,
> very widespread presence of madness. . . . Everyone knows who the
> ringleader is: the narrator. How is the narrator mad? He is a very
> bizarre narrator. Totally bizarre! He has no organs, he can't see, he
> does not understand anything, he does not observe anything, he
> knows nothing; when something is shown to him, he looks but does
> not see; when someone makes him feel something, they say: but look
> how beautiful this is, he looks and when someone says: here, take a
> look—something echoes in his head, he thinks of something else,
> something that interests him, something that is not on the level of
> perception, not on the level of intellection. He has no organs, no
> sensations, no perceptions: he is nothing. He is like a naked body, a
> vast undifferentiated body.[14]

It is precisely the combination of innocence and madness that is ascribed to the narrator's body, which feels impressions, memories, encounters, perceptions, and thoughts—but cannot understand them at first. It is safe to say that, whether due to madness or to innocence, *the narrator is a being who exists without presuppositions.* He presupposes absolutely nothing—not even his own sex!—not even the vaguest idea emerges at the basis of each impression or thought. Therefore, the narrator does not understand what he sees, what he feels, what is said by the characters, and this constitutes the basis of the search that Deleuze describes in his work as an apprenticeship of signs, since it is by developing and interpreting these impressions and signals that the Proustian experience of the world is woven together in the great web-body of signs.

Therefore, if it is not Marcel Proust who is mad, and the narrator is not made to be organically a representation of Proust, then there is the presence of something else, a presence of madness that is distributed across the characters of the *Recherche,* something that moreover cannot simply be reduced to language even though it is also something that cannot exist apart from language. Deleuze describes the subject of the narrator according to two different images: he is a spider; he is a vegetable. As a spider, he casts a web and perceives things only by signals, small vibrations. In another place, he is described as a kind of vegetal consciousness, which perceives or feels only what constitutes its immanent environment. "An orchid presents an image of the wasp drawn on its flower, with its antennae, and the insect comes to fertilize this image."[15] This is the manner by which the flower perceives the wasp that has no resemblance to empirical conscious, to the *cogito,* that Deleuze finds in Proust's method, which he in turn seeks to apply to Philosophy as a means of liberating it from the traditional image of thought.

Here, in both images we are presented an image of the subject of writing, of a text that is composed by weaving together signs, in other words, by a language of flowers or grass. Deleuze describes this spider or plant consciousness that he finds immanent to every moment of the text, constituting the form of presence of the narrator, the presence of another consciousness that must be described not as the consciousness of the empirical self but instead as a consciousness that can exist only in writing, in literature. To call it madness is only to highlight the strangeness and otherness with regard to the empirical consciousness. What is the consciousness found in literature but something that is partly organic, but also partly vegetal? In other words, how does perception take place in the process of writing? When the narrator describes a scene or event, we often represent these signs as perception in analogy to the common senses. But this is not how they are made. Rather, they are woven into a text constituting a body that first captures these impressions and converts them into signs, a body that also senses and feels but is not organically composed.

It is absolutely a prejudice to ascribe the presence of conscious perception that appears in writing to empirical consciousness, *which would be madness.* This is a very simple point, but one that is often overlooked in the history of criticism. In Kafka, most famously in "The Metamorphosis," Gregor Samsa is described from the perspective of waking up to discover that he is a beetle. But who is this "I" doing the describing, that is actually floating somewhere in Gregor's room and observing the events from different vantage points, including Gregor's own thoughts and physical experiences of pain. For example, Gregor suddenly falls from the bed to the floor. The narrator reports: "There was a loud thump, but it wasn't really a loud noise."[16] From which perspective might we understand this statement? Literary criticism has been drawn to describe this perspective occupied by the written narrator from different points of view (omniscient, partial, subjective), but in no way can this consciousness be likened to the empirical self. To understand this fact, however, we must learn to become a little stupid, forgetful of our habits and prejudices, or even a little mad like Proust's narrator. Yet the fact that this form of consciousness exists as a definite form of possible experience constituted by signs means that writing offers another possibility for human existence that is not possible for the simple empirical self, a means of occupying both objective and subjective points of view, another manner of perceiving, feeling, experiencing, and thinking.

The problem that Proust poses for us to consider is that the narrative consciousness is named in relationship to the empirical subject of Proust himself, as Marcel, and yet this would have to be another Marcel that is different from Proust, the author, one that offers Proust a method to distance himself from his own experience by passing through this strange consciousness born of writing. For example, every time I read a writer, and by this I mean when I read all their published works, their letters and diaries, their little notes to editors and lawyers, their grocery lists, I have the feeling that I am becoming a part of their consciousness, that I am inhabiting them and seeing things as if from inside their subjective perspective. I have the feeling of a familiarity that is bought by years of research. But this is just an illusion. Deleuze appears to offer a more accurate picture of this experience, which becomes the basis for the interpretation of the presence of the narrator in *Proust and Signs*: I am caught in their web, trapped in the intricate lacework of their signs. The only approximate representation of knowing their consciousness is the image of a spider dragging its heavy body toward me and in one terrifying moment wrapping me in its abdominal cord and drinking all my blood. This is a better representation of the experience of literature, or what a literary machine produces in me, which entails some kind of madness and obsession with a completely other consciousness, which is more likened to the consciousness of a spider or a plant.

Before turning to describe the components of the Proustian literary machine (what traditional literary critics usually call "the Proustian experience," but this is strictly an anthropomorphism), let us briefly turn to the conclusion of part one, written at some point between 1962 and 1964, where we find one of the first mentions of "the image of thought" in Deleuze's philosophy. Here we are given a more precise understanding of the problem of presupposition in philosophy, and why modern philosophy can no longer presuppose an image of thought that appears in natural consciousness. "Proust's work," Deleuze writes, "vies with philosophy. It sets up an image of thought in opposition to that of philosophy. He attacks what is most essential in a classical philosophy of a rationalist type: the presupposition of this philosophy. The philosopher readily presupposes the mind as mind, the thinker as thinker, and the subject as a being who wants the truth, and who naturally seeks the truth in consciousness. He assumes in advance the goodwill of thinking; all his investigation is based on a "premeditated decision."[17]

In this passage Deleuze is referring to what he will later define, in the chapter "Image of Thought" in *Difference and Repetition,* as the "subjective presuppositions," "under the double aspect of a goodwill on the part of the thinker and the upright nature of thought itself."[18] In the later chapter, Deleuze rigorously shows that this subjective presupposition, itself a form of prejudice, is implicitly borrowed from the idea of a common sense *(cogitatio natura universalis).* In other words, the classical philosopher sets off in search of something that is already presumed to be in agreement with his foreknowledge of it, something that is already accorded a nature that is disposable to being discovered or revealed, and, as Deleuze says, something that the classical philosopher claims to belong to him by *a kind of right.* Classical philosophy calls this something = x, "truth," which it sets off in search of by means of a "premeditated decision" (or method). But this would be a lot like setting out on a search for buried treasure armed with the foreknowledge of its gradual discovery, if only because you already have an idea of where it is hidden because you first buried it there, and you drew a little map for yourself as a reminder. In both these chapters, of course, Descartes will constitute the prototype of the classical philosopher of the rationalist type who sets out on a search for what is called "Truth" by means of a premeditated decision. If we remember from the opening of the *Meditations,* this trip is planned out well ahead of time: he waited until he was mature enough to take the trip, being in "secure possession of leisure and in a peaceful retirement," and even sets aside a full week (except Sunday, of course) to apply himself freely to "the overthrow of all his formerly held opinions."[19]

What is wrong with this image? On the first day, the narrator of the *Meditations,* the *cogito,* is quickly able to strip away all "objective presuppositions"—and here it is important to point out that the philosophical *cogito* as a Body without Organs is first given by Descartes: it has no natural organs of perception (no eyes, no ears), no external limbs or body at all, no feelings other than those that are necessary for the search itself; no memory, and even no extension (because even the earth and the sky are vanished as fictions created by the mind). However, on the second day of the meditations, after getting a good night's sleep having been exhausted by the previous day's expeditions, Descartes's narrator suddenly awakens to find that it is deep water, because it must now even doubt its own nature as a human being, or an *animal rationale.*

> I suppose, accordingly, that all the things, which I see are false (fictitious); I believe that none of the objects which my fallacious memory represents ever existed; I suppose that I possess no senses; I believe that the body, figure, extension, motion, and place are merely fictions of the mind. What is there, then, that can be esteemed true? Perhaps this only, that there is absolutely nothing certain.[20]

It is here that the "Body without Organs" historically first appears as the being who says "I think," but whose form of existence can never be proven and so must be submitted to a radical *epokhē* (as phenomenology will later label this method of suspending all objective presuppositions in order to finally begin as a purified *cogito,* that is, as a firm and immovable point from which thinking begins). To be fair to Descartes, everything cannot be said to have been predetermined in advance. He did not know that on the morning of the second day he would find himself in such deep water and suddenly have to deny his own human nature, all of his past memories, all sensation and feeling, all capacity to move around and occupy a place on the earth. Even the initial conditions of his search, his leisure and his peaceable retirement, seem absent on this morning. And yet, as Deleuze will show, this search was already betrayed from the start, even before it began.

Why? First of all, because one does not seek the truth only under the best conditions possible and in a pleasant state of retirement from the activities of the world (from all labor, need, desire, war, or natural disasters); there are other situations, more frequent, that are not so amenable, as when one is forced into thinking by something that is immanent and yet cannot be altogether thought. This might provide a better occasion for the event that causes thinking to occur; as Deleuze writes, "The act of thinking does not proceed from a simple natural possibility."[21] Secondly, Descartes is capable of removing all the objective presuppositions from thought, but even before he begins he does not place in question his own subjective presuppositions that thinking is by nature good and that the good nature of the thinker desires truth, even though he raises these subjective presuppositions at the end of the first day when he realizes that the path laid out for thinking is "arduous" and that the natural *cogito* so resists being filled with a feeling of indolence that it almost leads the narrator back to the ordinary course of life, to his leisure and his peaceable retirement: "just as the captive who perchance was enjoying in his dreams an imaginary liberty, when he begins to suspect that it was but a vision, dreads awakening, and [out of fear] conspires with the agreeable illusion that the deception may be prolonged."[22] In fact, Deleuze will highlight the nature of this fear and the conspiracy with illusion as the real subjective condition of thinking that must be presupposed in place of the essential good nature of the thinker and the upright nature of thought. Here we are given the essential image of stupidity and ill will as the preconditions of a modern image of thought:

Not an individual endowed with good will and a natural capacity for thought, but an individual full of ill will, one who does not manage to think, either naturally or conceptually. Only such an individual is without presuppositions. Only such an individual effectively begins and effectively repeats.[23]

Finally, although certainty, or the desire for certainty, is a representation of the truth under the conditions that everything can be doubted, it is already secondary to what causes us to seek the truth in the first place; moreover, it distorts the nature of this causality by already representing it as something that will extinguish this movement: it conceals or distorts the real causality of thinking by providing thought with an image of its end or its goal. Consequently it is the poet and the writer, and not the philosopher, who learns, rather than understands, that thought is nothing without something that forces and does violence to it, and this force will not be revealed as either uncertainty or simple doubt. Therefore, if we replace the certainty of truth with another object, the past, and another kind of certainty, real experience, then we have an idea of the Proustian search that Deleuze will say "vies with philosophy." Here, the Proustian narrator still seeks the truth, but the truth is not represented in advance as an object that wants to be found. The search for "time lost" does not begin in such a premeditated fashion, nor is there any preguarantee that time will be found; most importantly, the only presupposition is the fact of having lost it—it has not purposefully been buried only to dig it up again later on, because it is not simple recollection or memory—and the forcefulness of this loss itself is the causality that sets the Proustian narrator on a search, which begins the adventure of thinking by tracing the signs and developing them.

Perhaps no better image of the conditions of the search can be provided than the following long passage from the third volume of the *Recherche*, which Deleuze quotes in its entirety as if to underline that it needs no further philosophical interpretation:

The truths that intelligence grasps directly in the open light of day have something less profound, less *necessary* about them than those that life has communicated to us *in spite of ourselves* in an impression, a material impression because it has reached us through our senses, but whose spirit we can extract. . . . I would have to interpret the sensations as the *signs* of so many laws and ideas, by attempting to think, that is, to bring out of the darkness what I had felt, and convert it into a spiritual equivalent, . . . Whether this was a matter of reminiscences of the kind that included the noise of the fork or the taste of Madeleine, or of those truths written with the help of figures whose meaning I was trying to discover in my mind, where, like steeples or weeds, they composed a complicated and elaborate *herbal*, their first character was that I was not free to choose them, that they were given to me as they were. And I felt that this must be the mark of their authenticity. *I had not gone looking* for the two cobblestones in the courtyard where I stumbled. But precisely the *fortuitous, inevitable*, way in which sensation had been *encountered* governed the truth of the past that it resuscitated, of the images that it released, because we feel its effort to rise toward the light, because we feel the reality of the joy of reality regained. . . . In order to read the inner book of these unknown signs . . . no one could help me by any rules, such reading consisting in an act of creation in which nothing can take our place or even collaborate with us. . . . The ideas formed by pure intelligence have only a logical truth, a possible truth, their choice is arbitrary. The book whose characters are figured, *not traced by us*, is our only book. Not that the ideas we form cannot be logically exact, but we do not know whether they are true. Only the impression, however paltry its substance seems, however unlikely its traces, is a criterion of truths, and on this account alone merits being apprehended by the mind, for only the impression is capable, if the mind can disengage the truth from it, of leading the mind to a greater perfection and of giving it a pure joy.[24]

It is important to notice the words and phrases that Deleuze emphasizes in reading this passage: *necessary—in spite of ourselves—signs—herbal—I had not gone looking—fortuitous—inevitable—encountered—not traced by us*. This is the same kind of paratactic utterance that appeared earlier in Heidegger, but we can take it as indicating the formula of Proust's method, which is complicated and herbal (vegetable) and is composed of only those impressions and signs that his narrator "had not gone looking for," and therefore is not created to include all impressions and signs. Hence, the book or the literary machine, as "an involuntary machine of interpretation," will be a filter of sorts that first determines what impressions and signs are necessary to include and those that are merely possible and intelligible, and thus are not included—for example, the "two cobblestones" where he tripped are included because they are necessary and not merely possible perception, and constitute the signs of a real encounter or accident. The sign is created as the "spiritual equivalent" of the idea of the Past, beginning from impressions and developing these into signs that are "immanent" to the Past—not simply to the past of memory, but to the force of the past that causes each present to swerve toward it and often to become lost. Thus, each sign produced (remembered/created) by the machine will present what Deleuze later calls a "crystal image" of the moment when time is split into two unequal parts: one part rushing headlong toward the past where it becomes lost in relation to the memory; another part surging forward in relation to the past it will become in the sudden discovery or revelation of its impression that was hidden in some "material object."

> And so it is with our own past. It is a labor in vain to attempt to recapture it: all the efforts of our intellect must prove futile. The past is hidden somewhere outside the realm, beyond the reach [in some material object] . . . which we do not suspect [i.e., "had not gone looking for"]. And as for that object, it depends on chance whether we come upon it or not before we ourselves must die.[25]

The method that Proust devises for his search of this lost time, more a set of presuppositions for how the literary machine will work than a set of rules or axiomatics, can be contrasted to that of Descartes almost point for point. The method would proceed by interpreting the impressions of sensation as signs of laws and ideas; in contrast to Descartes, the writer or artist does not seek to bracket sensation first in order to determine the laws and ideas of the mind as pure *cogito*. Sensation is first and becomes an impression that is necessary and exists in spite of ourselves; thinking comes afterward, in working over these impressions to discover their law, that is, "to bring out of the darkness what I had felt": the living being of sensation itself, but which can be really experienced only through an artificial and organic body created by the process of writing. Elsewhere, Proust will define the book, in purely machinic terms, as a telescope for looking into ourselves—however, through its apparatus this telescopic machine would cause the appearance of a sensation, a sensation that would not appear otherwise to natural perception.

To conclude our discussion of Proust's literary machine, I will briefly turn to the second part of the 1970 French edition, where we are given both the definition of the literary machine as well as an image of the narrator as a Body without Organs that corresponds to what I have already described as the new image of thought: immanence. Here the Body without Organs becomes a being of pure sensation (no eyes, no ears, no memory, and above all, no thought), that is to say, a completely different Body without Organs than the one Descartes devised for philosophy, and therefore a completely different image of thought. In *Anti-Oedipus*, Deleuze and Guattari define a machine as anything that interrupts a flow. Here the machine (the book, the involuntary machine of interpretation) is a spiderweb—it is a vast and complicated partly animal and partly herbal web that interrupts the flows of signs and impressions that get caught up in it; and the narrator is the spider that drags its heavy body to the place of the interruption and spins by means of its abdominal fluid a cocoon around the impression it finds there (i.e., to develop the impression into a sign) in order to finally drink its blood (extract its essence, its spiritual idea). Is this being malevolent? Is the being of a spider malevolent for drinking the blood of the fly? In this question we find the image of thought divorced or separated from the idea, the prejudice actually, of a moral image of thought. In other words, it is in the Proustian image of thought, rather than the Cartesian, that we find a thinking that is capable of doing away with the subjective preconditions of good and common sense that still retain an anthropological prejudice of the *cogitatio natura universalis*. This is why Deleuze often refers to the being of the narrator as "in-human"—not in any monstrous sense of horror, but in the same way we would refer to the being of a spider as nonhuman without implying any judgment, except that it was a being of nature.

And yet the Proustian spider-narrator is not a being of nature, but a purely artificial being, a created being. Thus, in the conclusion of the second part, after diagramming the components of the literary machine and describing how it works, Deleuze concludes by defining the nature of the being that is found at its center, like a spider in an intricate web it has created:

> The *logos* is a huge Animal whose parts unite in a whole and are unified under a principle or a leading idea; but the pathos is a vegetal realm consisting of cellular elements that communicate only indirectly . . . the bumblebee that constitutes the communication between flowers and loses its proper animal value becomes in relation to the latter merely a marginalized fragment, a disparate element in the apparatus of vegetal reproduction.[26]

Partly animal, partly vegetal or herbal, the process of writing and the being of the writer are compared to a bumblebee that loses its own proper animality by becoming part of the reproductive apparatus of the flower. In the same way, we can say that the writer also loses his or her proper human value (i.e., the attributes of a self or an individual) in becoming part of another reproductive apparatus, which is no longer that of the self or the individual, but rather the expression of an impersonal, and in some sense inhuman life. Is this the nature of the being that Deleuze proposes to replace the classical philosopher, who would become the marginalized and disparate element of a vegetal image of thought? In the next chapter, in order to respond to this question, I will continue to explore the nature of this being, and of the new image of thought, in the "rhizome." Although the rhizome appears like a plant or a weed, in actuality it refers back to this partly vegetal and partly animal writing machine that was first created by Proust.

2

NOTES FROM A
THOUGHT EXPERIMENT:
WHAT IS A RHIZOME?
(CA. 1976)

- The Cartesian Body without Organs
- Three Images of the Book System
- The Method of an "Anti-Method"

In 1976, four years after their first work together, *Anti-Oedipus* (1972), and one year after the publication of *Kafka: Toward a Minor Literature* (1975), Deleuze and Guattari publish *Rhizome: Introduction,* which later becomes the introduction to their second volume of the *Capitalism and Schizophrenia* project, *A Thousand Plateaus* (1980).[1] Again, this work will concern the questions I raised in the Introduction: What kind of image is to be deduced from thought? How can thinking be determined by the image, and where does image first acquire its power over thought—that is, to induce what is called "thinking" to occur within the subject? Following the thesis offered in chapter 1, I would argue that concept of the rhizome represents the literal translation of the Proustian image of thought into modern philosophy, an image of thought that takes the form of a vast and intricate *herbal* (as Proust says). More importantly, it represents an externalization of the machinic dimension of Deleuze and Guattari's philosophy, a machine that literally presents us with the following situation: Contemporary philosophy is an assemblage that presupposes a new image of thought on the plane of immanence. However, this relationship is now portrayed as a relatively unlimited number of plateaus that populate this plane and constitute its regions, its moments, its temporary archipelagoes, as in the case of the spider web in Proust, "the huge animal *logos* whose parts unite in a whole and which are united under the principle of a leading idea," the idea of rhizome. Here, the plane of immanence (or the world of the idea) appears, not as a whole, but only as a "fragmentary whole" that is populated by a relatively infinite number of other planes or plateaus (relatively infinite because more plateaus can be added later, and there is no absolute number or limit that determines the composition of the whole, somewhat like moments and events that constitute the plane upon which "a life" appears). Therefore, plateaus are the surfaces and volumes, whereas the plane itself is formless; they are concrete assemblages of concepts and signs, and function as configurations of a philosophy machine, "but the plane is an abstract machine of which these plateaus are the working parts."[2] Because this may seem more than a little abstract, at first, in this chapter I will spend some time "unpacking" (as Whiteheadeans would say) all of these principles in order to trace out the new image of thought that Deleuze and Guattari now presuppose.

My first observation would be that, in a certain sense, the axiomatic statements and principles concerning the rhizome might be understood as corollaries to the method given in Descartes's *Meditations on First Philosophy,* but only in the sense that one of the explicit goals or tasks is to determine the necessary and the contingent attributes of an image of thought. Consequently, the first thing that the concept of a rhizome opposes is the form of the book as a necessary attribute of thinking or philosophy. It is difficult to say exactly when the book became the dominant form of philosophical expression, but it is essentially related to the rise of the novel in literature at the beginning of the nineteenth century (if it does not even constitute its implicit presupposition of the Romantic moment). In the book, the event of thinking was reconstituted as a narrative adventure, with a narrator and different characters. This was a different form than we already saw in Proust, who set out to destroy the form of the novel and who became the most severe critic of the genre for essentially fictionalizing real experience and turning it into a Romance. In the region of philosophy, perhaps we can identify Hegel's phenomenology as being the greatest philosophical romance, and it represented in its time a revolutionary expression by setting the movement of thought (the subject of Mind or Spirit) within a narrative adventure spanning an entire History that has a definite beginning and end. However, as in the case of Proust, Deleuze and Guattari will argue that this form has become too fictional and even a mythic vehicle of expression. In place of the form of the book, with its interior volume that represents the interiority of the Self, and which has the author as its Individual subject of enunciation, Deleuze and Guattari will oppose the form of the plateau, which is a flat surface without depth or volume, later described as either smooth or striated in distinction.

It is difficult to see, at first, how a plateau could easily represent the interiority of the Self, of a thought seeking to express the interiority of a subject (an author-God, an individual person), and this becomes the first major axiom that separates thought from its earlier image of the book: the interiority of the book has no essential or necessary relationship to the interiority of the empirical subject, but rather is composed of a flat surface in which one side faces (either facing upward or outward) and the other side remains implicit and virtual, and presupposed, facing toward the plane of immanence or "Body without Organs" (as Deleuze and Guattari define it at this point). For example, it is more like what happens in a close-up in film where thinking is implicated by a sign that emerges on the face of the other person; we often do not grasp what the person is thinking, only that he or she is thinking by grasping the nature of the signs that appear to indicate "pensiveness." This might be a better expression of the reality of thought, in which our knowledge of thinking always comes after the explicit signs of thought, and usually involves the advent of other signs that seek to express what is virtual or implicit on the first level, than the way thinking is represented in a book as the representation of an internal activity that takes place inside the subject who says "I think." So, first of all, in destroying the book as the natural presupposition of an image of thought, Deleuze and Guattari argue that "a book has neither object nor subject," and "to attribute a book to a subject is to overlook the working of matters, and the exteriority of their relations. It is to fabricate a beneficent God to explain geological movements."[3]

This destruction of the natural presupposition of the book and the individual subject who appears as its author-God is already further complicated by the fact that Deleuze and Guattari are writing together. This is not so simple as it seems, and cannot merely be reduced to the "two body problem" that has troubled the reception of their theory. Rather, it is the very presence of two "speaking-subjects" that causes the normative rules by which written expression is usually encoded as individual enunciation to go awry. Moreover, because the writing machine they have created together to replace the individual subject of enunciation violates all the normal, hermeneutical protocols of reading, this has also produced in the field of commentary a kind of redoubling of the codes and axioms that constitute the subject of authors—Deleuze *and/or* Guattari. Therefore, it is from the position of "the reader" that these codes are enforced, in a structural manner, and thus we have witnessed many times that it is the subjects of the reader and hermeneutic interpreter who have returned to re-impose a form of communication that remains implicit in the image of the book—even to the point of judging *A Thousand Plateaus* as a badly botched or imperfect book! From this fact, in reading Deleuze *and* Guattari, a kind of collective madness has come to characterize the reception of their work together: Who is speaking now? Whose idea or thought is this? Deleuze's or Guattari's? That is, which subject can we (as readers) attribute this particular idea to with our belief in authority? More often than not, by far the worst culprits of this kind of practice have been the specialists and expert readers of Deleuze and Guattari's work—and particularly academic philosophers!—as well as certain contemporaries like Badiou and Derrida, who have gone so far as to completely ignore Guattari as an eccentric and bizarre presence of madness under the banner of individual authority that is usually accorded only to Deleuze (the pure philosopher).[4] What these readers do not seem to understand is that, as in the case of the Proustian narrator, this presence of madness and eccentricity is carefully distributed across the multiple points of enunciation in *A Thousand Plateaus* as an effect produced by the specific invention of a writing machine according to the vegetal structure of a rhizome, and no longer according to a linguistic structure of individual enunciation.

As Deleuze said earlier in *Difference and Repetition,* concerning the nature of the subjective presuppositions, the reader should also not be understood as a subject of goodwill and the guarantor of the upright nature of the thinking that appears in a book, but potentially as maleficent being who appears only to impose his or her own ideas on the matter of expression.[5] I would even go as far to say that because of the subjective presuppositions of the philosophical reader, Deleuze *and* Guattari's great work of philosophy has not yet actually been read by anyone, with the possible exception of its translators! By this, I do not mean to assert that the translator is "a good reader," as opposed to the hermeneutic critic or Deleuzian specialist, who are "bad readers"; only that the translator can be defined a "faithful reader" in the sense of only constituting a moment internal to the writing machine itself, defined earlier as "the involuntary machine of interpretation." All extrinsic interpretation, on the other hand, approaches a writing machine from the outside, considering it an integral whole without external relations (i.e., a system of thought); in fact, most voluntary interpretation first approaches a writing machine by disassembling its parts in order to study them, but this only causes a writing machine to break down and no longer function. Nevertheless, this produces an effect that is usually associated with meaning that serves as the primary goal of all successful interpretation.

Deleuze and Guattari had already foreseen this, which is why they introduce their plan of assembling *A Thousand Plateaus* by immediately calling attention to this fact, by making it explicit and undeniable that "the two of us wrote *Anti-Oedipus* together. Since each of us is several, there is already quite a crowd. . . . Why have we kept our own names? Out of habit, purely out of habit."[6] Moreover, they immediately go on to confess that they have even developed a secret code and "assigned clever pseudonyms to keep us from being recognized."[7] At this point, the hermeneutic critic and traditional interpreter might become dizzy, because this statement implies that every appearance of another name, every mention of an author who is referred to or cited in their work, functions as a pseudonym of either Deleuze or Guattari, by means of a cipher that they keep to themselves in order to keep things straight for purely pragmatic reasons. One might ask: Who is Kleist, who appears so often like a character in this work and is associated with the concept of the "war machine"? And what about Kafka, who is associated sometimes with the idea of a "revolutionary becoming" and sometimes with "a depressive position in relation to the law"? Of course, we know, every time there is any mention of Proust, it is Deleuze who is speaking. But who then is Nietzsche, especially when the latter is heard to exclaim, "I am all the names in History"? Who then is Schreber? Who then is Artaud? Finally, who is the "wasp," and who is "the orchid"? It could very well be that each identifies the idea or thought of the other with names that only they would know. This could quickly be turned into the most marvelous game that Lacan once called "hunt the slipper." Who is speaking? And yet, in the very first passage of this work we are already told that it does not matter, and that they invented this manner of speaking, not in order to reach "the point where one no longer says I"—and in this sense, Deleuze and Guattari do not want to continue the game that was first invented by Beckett—but instead "the point where it is no longer of any importance whether or not one says I."[8]

However, this is not exactly true either, because it is not a realistic portrayal of the subjective processes that were involved during the process of collaboration. In fact, the question "Who is speaking?" was frequently a point of contention during the process of writing *Anti-Oedipus*—even intense ambivalence, paranoia, and jealousy—mostly on the part of Guattari, as the recently published letters and diaries vividly portray. As an example, the following diary entry from June 10, 1972:

> The writing machine is getting more complicated. I can get through it all on the condition that it keeps on working beyond me, I'm supported by someone who types, corrects, reads, waits. I will keep giving these texts to Fanny and, at the end of the chain, Gilles. I can tell they don't mean anything to him. The ideas, sure. But the trace, the continuous-discontinuous text flow that guarantees my continuance, obviously he doesn't see it like that. Or he does, but he's not interested. He always has the *oeuvre* in mind. For him, it's all just notes, raw material that disappears into the final assemblage. That's how I feel a bit over-coded by *Anti-Oedipus*. . . . What I feel like is just fucking around. Publish this diary for example. Say stupid shit. Barf out the fucking-around-o-maniacal schizo flow. . . . And I have to make a *text* out of that mess and it has to hold up: that is my fundamental schizo-analytic project.[9]

It is clear from this passage that the writing machine that Deleuze and Guattari construct has two aspects (or images) that serve as the conditions of its production, which I call "a body-image" and "a brain-image": First there is the body-image, defined as a schizo-flow of "the continuous-discontinuous text flow *that guarantees my continuance,*" because "I write in order not to die" (a "Guattari-image"), and then a brain-image that later organizes every flow into a final assemblage, giving all the various text flows the finality of a common project, or oeuvre (a "Deleuze-image"). But this particular writing machine needs both aspects to function, according to the image of thought each aspect presupposes as a condition for the other to work. The body-image is no less a brain composed of "neurological-vegetative" connections; the brain-image has a body, which organizes these flows into distinct forms and perceptions. What is most crucial to point out about this process is its difference from a normal conception of a writing process presupposed from the perspective of an individual consciousness of an author; in other words, when Deleuze begins to write, he already depends upon the text flows that have been already been produced by Guattari, and not upon the abstract flows of ideas and thoughts floating in his own head. It's a completely different image of thought. (In fact, would this not be a better image of writing than what is presupposed by extrinsic interpretation?) Therefore, it's absolutely ridiculous to ascribe the total functioning of the writing machine to one aspect (i.e., a "Deleuze-image").

Returning now to the general definition of the book as a machine or an assemblage, Deleuze and Guattari will immediately point out that historically there are three kinds of book machines, each of which structures (in the manner of a system) or even produces (in the manner of a machine) three distinctive images of the thought:

1. First, the "root-book, the tree book" *(livre-racine),* which is "the classical book, as noble, signifying, and subjective organic interiority," that is to say, in which the interiority of the book's volume is identified with the interiority of mental space and is homogeneous with the interiority of the world.[10]

2. Second, what they define as "the radical-system, or fascicular root" *(le système-radicelle, ou racine faciculée)*, which can be identified

in some ways the postmodern textual metaphors of grafting and weaving of traces of the absolute book together into an infinite process of textuality (Barthes), or into an unlimited, but nevertheless finite, text (Derrida). However, they also argue that this new system produces a "strange mystification" that occurs as a result of this absolute book constituted by fragments of an impossible totalization, because the image of totality negatively subsists in the temporal form of an infinite deferral and delay enacted by the process of rewriting, reweaving, and grafting of all of the fragments and missing parts in a "Total Work or Magnum Opus." Here, we might perceive an implicit reference to the textual systems of philosophy created by Barthes and Derrida, and in a different sense, the absolute volumes of Mallarmé and Joyce. As they write: "The world has become chaos, but the book remains an image of the world: radicle-chaosmos (*chaosmos-radicelle*) rather than root-cosmos (*cosmos-racine*). A strange mystification: a book all the more total for being fragmented."[11]

3. The third system is the "rhizome proper," which is made or produced by subtracting this final image or higher dimension of unity or totality: transcendence. As in the system devised by Proust, the spider, the rhizome is partly animal and partly vegetal; it is described as a swarming of rats in a pack form, or as a system of tubular stems in a patch of weeds. What is subtracted is a vertical dimension that allows its form to be grasped from another perspective that is posed as its higher unity. Again, it is a flat surface composed horizontally that remains perfectly abstract in that it is drawn in relation to a plane of immanence that, in turn, it does not seek to represent as an image of the world. It is purely immanent to the plane on which it appears as a plateau or partial region of the plane, like the manner in which weeds appear like patchwork on a meadow.

Concerning this third and final book machine, which is approximate to the image presupposed by *A Thousand Plateaus,* Deleuze and Guattari immediately say that it is always in danger of becoming too abstract and, thus, of convincing no one. But this is due, not to its own consistency, or lack of reality, but instead to the fact that "too many people still have trees growing in their heads."[12] For this reason, the rest of the introduction makes an effort to provide certain concrete axioms that will define how this system works. In other words, these propositions actually perform how the rhizome as book machine works in the very process of describing its major principles or rules of composition and construction. What is most important, first of all, is to grasp the purpose of the rhizome system. It does not exist in nature, even though it is comparable to certain natural formations such as weeds and mobile bands, packs, swarms, the "Brownian motion" of dust particles in a slant of light, or as Leibniz once said of the monads, "a squirming of fishes"; however, it must be invented and in a certain sense this must be discovered by means of experimenting, by trial and error, like most technological inventions.

Why are things invented in the first place? On one level, it is only to find a solution to a problem, a new way of doing things, to make life easier, to cure or to improve upon a previous technology (e.g., walking is supplemented by the horse, the wheel, later by the flying wing and the spaceship, but also by the telephone and the Internet). But certain new technologies also respond to a kind of social need for liberation, or to escape from a dominant form of organizing collective desires. Deleuze and Guattari invent the rhizome system as such a means of escape: from the previous two book machines that have served to create what they call "a Dark Age in thinking." As they write later on, "Grass is the only way out. . . . The weed exists only to fill the wastelands left by cultivated areas. It grows between."[13] At first, it is easy to perceive the difference between a tree-book system and a rhizome: the former sinks its roots in the very depths of the earth, which is below the level of perception, closest to an origin deep in the past; it contains or expresses a dimension of verticality that arranges a hierarchy. It resembles Aristotle's system of philosophy in which metaphysics is located in the upper branches of the tree of knowledge, with physics comprising its subterranean root system. However, it is difficult to grasp the differences with the fascicular-book system (i.e., infinite textuality), since it is only based on the absence of the root, even though the problem is that the memory of the root remains as a kind of ghostly supplement, a phallic cutting that continues to be grafted onto any assemblage and that still determines the unity and identity of any multiplicity. It becomes much more dangerous for this reason, because every multiplicity is made to circulate around a missing unity, an absent meaning, a far more demanding and more "extensive totality." In

this image we might even determine a certain representation of immanence that was revealed by modern philosophy itself, except it constituted
this immanence as a great secret or a conspiracy of History, or finally,
in the position of "the Real." Consequently, this plane still functions like
a transcendent plane (*the* Being of beings, *the* Structure, *the* Real), even
though this plane was no longer located above things, but rather beneath
them and before them as the form of their totality, which is nevertheless
absent from any given multiplicity.

As opposed to what might be called a phallic organization of the
image of thought, Deleuze and Guattari begin by proposing one simple
rule: "subtract the unique from the multiplicity to be constituted." Instead, *make a multiplicity using only the number of dimensions one already has available, without needing to add one dimension that is not yet
present and functions as a hidden point of unity.* Consequently, this relates to the first and second principles of the rhizome, connection and
heterogeneity, according to the axiom that "any point of a rhizome can
be connected to any other, and must be."[14] How will this help? "A rhizome ceaselessly establishes connections between semiotic chains, organizations of power, and circumstances relative to the arts, sciences, and
social struggles."[15] This must first be thought in relation to the new
image of thought Deleuze and Guattari are proposing for philosophy:
everything can be included, every semiotic chain, every statement, every
flow. There is no proper territory, and moreover, no proper language.
Signs of art can be placed in conjunction with signs of politics or organizations of power (as they do in the case of Kafka); signs emitted from
real social struggles can suddenly be made to express philosophical
thoughts if they are connected to the right machine. Again, there is no
proper philosophical language, no root language or mother tongue, as
there was in the case of Heidegger. However, this is also different from
saying that "everything is political," because here the political takes on a
static and transcendent value, as if redeeming the purely personal and
private matter by giving it the Universal form of a social struggle. This
can too easily become a dominant form and an oppressive value, like
what happens today in literary criticism under the terms of "political
reading," when only certain identities and contents are qualified as
having a political value. However, what is more important to note under

the terms of this regime of interpretation is the redundancy of these values or signs (the body, gender, sexuality, race, class, ethnicity) as if the organization of power operates only through these signs and does not also produce new political contents, those that correspond to different social struggles that are not yet "recognized" as political and are fated to remain invisible and unconnected. But that is not how private statements become politicized, or rather, that is not how the organization of power first appears connected to what was formerly a private matter like sexuality or child rearing in a family. In thinking these connections, in analyzing them and linking them together, philosophy can now make the most surprising discoveries (as in the case of Foucault). A discourse on masturbation in the nineteenth century, for example, can suddenly have the most surprising consequences for the philosophy of neoliberalism. What was not connected at first now is seen to be connected in the most surprising manner to other heterogeneous social assemblages like the clinic or the social welfare state, or to a discourse on public hygiene and the differences between classes.

The third principle is the principle of the multiplicity itself. If there is no single language in which everything is coded, only multiple languages and sign regimes, then there is also no supplementary dimension over and above these lines. This is the rule against the notion of "a Structure," which turns out to be only one code that overcodes everything. For example, when Lacan said, "The Unconscious was structured like a language," this was often taken as a machine for overcoding everything using a linguistic code. This has often been the complaint against post-structuralism for turning everything into a text, including the reality of social struggle. But Marxism was no different, because it overcoded everything simply by employing a different system of linguistic and semiotic values: base and superstructure, either direct or overdetermined with ideological signs functioning as mediators between the two levels. As Jameson said, totality is not a text, but is mediated by a system of signifying values. In place of an underlying Structure, therefore, Deleuze and Guattari propose a "plane of consistency" that increases with the number of the connections made on it. It is defined as the "outside" of every concrete multiplicity, but it is not determined by a Structure. In fact, as an evolution of the concept of machine first proposed by Guattari in the 1969 essay "Machine et structure," and of "the literary machine" in Deleuze's new edition of *Proust and Signs* the following year, the rhizome represents a decisive break with all notions of Structure and even forecasts the recent turn to the subject of the brain in modern neurology and biology by contemporary philosophy and logic, which is described as an "a-centered and probabilistic system," as I will return to discuss in the Conclusion.[16] As Françoise Dosse observes, from a point very early on Guattari often turned to modern biology, rather than to linguistics, to find more useful language for modeling structures. As he describes in one of the letters to Deleuze in the process of writing *Anti-Oedipus*:

> Cerebral writing is directly grasped from that which, from an exterior perspective, is *diagrammatic*. It is the organ of machinic affiliation. Thus, cerebral writing is that which can be directly grasped in the body's systematic machines: perception, motor systems, neuro-vegetative [systems], etc.[17]

As Deleuze and Guattari write, concerning the ideal book that could be produced from the principles of the rhizome, it would presuppose only a plane of consistency that is relative to the number of connections that could be made on it; to compose the book would be to lay everything out on a plane of exteriority of this kind, "on a single page, the same sheet: lived events, historical determinations, concepts, individuals, groups, social formations."[18] Of course, what they are describing is the ideal book they are actually trying to compose as *A Thousand Plateaus*, according to the first and second principles that everything can be connected to everything else at any point, and must be. Here we are reminded again of Proust's image of the book as a spiderweb in which signs and impressions are incorporated, even though it does not pretend to include all signs, as does a Structure.

Finally, the remaining three principles they discuss follow from the first three and can be understood as inferences or *disputations*, as in Scholastic method. The principle of a signifying rupture repeats the principles of connection and heterogeneity. What Deleuze and Guattari call the principles of cartography and decalcomania repeats the argument of the notion of a plane of consistency that "is not amenable to any structural or generative model."[19] Instead, the image of thought presupposed by the rhizome system is that of a map and not that of tracing a preexisting structure or genealogical inheritance. Thus, it would oppose the systems proposed by structuralism and psychoanalysis, as well as the philosophies of Heidegger and Derrida, or any system of philosophy that proposes to "trace out" the "History of Metaphysics," even if the objective of this tracing is to de-center this entire system and open a space for new signifying values to emerge. Ultimately, they argue against this method of *tracing* that has emerged in the modern period to determine the image of repetition and difference in modern philosophy. They write: "The tracing has already translated the map into an image; it has already transformed the rhizome into roots and radicals."[20] Here we can see the precise problem: the book machine as root system and the radical system as infinite textuality always return to extinguish the possible creation of the rhizome. They return again to reproduce hierarchies, or to dissipate the lateral movement of connections in a sterile form of a Structure. This was the problem Deleuze and Guattari already confronted in their critique of psychoanalysis, which tended to reproduce the same unconscious structuration in individuals, producing an incredible redundancy of significations and connections to social subjectivity: this way lies neurosis, that way phobia, and finally, a third directly to psychosis. In short, psychoanalysis prevents the patient from making any map of their own, of creating their own orientation toward reality. This will later become the basis of the emphasis on Kafka, whose literary process is often described as cartographic, making maps of the bureaucratic apparatus that in many ways are more accurate than the psychoanalytic tracings of the unconscious structures because these maps are also directly connected to political realities. After all, what are maps for? This is simple enough to answer: to find one's direction, to orient movement toward something. A map that appears on a placard in the shopping mall is a good example: first, you seek to find where you are ("YOU ARE HERE"), and only then do you seek to find where you are going. (Of course, sometimes you are looking for the nearest exit.) Literature, in comparison, most often provides such a map, and not a tracing of a Universal structure.

The remaining balance of the introduction to *Rhizome* is filled with the following sentiment: "We're tired of trees."[21] In other words, returning to what was referred to above under the tyranny of the "good reader," they are constantly making the argument that the image of thought they are proposing does not necessarily have to take the form of a tree. "Thought is not arborescent"; although the real problem to be confronted is that, again, "too many people have trees growing in their heads."[22] What follows from this point, therefore, is a literal transcription of the simple rules and axioms just outlined above into the flat surface or volume of the ideal book they are seeking to write together, recalling the above statements that it should be composed on a single plane, on a single page, including all kinds of heterogeneous impressions, signs, and elements drawn from everything around them. These are the instructions for the ideal reader (and not, it seems, for the expert reader or the Deleuze specialist):

> We are writing this book as a rhizome. We have given it a circular form, but only for laughs. Each morning we would wake up, and each of us would ask himself what plateau he was going to tackle, writing five lines here, ten there. We had hallucinatory experiences, we watched lines leave one plateau and proceed to another like a tiny column of ants. We made circles of convergence. Each plateau can be read starting from anywhere and can be related to any other plateau. To attain the multiple, one must have a method that effectively constructs it; no typographical cleverness, no lexical agility, no blending or creation of words, no syntactical boldness, can substitute for it.[23]

In conclusion, this is certainly a strange method for writing a book of philosophy, but the mention of a method again recalls the situation of Descartes's *Meditations on First Philosophy,* particularly in reference to waking every morning and continuing a thinking process on a plateau left off the previous day. Only in this case it is not one subject who awakens, and the process is described in terms of a writing process that attempts to connect one plateau to another in a somewhat random fashion. Therefore, in describing this writing machine invented by Deleuze and Guattari, as well as the new image of thought that it presupposes, I have reduced the rules of composition to three from the original six, only for the sake of economy:

1. In constructing any assemblage, subtract the unique from the multiplicity to be constituted, which also serves as the first principle of the rhizome (the rule against transcendence).

2. It is heterogeneous in the nature of its signs (the rule against a single or proper language of philosophy), because the rhizome system can be connected at any point to any other point and, therefore, must be connected in this manner.

3. The rhizome is reducible to "[neither] the One nor the multiple," which appears now as a false problem, because it presupposes a plane of consistency that is partial and is limited only by its relative outside and current number of connections (the rule against Structure).

The last thing to say about this new image of thought, as well as *A Thousand Plateaus,* is that if it seems too abstract, this is because there are too many readers today who continue to reinforce an image of thought that blocks or obstructs the connections. Something is usually called abstract only because the concreteness of the terms is missed, the relations between terms are not actualized. Abstractness, as in most abstract art, is usually due to the absence of a form or figure. In abstract painting, for example, it is the subjective disposition of the viewer who looks for the figure and finds that it is missing that is a cause of disorientation and the apprehension of a formlessness. Here the absence concerns an image of thought that is first presupposed by the classical book, which does not seem to appear at the basis of the book in this case, and this immediately provokes the judgment that it is too abstract, or too "postmodern." *Rather, I would argue, it is only the matter of a book that begins by forgetting the image of a book, and by constructing a different image as the basis for its semiotic organization.*

In truth, what is called a "plane" or a "plateau" is no more abstract than a book as a presupposition for thinking, any more than the cerebral image of the mind that is presupposed as the place where all thinking takes place—somewhere in the head of the natural thinker. However, both of these traditional images of thought, like the rhizome, are in no way natural and must be constructed by artificial means from the start. The problem is that classical philosophy has always presupposed its own image of thought as natural and universal, and has only reinforced this assertion by claiming that this image corresponds to common sense. However, the problem is the following: the form of immanence remains "outside" this image and gnaws away at it, causing the image of thought presupposed by philosophy to become sterile and in need of constant renewal. Real renewal can occur only through experimentation, and true experiments can often appear abstract and quite bizarre at first.

As I have already implied, Deleuze and Guattari's rhizomatic experiment might be judged today as a failure, given that it was perceived as too abstract and appeared to convince no one, particularly not philosophers themselves. Therefore, as a provisional transition to chapter 3, where I will offer a closer examination of what I call "the second literary machine" in Deleuze and Guattari's project (i.e., the Kafka experiment, or the burrow), I will conclude with the definition of the rhizome as the method of an anti-method offered by the French philosopher François Zourabichvili:

> The rhizome is therefore an anti-method, in which all would seem to be permitted—and in fact it does permit this, for this is its rigor—a rigor whose ascetic character the authors often stress under the heading of "sobriety" to their hasty disciples. . . . Thought gives itself over to experimentation. This decision involves at least three corollaries: 1) to think is not to represent (it does not seek an adequation with a supposedly objective reality, but a real effect that re-launches both life and thought, displacing their stakes, farther and in different directions); 2) there is a real beginning only in the middle [*au milieu*]—the word "genesis" recovers here its full etymological value of "becoming," without relation to an origin; 3) if every encounter is "possible," insofar as there is no reason to disqualify a priori some paths rather than others, encounters are not for all that selected on the basis of experience (certain arrangements and coupling neither produce nor change anything). This last point requires more elaboration. The apparently free play that the method of the rhizome calls for should not be misunderstood, as if it were a matter of blindly practicing any old arrangement in order to arrive at art or philosophy, or as if every difference was fecund a priori, following a *doxa* commonly held today. Certainly, anyone who hopes to think must

consent to a certain degree of blind groping without support, to an "adventure of the involuntary" and despite the appearance or the discourse of our teachers, this tact is the least evenly distributed aptitude, for we suffer from too much consciousness and too much mastery—we hardly ever consent to the rhizome. The vigilance of thought remains no less requisite, but at the very heart of experimentation: besides the rules mentioned above, it consists in discerning the sterile (black holes, impasses) from the fecund (lines of flight). It is here that thought conquers both its necessity and its efficacy, recognizing the signs that force us to think by enveloping what has so far remained unthought. Which is why Deleuze and Guattari can say that the rhizome is a problem of cartography [mapping], which is to say a problem of immanent evaluation.[24]

3

THE IMAGE OF THOUGHT
IN KAFKA, OR THE SECOND
LITERARY MACHINE
(CA. 1975)

- "Only Expression Gives Us the Method"
- "The Rhizome, a Burrow . . ."
- "Literature Is the People's Concern"
- A priori Innocence and the One

In chapter 2, I concluded with a quotation from Zourabichvili, who defines the rhizome as "the method of an anti-method," under the guiding principle of experimentation in thought that must be rigorously applied. At this point I will now return chronologically—defined only by year of publication—to the book written with Guattari a year before, *Kafka: Toward a Minor Literature.* It is here we first discover that the term "rhizome" appears to determine the particular image of thought in Kafka's writing, the thought emitted by what they call a "bachelor machine" *(machine célibataire),* which is proposed in relation to the experimental method of reading Kafka: the method of "anti-interpretation." Here the apparent contradiction between a method and an anti-method should not concern us too much, because Deleuze and Guattari claim that there is indeed a method determining their approach: expression. "Only expression gives us the *method.*"[1] To quote again the passage by Zourabichvili: "In this respect, the rhizome is the method of the anti-method, and its constitutive 'principles' are so many cautionary rules measured against every vestige or reintroduction of the tree and the One in thought."[2] Recalling the four principles outlined in chapter 2, which Zourabichvili refers to here as so many "cautionary rules" against "the One in thought" (i.e., transcendent organization of meaning, or structure), I will offer them again in a more pragmatic formula *(mode d'emploi)*: (1) Identify the One; (2) subtract oneself from the One; (3) enter into an assemblage at any point; and (4) use whatever you have to hand.[3]

The underlying principle of this method of "anti-interpretation" is that, in the form of the rhizome, thought gives itself over to experimentation, which is to say, it does not know what it is looking for in advance. It is according to this principle that Deleuze and Guattari's manner of "reading" Kafka is completely opposed to interpretation and is constituted by a number of simple rules that allow this reading machine to work, rules that I will describe later. Of course, we recall that in Proust the process of reading was described as an "interpretation of signs." Here, the book functions as a different kind of machine, the telescope of impassioned astronomy, made to allow certain signs and impressions to filter through so that they can be "interpreted"—in other words, so that their essences can then be extracted by "the involuntary machine of interpretation." However, this does not pose a contradiction to Deleuze and Guattari's own method, given that in this process "intelligence always comes after," including the intelligence that informs the meaning of these signs and extracts their essences. In Proust, intelligence (or meaning) does not exist beforehand, and in this case certainly does not exist in the mind of the author, Proust himself, since we have already described the nature of this mind above as partly vegetal and partly animal, the mind of a spider. Does a spider know beforehand the essence of the butterfly that will get caught up in his web, that is, before he blindly crawls to the point where it first feels its impression and then drinks its blood? This is the image of the involuntary, based upon an encounter that must first assume the form of a sign (the vibration or signal, the trembling of the web, the small disturbance of the surface of a Body without Organs), before it can become an object of interpretation and open to the play of meaning and sense. Here we might have a vivid example of a situation where intelligence comes after and presupposes nothing beforehand but a certain unconsciousness, even though in the machine itself (the web), there is the presence of an abstract rationality (although this could certainly not be determined by an image of human rationality), a machine that works precisely by allowing what was unconscious, at first, to be developed into a form of intelligence. Thus, what Deleuze calls "signs" in Proust are extremely contracted and tightly involuted states of ideas in pure duration:

> There is no more an explicit signification than a clear idea. There are only meanings implicated in signs; and if thought has the power to explicate the sign, to develop it in an Idea, this is because the Idea is already there in the sign, in the enveloped and involuted state, in the obscure state that forces us to think.[4]

Of course, one might argue that according to standard hermeneutic theories, intelligence also comes afterward in the form of meaning; however, in response to this objection, the problem in this case is that intelligence always assumes, if not the same form, then a relatively finite number of forms that can be reduced to two: the form of significance, the form of sense or meaning. In hermeneutics, intelligence always assumes these forms that are already known in advance, and most importantly, can even exist regardless of their contents. This is why there can be so many interpretations of the same work or author (particularly in the case of Kafka): an existential Kafka, a Marxist Kafka, a psychoanalytic Kafka, a Jewish Kafka, a Christian Kafka, a new historicist Kafka, and a postcolonial Kafka. Despite the fact that all these interpretations vary with regard to the contents, the particular signs or statements that are included as the interpretative matter, the form of significance that concerns the Whole, the image of the work and of the author, or as we say, "the Meaning" as the overall form of intelligence that captures its sense, is relatively similar in all these theories, if not the same. It is ironic to see that Deleuze and Guattari's work has been received in some literature departments as "yet another interpretation" of Kafka, in the sense that it was strung up on the same tree along with every other major interpretation, an interpretation that moreover has been crucified repeatedly for its bad sense and its misreading of Kafka's works, for example, for not knowing the German well enough, for failing to pay attention to certain signs, for misunderstanding the word "minor" when everyone knows what Kafka was saying was "small" *(kleine)*. And yet, given the fact that it has been made to "work" like every other interpretation or hermeneutic theory of Kafka historically, one must question whether this is due to the reproductive nature of the tree or to some failure of Deleuze and Guattari's Kafka experiment? This will be the question that I will take up in this chapter.

Following the overall method of experimentation, therefore, let us then pursue the Kafka experiment by first paying close attention to how the process works. In doing so, we will attempt to follow the rules that were outlined in the introduction to *Rhizome* one year later, which I have earlier on reduced to 2 (or 2 + 1) for the sake of convenience:

> 1. The rhizome is reducible neither to the One nor to the multiple, but only presupposes a plane of consistency that constitutes its relative outside and current number of connections.
> 2. Thought can be connected at any point to any other point in an assemblage and is heterogeneous according to the nature of its signs.

It is important to point out again that *Rhizome* was written a year after *Kafka,* the work where they attempted to read Kafka together according to the principle of "anti-interpretation." Of course, this is just a guess on my part, based on year of publication; Deleuze and Guattari could have written both works at the same time, one work for each pair of hands, and *Rhizome* would constitute the method (or theory) of their practice of reading in the manner of a laboratory experiment. But this perfectly fits my earlier thesis, as well as the major principles I have already outlined above, because this would mean that the theory *(Rhizome)* actually comes after the practice *(Kafka)*. Theory always follows practice, which reverses the usual order presupposed in most theoretical models, where the theory comes first and already projects an image of the practice to follow. This is Deleuze and Guattari's stated critique of all hermeneutic theories, in particular, but also of the image of thought that is presupposed by "Theory," including Marxist literary theory, psychoanalytic theory, and most importantly, all linguistic theory and theories of language that already presuppose an image of actual statements and signs.

Consequently, if *Rhizome* is to be understood as the outline of a method that was first invented to read Kafka, then the fact that it appears a year later as an introduction to *A Thousand Plateaus,* very simply as a description of what they are doing in practice, then we might very well understand this later work as an "applied rhizomatics." Here, it is most important to realize that this order is inherently logical, in addition to simply following an empirical order of things, as in the logical order in any experimentation. First, you conduct the experiment according to certain rules or presuppositions that are constructed in the process of creating the experiment, and then you describe the outcome and report your findings, which are usually the basis for future experiments that will verify the findings. This is the simple empirical procedure that can also be found to determine the nature of the experimentation that Deleuze and Guattari propose between the Kafka experiment and the findings reported in *Rhizome,* which forms the condition of the other experiments performed in *A Thousand Plateaus* according to the same method. Each time, however, or within the instance of each experimental plateau (or *milieu*), the method will change depending on the number of planes and connections, because each plateau is a multiplicity that is constituted only by the number of connections; to subtract one is to change the nature of the multiplicity.

After defining the conditions of the experiment proper, let us determine then how it begins. As with any experiment, you begin with what is called a hypothesis, which is a theoretical presupposition of a different order than a hermeneutic presupposition. What is the hypothesis proposed as the condition of the Kafka experiment? In reading the first lines, we already find it there in the second sentence: "The work is a rhizome, a burrow."[5] This is the first appearance of the word "rhizome" in Deleuze and Guattari's philosophy, but again, because this word has already been overdetermined by subsequent readings that have locked in its significance, and in a certain sense have already interpreted this significance for Deleuze and Guattari's entire body of writings, at this point we must keep in mind that as readers, we do not know what a rhizome is, what it means, or more importantly, how it is to work. In other words, we must pose the question of the rhizome again without presupposing its meaning in order to maintain, even only theoretically, a certain condition of stupidity. At first, this approach might appear like something straight out of Beckett:

A: What is a rhizome? I have never seen or heard of one before.

B: I don't know, but I think it refers to some kind of grass, or weeds.

A: What's the difference between grass and weeds?

B: I don't know, really. Could be the same thing . . . a rose by any other name.

A: Are you saying that roses are, in fact, rhizomes?

B: Absolutely not, that's silly. They are flowers.

A: But why did you mention roses then?

B: I was speaking of metaphors.

A: Oh, but what does it have to do with Kafka?

B: I don't know, it's a very strange term, but these philosophers are particularly well known for their wild assertions, bizarre associations, and strange terms—Bodies without Organs, Desiring Machines, Schizophrenic Desire, Becoming-Woman, etc.

A: Sounds like a bunch of non-sense to me.

B: Make sense who may.

To be more precise with our terms, therefore, let us provide the botanical definition of rhizomes, since dictionaries and herbarium manuals existed when Deleuze and Guattari were writing and this would be an allowable move. Here, I offer the following definition from Wikipedia:

> Rhizome (from Greek: ῥίζωμα, rhizoma, "root-stalk") is a characteristically horizontal stem of a plant that is usually found underground, often sending out roots and shoots from its nodes. Rhizomes may also be referred to as creeping rootstalks, or rootstocks. In general, rhizomes have short internodes; they send out roots from the bottom of the nodes and new upward-growing shoots from the top of the nodes. *It is a method of asexual reproduction for plants.* A stem tuber is a thickened part of a rhizome or stolon that has been enlarged for use as a storage organ. In general, a tuber is high in starch, for

example, the common potato, which is a modified stolon. The term tuber is often used imprecisely, and is sometimes applied to plants with rhizomes. Some plants have rhizomes that grow above ground or that lie at the soil surface, including some Iris species, and ferns, whose spreading stems are rhizomes. Plants with underground rhizomes include ginger, bamboo, the Venus Flytrap, Chinese lantern, Western poison-oak, hops, and turmeric, and the weeds Johnson grass, bermuda grass, and purple nut sedge. Rhizomes generally form a single layer, but in Giant Horsetails, can be multi-tiered. Farmers and gardeners who propagate the plants by a process known as vegetative reproduction also use the rhizome. Examples of plants that are propagated this way include hops, asparagus, ginger, irises, Lily of the Valley, Cannas, and sympodial orchids.[6]

Even though we now know what the term "rhizome" means in botany and agriculture, this will not help us determine what the rhizome means in relation to Kafka, or how it pertains to writing and literature. For this, we will need a second term that established this connection. The second term is "burrow," which moreover establishes an equivalence or a literal connection: RHIZOME = BURROW. More specifically written, "This work is a Rhizome, a Burrow." As we know from reading Deleuze and Guattari's work where similar statements are made, the use of indefinite articles is always important; it implies that they are not speaking of a metaphorical equivalence, or simile, because the work is not said to be "like" by means of resemblance or analogy. Moreover, any reader of Kafka will already recognize this term as belonging to the work itself, particularly in the story "The Burrow," which is what allows them to establish this literal connection or equivalence, and then already to multiply its associations in referencing other places in Kafka's body of work and defining them as different kinds of burrows: *The Castle,* the ship and the hotel in *Amerika,* the series of rooms found to be adjacent to the courtroom in *The Trial*; basically, any place in Kafka's work that is described as having multiple exits and entrances. But the funny thing, which only the experienced reader of Kafka already knows, is that this pretty much describes every place in Kafka's work, because every room is always described as having doors by which one enters or leaves (or through which one is prevented from leaving) and windows for entering and leaving as well (or for looking through, either in the moment of being watched, like in the beginning and the end of *The Trial,* or in the dream of jumping out, as in "The Judgment").

Let us stop this train of associations and immediately call attention to something that occurs in the above equation: rhizome = burrow. Here we might notice that something is different, something not immediately apparent, which is added by the term "rhizome," and which in some way interprets the animal sign of the burrow to have a vegetable meaning, referring to the asexual manner of its reproduction. Thus, burrows are said to reproduce in Kafka's writings in the manner of underground rhizomes (e.g., ginger, the Venus Flytrap) or weeds (Johnson's grass, Bermuda grass). Where does this equivalence come from, since it appears as a forced equivalence or catachresis? This interpretation is not allowed by the machine that Deleuze and Guattari construct; it is a literal equivalence that, moreover, must already be part of the assemblage. Nevertheless, we must acknowledge that even though the second term ("a burrow") is readily apparent in Kafka, the origin of the first term of the equation ("a rhizome") is difficult to discern. Where does the term come from? As I have already argued, it comes from or is introduced by the description of the literary machine in Proust, and from the final description of the writing machine itself as partly vegetal and partly animal. I recall the following sentence offered in the conclusion of *Proust and Signs,* which I will return to discuss in greater detail below: "The *logos* is a huge Animal whose parts unite in a whole and are unified under a principle or a leading idea; but the pathos is a vegetal realm consisting of cellular elements that communicate only indirectly."[7] Thus, according to this reading, in some ways the rhizome can be understood as a foreign idea, or the introduction of a foreign sign that might even belong to another language, concerning a basic presupposition drawn from Deleuze's earlier understanding of the nature of the literary machine and how it functions. It is a sign plucked from Proust's web that is introduced into Kafka's burrow, creating the conditions of a hybrid construction. As we will see, this is not as frivolous as it might appear at first, because the very nature of the literary machine changes by adding a new connection and, thus, a new entrance into Kafka's work.

By the way, spiders create burrows too, so perhaps the equivalence is not so foreign. In Proust, we recall, the narrator is a spider who emits a spiderweb from his abdomen, the system of writing that determines the nature of the work. This already provides another presupposition: the figure of the narrator in Kafka is more likened to an animal who builds a vast burrow, a network of connecting subterranean passages for refuge and for safety, as well as for flight. The Kafka narrator is an animal that creates a burrow and lives somewhere in the center of it like the spider lives in its web. A burrow is a hole or tunnel dug into the ground by an animal to create a space suitable for habitation or temporary refuge, or as a byproduct of locomotion. Burrows provide a form of shelter against predation and exposure to the elements, so the burrowing way of life is quite popular among these animals. But, I might also say, among writers too! In other words, is this not the best definition of the modern writer: an animal who burrows into language and creates a subterranean system of signs for refuge and safety from external predators? Moreover, is this not the image that Kafka himself gave to his own writing system? In the letters, he escaped from family members and his fiancée, and even talks at some point of burrowing into Felice's underwear drawer and hiding among her pretty things. In the diaries, he found refuge in this system from how he was determined as an individual by family and society. In the stories and tales, he escaped from the condition of being human; in the novels, he escaped and found temporary refuge in hallways and passages between each chamber and adjoining room. *The Castle* is described as a giant burrow of passages in which there is no outside; this is one reason why K. cannot get to the Castle by walking across the surface of the earth in a single straight line; he must take the tunnel and enter through the circular labyrinth.

But what happens when a foreign spider is introduced into the web of another spider, when one writing system is combined with another, as in this case? In the first sense, introducing the Proustian spider into the Kafkaesque burrow provides us with two corollary but nevertheless competing images of the system of writing, two different literary machines that are combined in an equivalence: a rhizome, a burrow. This is the basic presupposition of the hypothesis that Kafka's literary machine must be found to work in some way that is equivalent to Proust's, but according to a different machinic set of rules that will determine the "style" of each work. Here I recall that in the conclusion of *Proust and Signs*, Deleuze defines style as precisely as "the unity of the work" that allows it to communicate and makes us communicate with it, by means of the machines that it organizes within each other. This communication is not interpretation and does not take the form of interpretation, which only grasps a meaning that is already there before our communication within the work. Thus, as Deleuze writes, it would be a kind of communication that would not be posited in principle (like the prejudice of "communication" in language), but rather "would result from the operation of machines and their detached parts, their non-communicating fragments."[8]

The connection to Proust's literary machine is important, because it provides an important condition of Deleuze and Guattari's particular approach to the question "What is literature?" Against those who would oppose this question on the basis of a prejudice concerning either author, or against a notion of modernist literature in general, they would defend themselves by saying that this already is a badly posed question, and that they are speaking only of a particular literary machine, in the same manner that one might refer to a particular "rhizome," or a particular "burrow." In any case, such objections are not that critical, because Deleuze and Guattari then go on to test their hypothesis by describing the components of the literary machine that works only in the case of Kafka's writings. For example, the Kafka machine *does* work, and it produces something fundamentally different from the Proustian machine, a different experience fabricated by a machinic production of impressions and signs. The first task, therefore, will be to create a diagram of the machine and determine its components. They begin simply, in the milieu of the burrow, Kafka's literary machine, making connections point by point. Here, we remember the first axiom of the rhizomatic method: any point can be connected to any other point whatsoever. Consequently, as they say, "We'll start with a modest way" with these two elements: the portrait or photo, and the bent head.

They begin in the exact middle of *The Castle* (the burrow), but these signs immediately proliferate and connect to other places in Kafka's work: the portrait of the woman in furs in Gregor's room in "The Metamorphosis," the bent head of the father in a porter's uniform in the same story. The portraits and photos in Kafka's work multiply, as does the bent head, which is also found in the diaries, the letters, and the novels. For example, in the diary entry that recounts the completion of his very first story, "The Judgment," Kafka describes himself as suddenly being able to straighten his own posture and sit straight; likewise, in "The Metamorphosis" the sister is finally able to stretch out her young body, to the family's great joy. Here we have a variation on the bent head posture, which also gives us more information on the subterranean tunnel system, which has low ceilings and is cramped, causing the characters to slouch down as if walking on all fours. Only in a place outside the burrow, which appears infrequently in Kafka's stories, can the characters stand up on two legs like human beings. Deleuze and Guattari write: "The head that straightens, the head that bursts through the roof or the ceiling, seems an answer to the bent head. We find it everywhere in Kafka."[9]

Here we are reminded of one of the principles of *Rhizome*: use only what is readily available and connect to it. Consequently, it is crucial to note that the "straightened head sign" is not immediately interpreted by Deleuze and Guattari (for example, as transcendence or liberation), because this would suppress the literal meaning and replace it with a symbolic value. There are associations, of course, but this has to do with the feeling of no longer being confined by a cramped space, or of stretching out to a point where the muscles are livened and a feeling of extreme pleasure fills the body with satisfaction, as in the passage from Kafka's diary about writing all night, hunched over in the writing chair at his desk, and then at the moment of completion, the feeling of raising one's arms and stretching. This sensation may very well express an intensity that also connects to political liberation; but without the literal connection to the body, its sign loses a specific intensity and becomes too abstract.

As in the case of reading Proust, the second step is to develop these multiple impressions into signs that will contain them and determine their expression. At first Deleuze and Guattari make the following hypothesis: "The straightened head is the form of content, and the musical sound is the form of expression."[10] Thus, the straightened head functions like a musical sound in Kafka's works, a refrain or ritornello in a Kafka symphony. It expresses something completely different from the bent head-portrait-photo, which functions by means of representation alone. But then, they immediately reject this hypothesis as being "not quite right." It is not about music as a semiotically formed substance, which would simply turn music into a metaphor. Therefore, "it isn't a composed and semiotically shaped music that interests Kafka, but rather a pure sonorous material."[11] What do they mean here? This is where most interpretations of Deleuze and Guattari's reading of Kafka go astray, and this will determine how the concepts they propose of a "minor literature," or of a "becoming minor," have become simply representative categories, like portrait-photos or snapshots of literary works that express the bent-head of the minority, ethnic, or postcolonial writer.

In responding to this question, they immediately go on to provide multiple examples of all the sounds they find in Kafka's writings—I will not list them all here—as if they are trying to classify and illustrate all the sounds an instrument can make without regard to playing a tune or a composition of music. Listen to the instrument itself, they say. What noises does it make? What are the possible sounds that define it? What are the sonorous qualities? Here we discover the question of style in contrast to the Proustian literary machine, which is defined as a telescope for viewing into ourselves; Kafka's literary machine is a kind of musical instrument and this will define what it produces, as well as the difference in style. Different musical instruments produce distinctive sonorous qualities that will determine their distinctiveness. A guitar or a banjo expresses different sonorous qualities than a violin or a trombone. Is this a good way of defining style in writing as well? Moreover, in listening to Kafka, in trying to determine the distinctive sounds that will characterize this particular writing machine, Deleuze and Guattari find a distinctive sound that appears like a low humming that is "generally monotone and always non-signifying." It is this sound that one can hear beneath Gregor's voice and equally in Josephine's song. "In short," they write, "sound doesn't show up here as a form of expression, but as an unformed material of expression, that will act on the other terms."[12] But is this not merely noise, or rather silence, someone might ask? No, because noise already presupposes music, just as silence presupposes language as a semiotically formed substance. Their argument is that in Kafka the material of writing, and perhaps writing alone, is capable of emitting this particular sound as an unformed material of expression, and this sound defines Kafka's literary machine more than any other characteristic or quality.

Now that we have defined this sound particular to Kafka's literary machine, the sound of an unformed material of expression, let us now turn to the concept of minor literature to see how this sound turns up there. Here we are not seeking to interpret what the sound means, but simply to test Deleuze and Guattari's hypothesis that what this sound expresses is essential to their method of reading Kafka. Again, "only expression gives us the method." In the chapter on the question "What is a minor literature?" we find this sound immediately connected to what they define as "collective assemblages of enunciation." In a certain manner this connection already makes sense, because the question of minor literature is attached to the expression of a people, that is, to an unformed material of expression (i.e., a collective enunciation that is missing). Here we remember that language is already described as a deterritorialized sound that is then reterritorialized in the form of sense (i.e., semiotically formed expression), which is both physical and abstract (or symbolic). Language shapes the mouth as much as it defines a form of expression as a collective unity of a language. The modern writer enters into this reterritorialized sense in order to discover new means of expression in this relationship. In fact, the entire chapter on minor literature turns out to be a treatise on linguistics, or an anti-linguistic theory, based on what writers actually do in language, and certain writers more than others. Artaud and Céline are given as examples of "minor writers" in the French language. What is it exactly that these writers share with Kafka? What is their method of creating a minor literature, each in his own situation and respective language?

Again we come back to this sound, the sound of an unformed material of expression that is connected to a collective assemblage of enunciation: Artaud's scream, Céline's obscenity. If it sounds here like I'm just stringing phrases together, it is only because I am trying to remain on the literal level of the descriptions that are given and not trying to interpret them immediately, saying this sound means that symbol or its equivalent. At this point, however, we must come back to the concrete situation of the writer. What is each writer trying to express, if not a certain need to escape the situation of a major language defined by previous literatures, by a previous generation of writers, to cause the art to progress by means of finding new expression that is invented from unformed materials and sounds (unarticulated blocks of expression and memory alike). In this regard, writers and musicians progress in the same fashion using different materials. In creating new music, musicians seek to deterritorialize previous musical forms, often by introducing what might sound at first like unarticulated blocks of sound. Why would literature progress any differently? Introducing into language what might initially appear as unarticulated blocks of expression into root language, creating new semiotically formed substances. According to Deleuze and Guattari, this is precisely what Kafka did: "He will pull from it the barking of a dog, the cough of an ape, and the bustling of a beetle. He will turn syntax into a cry that will embrace the rigid syntax of this dried up German."[13]

Nevertheless, one might ask, "How is this at all revolutionary?" as modern literature is so often assumed to be. In other words, how do we connect these distinctive sounds to the conditions of collective enunciation? If the form of expression alone is revolutionary, as in the case of much modern music or art, this does not immediately lead to a change in the form of content, just as the pure sonorous quality of a "straightened head" does not immediately cause the subject to become liberated. It is for this reason that much of the innovations of modern art and literature appear too abstract, too intellectual, too "modernist," and the real problem that Deleuze and Guattari are addressing is how to connect these technical and formal innovations to the level of contents and to the collective assemblages of enunciation that determine these contents. This, in fact, is the same question that Sartre asked in "What Is Political Literature?," although Deleuze and Guattari's answer will be quite different, as I will show in chapter 4.

The image presupposed by many of the critical representations of modern literature, and presupposed even more today in relation to what is called minority writing, is an image that expresses the relationship between the form of expression and the form of content either as being immanent to a collective subject or as distorting or concealing this immanent relationship, as in much of Marxist criticism of literature. Deleuze and Guattari were not writing in a vacuum and they were certainly aware of these critical representations of modern literature, as well as of certain modern writers such as Kafka in particular. The question they ask is: How do modern literary works communicate, and how do they become "a concern of the people"? The answer they give at first is: not very well. Modernist works, especially, have been trapped by stale and purely formal innovations of expression, regardless of the differences in content. But here is the point: the matter for the writer is to liberate expression, to create new possibilities through unformed material, and not at first to liberate the subject as it is defined elsewhere by collective assemblages of enunciation. There has been an unrealistic demand placed on the modern writer, one that distorts the real situation of writing itself by making it already a transcendent or mythical portrait of the social situation of the subject. They write:

> We find ourselves not in front of a structural correspondence
> between two sorts of forms, forms of content and forms of expres-
> sion, but rather in front of an expression machine capable of disorga-
> nizing its own forms . . . in order to liberate pure contents that mix
> with expressions in a single intense matter. . . . Since content is
> presented in a given form of content, one must find, discover, or see
> the form of expression that goes with it. That which conceptualizes
> well expresses itself. But a minor, or revolutionary, literature begins
> by expressing itself and doesn't conceptualize until afterward ("I do
> not see the word, I invent it").[14]

In other words, as in the case of the principle of the rhizome, they begin, not by theorizing the situation of modern literature as a whole, like Marxist theory, but rather by describing literally the components of expression that belong to Kafka's work, in order to connect form to content, and the literary machine to real collective assemblages of enunciation. When Kafka was writing, the Czech people faced a situation similar to the situation Kafka faced as a writer. A writer faces a real situation that is fundamentally the same as the situation of a people, and this situation cannot be defined by representation. A writer does not seek to "represent" a people; this critical presupposition very much distorts the nature of the literary process, of the writing machine and how it works. Consequently, "living and writing, art and life, are opposed only from the point of view of a major literature."[15] Deleuze and Guattari, on the other hand, provide another definition of what the writer and the people share—a line of escape. Each, in their own way, and using whatever means that are available to them, whatever means that they can invent, to escape their own situation: the writer attempts to escape the situation in which a previous generation of writers and a previous major literature determines her as a "writer"; a minority seeks to escape the situation of being a collective subject defined by a major form (a nation, a class, a race, etc.). Here, the situation faced by so-called minority writers and by minority peoples is ever more evident, but the means of escape that centers around the invention of a new means of expression in each case is also evident. The situation of "becoming minor" defines both the writer and the people in a mutual effort to escape the definition of a major form. Writers are oppressed by their own major forms, which determine them as writing subjects, no less than a collective subject is oppressed by the major forms that determine its own particular situation as subjects, in yet a different sense and according to a different regime of what Deleuze and Guattari will call "order words" *(mots d'ordre)*. However, these two situations, or two states of being a subject, are not the same; most importantly, *one situation should not be taken as a metaphor of the other,* as has been done in the history of modern literary interpretation.

Throughout the preceding discussion I have argued that the development (if not evolution) of the concept of the literary machine must be understood as the combination of two specific literary machines: the complex vegetal *logos* of Proust and the burrow or animal *logos* of Kafka. Let us now explore a subterranean and common theme that links these two machines together and gives them a social function. The theme is guilt, which is present in both authors' works to different degrees and according to different subthemes. Nevertheless, for both writers the theme of guilt is only apparent and in some ways hides or conceals a more profound meditation. In other words, in both Kafka and Proust we find only an apparent and statistical guilt of the subject, which has not yet been internalized. In Proust's case, the apparent guilt of being a homosexual and the statistical guilt of being a member of "an accursed race"; in Kafka, the apparent guilt of being a bachelor and the statistical guilt of being a Jew living in the Hapsburg monarchy. The theme of guilt, however, in both cases is immediately linked to the form of the Law; in one case it is only apparently the Law of the Father that condemns the son and bachelor as a guilty member of the family; in the other case, it appears as a sexual law that condemns the homosexual as guilty of belonging to another species. "In Proust," Deleuze writes, "the theme of guilt remains superficial, social rather than moral, projected onto other persons by the narrator, rather than internalized within the narrator himself."[16] In Kafka one might find that the opposite is true, but again this is equally superficial and only apparent; Kafka's narrators often begin in a position of apparent guilt (which, as in the case of Proust, is only statistical and formal guilt) but have yet to internalize its image or its sentence. This progression is evident from the very first story, "The Judgment," which begins with the apparent guilt of Georg, who is "avoiding the reality of his own dependence and failure" by displacing this onto his imaginary friend, and ends with the Father's revelation of this self-deception and a sentence of death by drowning. However, in both cases the law appears only in response to a particular problem, of a world devoid of *Logos*, no reference to the Good, composed only of fragments of a totality that is no longer whole, and so it becomes identified in each case with a process of violently forcing these fragments into place. It is only in this context that the depressive and the schizoid (or paranoid) position of the writer takes on a larger social and political meaning as concrete responses to the condition of the law.

The question we need to answer is why the writer is so often represented subjectively from either a depressive or a paranoid-schizoid position in society, as if to answer the question of why the writer appears strangely apart or separated from the social (the condition of a "bachelor").[17] Returning again to *Proust and Signs,* Deleuze makes the following claim concerning the relationship of Kafka and Proust:

> Modern consciousness of the law assumed a particularly acute form with Kafka: it is in "The Great Wall of China" that we find a fundamental link between the fragmentary character of the wall, the fragmentary mode of its construction, and the unknowable character of the law, its determination identical to the punishment of

guilt. In Proust, however, the law presents another figure, because guilt is more like an appearance that conceals a more profound fragmentary reality, instead of being itself this more profound reality to which the detached fragments lead us. The depressive consciousness of the law as it appears in Kafka is countered in this sense by the schizoid consciousness of the law according to Proust.[18]

Moreover, we will find a similar formulation of this relationship in *Anti-Oedipus,* written around the same period as the above passage: "In Kleinian terms, it might be said that the depressive position is only a cover-up for a more deeply rooted schizoid position."[19]

I have already argued that Deleuze and Guattari's concept of the literary machine was historically an amalgamation of two specific literary machines, those of Kafka and Proust. Around the theme of guilt and the law we see the secret affiliation and even the patch of code that connects them together precisely as one machine. Kafka's machine functions only from an apparent and all-too-visible depressive formation with regard to the fragmentary construction and the unknowable character of the law, that is to say, as a "cover-up" for the more profound reality discovered by Proust—for whom, Deleuze and Guattari write,

> the rigors of the law are only an apparent protest of the One, whereas their real object is the absolution of the fragmented universes, in which the law never unites things in a single Whole, but on the contrary maps out the divergences, the dispersions, the exploding into fragments of something that is innocent precisely because its source is madness.[20]

Therefore, once this secret code is established in place as the interpretation of the literary machine, around the period of *Anti-Oedipus* and then later on in *Kafka,* it even appears as if Kafka occupies or produces both positions and emits both the depressive and the schizoid series in relationship to the modern form of the law. Thus, in *Anti-Oedipus* Deleuze and Guattari write:

> The two features that Kafka so forcefully developed [are]: first, the paranoiac-schizoid trait of the law (metonymy) according to which

the law governs nontotalizable and nontotalized parts, portioning them off, organizing them as bricks, measuring their distance and forbidding their communication; henceforth acting in the name of a formidable but formal and empty Unity, eminent, distributive and not collective; and second, the maniacal depressive trait (metaphor) according to which the law reveals nothing and has no knowable object, the verdict having no existence prior to the penalty, and the statement of the law having no existence prior to the verdict.[21]

However, three years later in *Kafka*, we discover this statement that returns again to the paradigmatic status of "The Great Wall of China," showing how a paranoid unity ultimately resolves into a schizoid form of unlimited fragments, which is the form of the rhizome:

Paranoid law gives way to schizo-law: immediate resolution gives way to unlimited deferral; the transcendence of duty in the social field gives way to the immanence of desire that wanders all over this field. This is made explicit in "The Grate Wall of China," without being developed in any way: there are nomads who give evidence of another law, another assemblage, and who sweep everything in their journey from the frontier to the capitol, the emperor and his guards having taken refuge behind the windows and screens. *Thus, Kafka no longer operates by means of infinite-limited-discontinuous but by finite-contiguous-continuous-unlimited.*[22]

In commenting on the above passage, let us first recall now that in the last chapter I showed how proper names function in Deleuze and Guattari's works as signs indicating sometimes their own names or positions. In this case, we see the coupling of the overt depressive position with the covert schizoid position—that is, *the machinic coupling of the unconscious positions of Deleuze and Guattari!* It is not in the self or the individual, but only in the machine they construct together, that an unconscious position can be produced in this manner, that is, in the same manner that Deleuze earlier describes in terms of the rigorous distribution of the general form of madness between the different characters in Proust's *Recherche*. One can only imagine, in Deleuze and Guattari's case, that this manner of producing the unconscious is liberating with regard to the poles that each one is assigned as an individual or a person: the paranoid-schizoid (Guattari) and the depressive (Deleuze). In this sense we might now understand the Kafka who appears in the works written together several years later, which can be defined precisely as the production of a *new Kafka,* expressed in the work as *a depressive position with a schizoid attitude.* (Simply put, they produce this "Kafka" by applying the first principle of the rhizome: "subtract the One.") This will also be my formula for reading the "becoming-revolutionary" proposed by Deleuze and Guattari: to liberate the modernist writer from his apparent and statistical depressive position by giving him a schizoid attitude. As I will try to show in chapter 4, this formula will have profound implications for contemporary literary machines as well, particularly those of so-called minority writers, and for the interpretation of the concept of a "minor literature," since it will be necessary to link the schizoid position to the collective image of a people. We need to remember the disjunctive synthesis of the two viewpoints: the depressive viewpoint hides or conceals the schizoid, which always seems to be lurking behind or just underneath the appearance of the first; consequently, the people will be found to occupy this schizoid position as well, just underneath the surface offered by the depressed and individual writer.[23]

In concluding my reading of *Kafka: Toward a Minor Literature,* I would simply suggest that perhaps this is the very precise meaning of "grass" (the rhizome) in their first sentence: "The work is a rhizome, a burrow." In other words, it is precisely the schizoid element of a Proustian machine that is detached and now mobile—which is the literal meaning of a schiz-flow—by being forcefully connected to the Kafka machine (of infinite debt and guilt) in order to produce a desired effect or product: *an a priori innocence in place of a priori guilt.* Of course, Deleuze and Guattari can be accused of constantly overstating their case, as in the catachresis of rhizome = burrow, even to the point of intentional misinterpretation; I would call it simply anti-interpretation. In other words, it is simply not true that the entire history of Kafka criticism got Kafka wrong around the themes of infinite or transcendental guilt and even the elements of theology that are certainly present throughout his works. In Deleuze and Guattari's schizoid version of the depressive Kafka, this often leads to wild and unsupportable reversals and the most bombastic statements, and even the most hysterical accusations against Kafka's interpreters, as in the case of the blame against Max Brod for organizing the sections of *The Trial* so that "the Cathedral" appears at the end, followed by the execution of K., rather than in the beginning or as a fitful dream that interrupts K.'s investigation. "Thus," they write, "we must follow the movement of The Trial at several levels, taking account of objective uncertainty about the supposed last chapter and of the uncertainty of the second-to-last chapter, 'In the Cathedral' was more or less poorly placed by Max Brod."[24]

As in the example of the passage above, Deleuze and Guattari's entire reading (I would prefer to call it "production") could be called patently artificial, mechanistically contrived, a fabrication, a pure construction. As I have tried to demonstrate, if there is any interpretation, it is intimately related to a foreign idea imported into Kafka's work from the earlier construction of Proust's literary machine that occurs in Deleuze's work and also in the many references to Proust that appear in *Anti-Oedipus*. Moreover, Proust and Kafka are two authors who have little in common, or only apparently have nothing in common, until they are connected together in *Kafka* in much in the same way that a wasp is connected to the orchid through a transversal and machine dimension in which the two parts combine to produce a whole that nevertheless remains an additional part. In Proust, the fragments are arranged in noncommunicating vessels or blocks, like sections of a spider's web, and the consciousness of the narrator is produced alongside these fragments in a manner that does not unify them in one vision. The spider is blind and can only feel the entire expanse of the web through its body; it feels the unity of all the fragments it has connected together in its great-expanded body, but this is produced not as a vision of the whole but only as a distinct perception of fragments that come near. The spider-narrator sits in the corner of its web and waits for the next "sign" of its prey, which must then be distinguished from all the other signs that disturb the web and cause it to tremble, like the falling leaves or drops of rain.

In other words, the Proustian narrator is a sedentary being: all the world literally approaches in order to be spun into his web (hence the description of the narrative consciousness as the view from the window of the train in which the landscape forms a whole that is continuous yet made up of noncommunicating posits of view that do not refer to the position of the narrator for their unity). Secondly, the Proustian narrator is immanent to the work and is always producing and adding new parts in the manner in which a spider builds its web, or, according to the vegetal metaphor, in the manner in which grass expands its territory in a constant patchwork. Thus, it seems silly to ask what is the unity of grass in the sense of relating a center to a periphery as in an animal organism; in the same way, it would appear silly to ask what is the unity or central perspective, or episode, that unifies the *Recherche*.

Let us return again to the key passage from *Proust and Signs*:

> The *logos* is a huge Animal whose parts unite in a whole and are unified under a principle or leading idea; but pathos is a vegetal realm consisting of cellular elements that communicate only indirectly, only marginally, so that no totalization, no unification, can unite this world of ultimate fragments.[25]

The image of the vegetal realm in this passage is a perfect description of grass, of the rhizome. Deleuze writes earlier on, "It is no accident that the model of the vegetal in Proust has replaced that of the animal totality, as much in the case of art as in that of sexuality."[26] In Kafka, on the other hand, the vegetal realm of the rhizome is also a "burrow," which is to say a vegetal realm with the animal-*logos* concealed inside. Consequently, it is precisely this tension between the construction of the animal-*logos* as a whole that is unified under a leading image of the Law (as in *The Trial*, and particularly the fables that appear as episodes in the unfinished novel, such as "The Message from the Emperor" and "In the Cathedral"), and the vegetal image of the rhizome, which in Kafka can describe the infinite succession of blocks or series that are not totalizable by the first principle (as in the example of "The Great Wall of China," but also in *The Castle*). This will constitute the specific tension that Deleuze and Guattari will seek to exaggerate and make more evident everywhere in their reading of Kafka writings: the vegetal proliferation of series and blocks to replace the animal-*logos* and the image of totality, much like the bricks and pieces that compose the unfinished Great Wall of China. However, I think it is crucial to notice that it is Proust, rather than Kafka, who provides the intuition of a method for producing the multiplicity from a Whole that is produced alongside each of the parts, even though a Whole neither totalizes nor unifies all the parts into the One.

Also, it is not by accident that, for example, Deleuze and Guattari very early on seek to discover the positive reality of the child's relation to the world of partial objects, and that this relation is primarily defined as machinic, or in purely machinic terms, keeping in mind that certain machines function by exploding as much as organizing a flow of energy into a productive continuum. Likewise, it is not by accident that Deleuze and Guattari also find that certain writers choose an intense curiosity with the positive discovery of the power contained in partial objects to reorganize the whole, as if these objects were capable of storing the energy of creation itself. What is Proust's *madeleine,* for example, but a partial object of this type, and moreover, a desiring machine that is connected by means of the mouth? Although the very first pages of *Anti-Oedipus* begin with the example of the partial object derived from Beckett, that of Molloy's "sucking stones," it is often completely misunderstood. The relation between the sucking stone and the partial object derived from the mother's body is even offered up as a joke at the very beginning of the novel (recalling here that Beckett was also analyzed by Melanie Klein). The mother's breast is dried up—she is either dead or merely desiccated, only her senile head remains—the sexes have been replaced by a series of more primary couples, all of which differ only by a detachment of a chain of associations (Molloy, Malone, Mahood, Moran, etc.). The literary machine often has as its goal the discovery of more primary couples, detached from the parents and even from the secondary sexual couples; thus, as we have also seen in Proust and Kafka, Beckett always discovers behind each couple a more primary couple that is nonfamilial and thus completely innocent. That is to say, *innocent a priori before the Law.*

The thinker and the writer (and in a certain sense the masochist) are united in their goal of producing a more primary couple, and the problem for each is to construct a mode of the couple in thought without sinking back into the puerile associations and clichéd assertions "about" sexuality, which only construct a way of thinking the couple or even of becoming a couple via castration (separation, sexual division, lack, extrinsic relationship between desire and its object). Thus, throughout

Deleuze and Guattari's work there is always this tendency of the writer to begin or to affirm the position of the bachelor, or of the thinker to begin from a depressed position of solitude, just as the masochist must begin from a perverse position at least with regard to the Oedipal organization of sexuality and "human desire." (Kafka offers us the most unique example of all three positions: depressive, schizophrenic, and the masochist.) But is this any different from those who begin or seek to begin again on the plane composed by their own sexuality, to become thinkers and artists, just as often as they become strangers and refugees (if not perverts and criminals, as in the case of Genet)? And yet, on the basis of the above dialectic, the path via sexuality is never the final answer and more often than not leads to sadness and failure, because the sexual pair always obstructs the more primary couple, and sooner or later becomes an image or simulacrum that blocks any access to this couple, since it is only a superficial path on the way to the primary social division: that of the species and an entire humanity.

4

A MINOR QUESTION OF LITERATURE, OR THE BACHELOR MACHINE (CA. 1975)

- "Between 'the Writer' and 'a People'"
- "What Is Writing?"
- "Why Write?"
- "For Whom Does One Write?"

—For Fredric Jameson

In the previous chapters I have covered, more or less, the "objective determinations" of the literary machines we have found to be working at the basis of Deleuze and Guattari's own collaborative project—that is, basically, the writing machine that they themselves were attempting to construct by borrowing different components from the literary machines of Kafka and Proust. Now, I would like to turn to "the subjective determination" of the agent *(agent)* that belongs to this assemblage *(agencement)*—who is often colloquially referred to as the writer. We recall that Kafka's literary machine (a burrow) was described as the hybrid of a vegetal system with an animal-*logos* either trapped or hiding inside. What are the subjective determinations of this strange animal-*logos* who dwells in a system of writing—or as Guattari says, "a machine," or a "written device"—and who, as in Proust, may not be said to actually exist otherwise?[1] This could be likened to the consciousness of the narrator in the *Recherche*, which Deleuze describes as being rigorously distributed among all the characters, thus producing the conditions of multiplicity, or a "polyvalent" collective assemblage of enunciation. It is on the basis of this discovery that Deleuze and Guattari will deny that there is anything like individual enunciation in Proust, and later in Kafka—perhaps in all literature, for that matter! No individual, no person. The animal we are trying to determine is already a multiplicity, or what they will call a "collective assemblage of enunciation." Therefore, it is around the subjective determination of the "being who writes," the animal that they identify as "a bachelor," and an objective determination of writing as "a collective assemblage of enunciation" *(agencement collectif d'énunciation),* that we must now turn to the question of what they call "minor literature," which in some way already presupposes this relationship, even though it has been badly understood.

In *Kafka: Toward a Minor Literature,* the argument that Deleuze and Guattari employ for determining this relationship, or this supposed equivalence between a writer and a people, is contained in the following description: "A machine that is all the more social and collective insofar as it is solitary, a bachelor, and that, tracing the line of escape, is equivalent in itself to a community whose conditions haven't yet been established."[2] In other words, the question "What is a minor literature?" already invokes the presupposed relationship that exists between the "writer" and a specific community, or "people," either formally or linguistically defined; determined by nationality, class experience, ethnicity or race, gender or sexuality; or with another kind of community *(Bund)* whose conditions of collectivity have not yet been established according to any of the terms above. Perhaps these conditions have been lost, according to a Marxian or postcolonial understanding (along with unfortunate echoes of a fascist or neonationalist understanding as well); or perhaps these conditions do not exist in the present because they belong, as Deleuze and Guattari often say, "to a people who are missing" (which, as we will see, does not presuppose that these conditions ever existed in the past and later succumbed to collective amnesia, historical loss, or political destruction). The formulas of a "solitary bachelor" and "a people who are missing" will be the subjects that preoccupy me in this chapter: who, or rather what, is a bachelor? Where are these people? Most importantly, how can literature (or writing) help us find these people, if it does not simply come down to a manner of creating them *with* literature, or *through* writing? Finally, can literature (alone) produce (or establish) the conditions of a people who can exist?

When posed in this manner, at first these questions might appear somewhat fantastical. Are we speaking about a purely fictional people, like Swift's invention of the Lilliputians, Brobdingnagians, and the Houyhnhnms? Are we speaking of a kind of people as a species of aliens who often appear in the genre science fiction—a purely utopian and enlightened folk who are missing only because humans are too barbarian? Both of these inventions (or "fabulations") entertain an essential relation to the notion of "a people" that appears in modern criticism. In fact, most criticism begins by presupposing a direct relationship between the "writer" and "a people," even though this relationship is never actually established as the condition of literary enunciation itself. *All criticism is still too theoretical on this question,* especially "political interpretation." But is this any different from the most common language acts? For example, I'm in a "foreign country" (let's say Korea), and I make the statement "I am an American" (in English, of course). In what way can it be established that the American literary tradition (e.g., Emerson, Hawthorne, Thoreau, Melville, Whitman, Crane, Faulkner, Cather, Salinger, Morrison, Pynchon, DeLillo—of course, I am leaving out important writers) has anything to do with the sense of this statement (*énoncé*)? This is not so easy to establish, but it is difficult to rule out altogether. Even if my Korean interlocutor has not read a word of Melville, for example, there may be an implicit, *yet nevertheless indiscernible,* connection between the statement "I am an American" and the statement "Call me Ishmael," or Bartleby's "I am not particular." In fact, the contemporary writer does not have to be born into the language and culture to create the possibility of collective enunciation, and not *for* minorities alone, because many of our best writers today often arrive from elsewhere, which is one of the defining conditions of what Deleuze and Guattari call a "minor literature." As they ask: "How many people today live in a language that is not their own? Or no longer, or not yet, even know their own and know poorly that major language that they are forced to serve?"[3]

Nevertheless, let us state again (once more!) that the presupposed relationship between the so-called writer and a, more or less, absent or missing people has attained the status of a myth that determines what is called "modern literature," a myth that, in the contemporary period, has become a pure and empty form of representation. Deleuze and Guattari state from the very beginning that this relationship should not—must not!—be understood in representational terms; a writer does not represent a people according to a dominant modernist representation of the writer as the authentic creator of national consciousness in exile, nor in the quasi-elective and public social function assigned to certain writers who are assumed to represent minority or subaltern experience (even though this experience is almost always addressed to a majority viewpoint). As Deleuze argues concerning the relationship between literature and life, "To write is certainly not to impose a form (of expression) on a lived content."[4] This is because literature (apart from other kinds of written expression) always involves a *becoming* that surpasses the lived experience of the writer determined as a subject or an individual; therefore, in order to further clarify the often misunderstood refrain, "the vocation of a writer is to create a language for a people who is missing," Deleuze will return later to add "not in place of" but rather "to the attention of . . ." in the sense of a "carbon copy recipient" (cc:) of an official document or public listserv.[5]

Following this understanding, I would suggest that there is a closer relationship than might be believed between Deleuze-Guattari's conception of the writer and Sartre's earlier response to the question "For Whom Does One Write?" Even though their respective methods of responding to this question are no doubt different, what Deleuze and Guattari call "minor literature," on the one hand, and what Sartre defined as "a literature of commitment," on the other, will be shown to bear a certain commonality in determining the conditions of collective enunciation. For example, the tenuous status of the relationship between the individual act of writing and what Deleuze and Guattari call "collective enunciation" can be thought in relation to the problem Sartre invoked in *Search for a Method* with his famous example of the black airman in World War II: a mechanic who works on fighter planes because he is ineligible to become a pilot (no doubt due to his race), who therefore steals a plane and flies into France, only to end up dying in a plane crash because he does not know how to fly.[6] The meaning of this act, of course, has only an indirect relation to the general situation of the colonized as Sartre defines it: "The general revolt on the part of all colored men against colonists is expressed in him by this particular refusal of this prohibition." However, the means of expressing his revolt is not immediately given in the insane act of stealing an airplane without even knowing how to fly it, in order to die in a nationalist war for the same colonialists he is supposedly rebelling against. As Guattari writes in his 1969 essay "Machine and Structure," "It is, in fact, impossible to systematize the real discourse of history, the circumstances that cause a particular phase or a particular signifier to be represented by a particular event or social group, by the emergence of an individual or a discovery, or whatever."[7] Consequently, even though no one can deny that this black airman's "suicidal act" is real, and that it therefore belongs to the "discourse of history," this act represented, not a general revolt on the part of all the colonized, but only a specific and individual refusal of his status as a subject that informs his "desire to fly" (and in some ways, this choice even seems perfectly Kafkaesque, much like the desire to become "a red Indian" in one of Kafka's fables). As Sartre writes, "this political position, of which he doubtless has no clear awareness, he lives as a personal obsession: aviation becomes his possibility and clandestine future."[8]

As a second point of comparison with Deleuze and Guattari's choice of Kafka as the author who will provide them with the blueprint for the "becoming-revolutionary" of literature, let us also recall Sartre's manner of posing the same problem by championing, through what he defined as a "progressive and regressive method," the most unlikely figure of Flaubert, the petty Bourgeois, who chose as his response a style of "Becoming-Woman" (in the famous example of "I am Madame Bovary"). As Sartre writes concerning Flaubert's project,

> This project has a meaning, it is not the simple negativity of flight; by it a man aims at the production of himself in the world as a certain objective totality. It is not the pure and abstract decision to write which makes up the peculiar quality of Flaubert, but the decision to write in a certain manner in order to manifest himself in the world in a particular way; in a word, it is the particular signification—within

the framework of the contemporary ideology—which he gives to literature as the negation of his original condition and as the objective solution to his contradictions.[9]

In this passage from Sartre, and also in Kafka, the question of "style" emerges as the single criterion for determining the "becoming revolutionary" of the writer; one might even say, in the case of Deleuze and Guattari, *style is equated with becoming.* It is, as Jameson will say later on, the "idea" (the "image" of the act itself), which later acquires a particular signification in the framework of an Ideology (e.g., modernism). However, the original "idea" (or image of thought) cannot be immediately reduced to an ideological expression, just as the idea of flying an airplane cannot be deduced from the general situation of all colonized. In this regard, Fredric Jameson was absolutely correct in his observation that the cases of Proust and Kafka (as well as other early modernist writers like Joyce and Durrell) are absolutely singular because there was no pre-given model or archetype for connecting the political and social subjectivity to the means of writing as a response to "an impossible situation":

> The first modernists had to operate in a world in which no
> acknowledged or codified social role existed for them and in which
> the very form and concept of their own specific "works of art" were
> lacking. . . . Such imitation was unavailable to the classical modernists,
> whose works designate their process of production as an analogical
> level of allegory, in order to make a place for themselves in a world
> which does not contain their "idea"; this formal auto-referentiality is
> then utterly different from the poems about poetry and novels about
> artists in which the late-modernists designate themselves in their
> content.[10]

For Jameson, this singularity accounts for the "singularity" of these original writers, as opposed to the late-modernist writers (like Beckett and Nabokov), whom he seems to discount where the vocation of the modernist writer in exile was already a cliché. Singularity, as opposed to particularity, is a word that I will return to discuss later in this chapter.

Of course, today the situation of "becoming a writer" is somewhat different from what it was for Flaubert, because its social meaning is

already given in advance as one possible objective solution to one's contradictions, which in some ways already limits this activity's significance because it is already too meaningful. In other words, the project
of becoming a writer has a meaning even before it is actually a project of
writing, or before the question of whether the particular work has merit
is even raised. In the case of a younger generation of minority writers,
where the vocation of the writer is already invested with a social and political value, this determines the meaning of this particular activity in
advance—even to the point of providing a prejudicial response to the
question "For whom does one write?" to apply to every particular case of
"minority writing." Where the model is already too determining of the
specific activity, the whole meaning of writing is often reduced to becoming a one-dimensional and clichéd matter of representation (allegory), and thus the question of style (what Jameson defines as signification
of an "idea" within the contemporary framework of ideology), as well as
the question concerning the specific circumstance (what most cultural
critics today call either "context" or "history"), is completely lost in a presupposition that never explains the real reason a subject chooses to write
as a peculiar means of both taking flight from and, at the same time, specifically engaging his or her particular situation (whether or not this situation is defined in sexual terms, ethnic terms, or in some other manner
yet to be identified by criticism as worthy of being called "political" today).

As a criterion by which many works of literature are selected to be
brought before an already specialized public and the court of professional and academic opinion, the "political" already names a value that
infuses the work with a ready-made signification, even when these significations are yet to be released from the work's blank volume. These
significations are usually released by the critic whose official role in the
process is to identify what is worthy of being expressed and valued,
worthy enough to be repeated and extrapolated within the critic's own
text. But this process usually obscures the criterion by which the writers
first choose to select certain themes (even when the theme is the act of
writing itself!), or choose to construct particular characters in a fiction
(when we are speaking of fiction and not of poetry), or, as Deleuze and
Guattari often describe one of the goals of this process, to produce certain particle signs and expressions that refer to purely intensive states of

being—"to make the sequences vibrate, to open the word unto unexpected internal intensities."[11] In short, the original meaning of the idea of style, which is often "to create an a-signifying and intensive utilization of language," is completely lost in the representation of its signification *for* the critic. Certainly, not all writers have a style, and it is obvious that most writers do not have any idea what they are doing, which is why relatively few writers manage to achieve this "becoming."[12] (As Deleuze will ask later, is this state of exception any different in any of the other arts, including philosophy, which is "the art of creating concepts"?) In other words, the mere act of writing, or of becoming a writer, is no guarantee that the process will be successful in producing new intensive states and subjective qualities.

In the case of "minority writers," therefore, we come back to the objective determination of the act of writing, which always precedes the subjective determination itself in every particular case, or the writer's own "idea" as Jameson defined it in the passage quoted above. If the meaning of this specific activity has become too abstract, it is because the answers to the questions "What is writing?" and "Why write?" and the representational framework in which the literature is read already gives "for whom one writes" in advance, and thus the content has already been abstracted and is immediately criticized for not being specific enough (i.e., the meaning and value of the work are given before the actual work itself). Of course, Sartre is right to point out that it is not the more or less abstract decision to write, but rather the decision to write in a certain manner, that constitutes the primary criterion for discerning the question of style (in Flaubert's case, the style of "Becoming-Woman," which is not simply a matter of "writing like women write" or even "writing as a woman") as one of how the subject of writing constitutes a movement that is both away from and toward the given situation of being a subject in other respects. In their reply to these questions, Deleuze and Guattari will argue that the statements emitted by a literary machine do not refer back to the individual subject; therefore, according to Deleuze and Guattari's major thesis concerning what they define as a "minor literature," the more singular the writer's expression becomes, the more the relationship between the writer and a people (in this case always meaning a virtual people) will become an intensive zone of mutual becoming, particularly in the way that new literary statements are sometimes taken up to express new possibilities of collective enunciation. Moreover, such a becoming is not of the writer and a people as actually existing subjects, but instead of the creative relation between so-called individual enunciation (which does not exist in the first place) and collective enunciation (which is a fabulation)—as in the case, for example, where the writer's description of his or her own situation (which is intentionally falsified) functions like a "childhood block of memory" or what Sartre called a "clandestine future," often in a manner that is difficult to predict.

The thesis concerning fabulation put forward in Deleuze and Guattari's *Kafka: Toward a Minor Literature* is the following: modern writers must invent their own style, which is sometimes related to the specific situation of a people. Simply put, the manner in which a writer describes his or her own situation can sometimes provide the conditions for collective enunciation, even when the objective determinations of the conditions are lacking (except in the specialized case of literary enunciation). What Jameson refers to as analogical actually refers only to the "idea" that does not belong to the framework of an existing language, or to a given world, and thus the means of expressing the idea must first be invented. For example, a writer who is determined by what today is called a "minority" or "postcolonial" situation must invent the means by a number of creative and purely "artificial" procedures to escape that situation via literature (which I would qualify to refer to a writing process that is not also specified in advance by the given situation of literature itself). The fact that the writing process is not completely specified beforehand—thus, it is not determined by the situation in the same way that the living subject is determined—means that there exists some degree of freedom in the process, even though this relative degree of literary freedom may be quite remote from the real situation experienced by the individual subject.

What would be the literary critic's role in all this? "Pay attention to the process!"[13] "Most importantly, pay attention to how it works!" Deleuze and Guattari give a much more succinct formulation of this axiom, which I addressed in chapter 3: "Only expression gives us the method."[14] Beginning from this axiom, we would need to place the question of expression at the center of our discussion of the literary process again. But what is expression? Of course, this question is not so simple. If the true task of the critic is to describe the writing process, first by understanding how it works, there is always a danger of falling into the trap of reducing the process itself to a purely formalist description of literary terms and procedures (metaphor, metonymy, allegory, narration and *récit*, etc.). The writing process cannot be understood simply as a set of superficial features or mere "effects," and this is not what Deleuze and Guattari mean when they say that expression will provide its own unique method, one that we might assume would be particular to every case. If this is true, however, and the writing process also functions by means of a subjective determination that belongs to a particular "writing machine," then how can we pretend to abstract from this larger determination of expression a "method" that could be applied to other writing processes, to other writers? Again, as Deleuze and Guattari first argue, Kafka presents us with a case perfectly suited to illustrate this critical problem, which is not the same problem for all writers (i.e., Kafka does not present us with a Universal case that can be applied to all other writers, to all literatures past and present, like "the Kafka theory of literature"). The problem that Sartre attempted to solve in the case of Flaubert with his "progressive and regressive method," and that Jameson later attempted with his theory of "mediation," is the same problem that Deleuze and Guattari also address with their theory of "minor literature."

If, as Deleuze and Guattari claim, Kafka's own process was specific to what they describe as a particular "writing machine," and later on as "an assemblage" *(agencement),* then how do we get from this statement to the claim that the case of Kafka is exemplary for the situation of minor literature in general? What seems to be missing is something that Sartre had defined as the object of his own search, a "progressive-regressive method" for moving between the subjective determination of a particular writer (e.g., the style of Flaubert) and the progressive determination of the writer as a "free alterity" who represents a "virtual people" (according to Sartre's own terms). Another way of understanding this reciprocal relationship, referring back to Sartre's example, is the relation between the black airman's "desire to fly" and his situation as a colonized subject. For example, what Deleuze and Guattari will define as Kafka's "bachelor desire" may indeed be comparable to the desire to fly an airplane, but how would flying specifically apply to other modern writers? As Deleuze and Guattari write, "as long as the form and the deformation or expression are not considered in themselves, there can be no real way out, even at the level of contents." Here we encounter the same problem that has determined Deleuze and Guattari's concept of "minor literature," when applied to other literatures, especially those written by minorities. And yet we also find here the problem of expression indicated above, one in which the "method" is not given beforehand, as is the case of a "theory" for interpreting different contents. In other words, this reverses the priority of understanding that operates in most theories of interpretation, in which the method (or the theory of interpretation) gives the expression (in this case, the meaning). What Deleuze and Guattari are trying to devise is a critical procedure according to which the method is singularly derived from the expression and only refers back to the expression. In other words, Deleuze and Guattari provide an "interpretation" of Kafka's literary machine that is so "singular" as to make it inapplicable to another work of literature. Only in this sense, I would argue, can their theoretical project be understood as "anti-interpretation."

It is for this reason that they are almost exclusively concerned with the question of how Kafka's literary machine works, in defining its component parts, its connections, its relays, its series and blocks, and finally, with describing the entire process of how it was assembled, beginning with the letters and ending with the novels (which is to say with the posthumous writings that continued to be assembled by others after Kafka's death). And yet, not only is Deleuze and Guattari's method determined by the expression, but we find that Kafka's writing machine is even more specific because it not only includes all the components that constitute his literary works (the diaries, journals, letters, short stories and fables, and novels), but as Deleuze and Guattari insist, must also be understood to include his bureaucratic and legal writings, his juridical papers, and his reports for the Worker's Accident Insurance Company.[15] Only by taking all his writings together as a whole, Deleuze and Guattari argue, negating the generic determination of what previously constitutes the conditions of literary statements, can Kafka's specific value as a writer be defined as occupying a border position between the literary and the social, or between the new technical machines and the machinery of the

State and the political forms of collective desire that are coming into view (including the collective desires that belong to the social formations of fascism and totalitarianism). This unique position provides his writings both with new contents as well as with the occasions for new forms of expression (such as the hyperrealism of the final novels).

> In Kafka's work, it is not a question of formalist or technical machines in themselves or of the juridical statement in itself; rather, the technical machine furnishes the model of a form of content that is applicable to the whole social field, whereas the juridical statement furnishes a form of expression applicable to any statement.[16]

In my view, here we have one of the most precise descriptions of Kafka's achievement of infusing the formal elements drawn from juridical language with new subjective qualities, particularly in *The Castle*. Given the position that Kafka occupied to be able to bring both literary and juridical statements into such close proximity in a work of art, I think it is safe to say that there is no other modernist writer who would be comparable in this regard.

Completely contrary to the first tendency, however, we also find in the concept of a minor literature an opposing current that would even define a universal trait or condition of modern literature, or at least the production of new literary statements in general. However, it is only in the last chapter, "What Is an Assemblage?," which in many ways replaces the earlier chapter "What Is a Minor Literature?," that we hear them speak of a general and nonspecific use of the concept. For example, at this point we should note that they often resort to the phrase "so-called minor literature," as in the following passage: "Let's return to the problem of the production of new statements and to *so-called* 'minor literature,' since this literature, as we have seen, is in an exemplary situation for producing new statements."[17] It is a pity that most critics, including most readers of Deleuze and Guattari, have never really gotten beyond the third chapter of the book, "What Is a Minor Literature?," to reach this point where the question of a minor literature is defined again by new terms and according to a new emphasis: as an exemplary situation for producing new (so-called literary) statements. What is the methodological status, at this point, of the theoretical statement, or rather, what they call the "Anti-method"? As I have already argued, the method being employed is simply inductive. According to an inductive method, one begins with a certain hypothesis that is then tested in a process of experimentation, which results in an analysis of the results and concludes with a judgment concerning whether the initial hypothesis was valid, leading to a new set of thetic principles that can be the basis for certain general conclusions, which must themselves be tested in a number of new experiments.

In this case, the initial hypothesis was that Kafka's work was "a rhizome, a burrow," and was composed by certain identifiable contents and forms of expression (the bent-heads, the portrait-photos, the musical sounds, the animal-becoming, etc.). The concluding hypothesis concerns what Deleuze and Guattari define as an "assemblage" *(agencement),* which is the specific object of the novels and seems to confirm the validity of the initial hypothesis. At this point, we arrive at two primary characteristics of a minor literature in general, which they define as "an exemplary situation for producing new statements." The first characteristic is that of "a clock that runs too fast," referring back to its prognosticating potential concerning "the diabolical powers knocking at the door" (e.g., fascism or totalitarianism); the second is that the literature produces statements that are intended for a people who are missing.[18] Concerning the first characteristic, I refer back to the proximity in Kafka's works between new juridical and bureaucratic statements and the new literary statements that seem peculiar to Kafka's style. However, at this point in Deleuze and Guattari's argument, the second characteristic now assumes the primary role in the identification of a minor literature, which is described in the following manner: "When a statement is produced by a bachelor or an artistic singularity, it occurs necessarily as a function of a national, political, and social community, even if the objective conditions are not given to the moment except in literary enunciation." This is stated even more directly in the following sentence: "a statement is literary when it is 'taken up' by a bachelor who precedes the collective conditions of enunciation."[19]

We should immediately note that the object of the definition has changed—no longer being in response to the question "What is a minor literature?" but extending to address the more general question "What are literary statements?"—and now bears on defining the subjective conditions of new literary statements, perhaps even the subjective conditions of all literature as such.

Let us summarize the logical progression thus far:

1. Minor literature is defined as an exemplary situation for the production of new statements.

2. The specific kind of new statements belonging to minor literature are defined as literary statements.

3. The character of literary statements is defined by their novelty (or singularity), but this novelty refers to the subjective conditions of the enunciation, which precede the objective conditions.

4. According to the criteria of the subjective conditions of enunciation, only bachelors produce literary statements (i.e., literature); or in other words:

5. Literature, more generally, can be defined as the set of all new statements produced by bachelors.

According to the final criterion above, what Deleuze and Guattari identify as a bachelor (or what they also call an "artistic singularity") refers only to the subjective conditions of enunciation, but these subjective conditions do not refer back to the individual subject of the writer. In some ways this progression again recalls Sartre's search for a manner of determining the relationship of the subjective form of the artwork and its relation to the objective or historical conditions, which he defines as a movement of "free alterity." This is why the subjective conditions for literary statements that define a minor literature do not necessarily correspond to the subjective conditions of being a minority or a member of a minority group. Why? There are two reasons. First, because this term "minority" actually refers to the objective conditions of the individual or subject who is identified as belonging to social, national, or ethnic identity (even when this objective determination is divided or reflected by the subject of enunciation itself); second, even these objective conditions are already too abstract and function formally as the subject of the statement according to juridical or statutory requirements. In other words, it is already at a position that is in some way twice removed from the subjective conditions of enunciation, especially literary enunciation (even though literary enunciation can and often does take these abstractions and fill them with new contents and forms of expression). On a very technical level, however, this illustrates the second definition of a minor literature as the production of new statements when the objective conditions are not given to the moment except in literary enunciation.

Recalling Sartre's own observations, even before we consider the particular social identity in question, there is already the objective determination of the writer qua writer, which is to say, the objective and historical conditions of literary enunciation determined by tradition (national, linguistic, popular, ethnic, or cultural), which the writer cannot choose to ignore entirely without losing precisely the objective determination of "a writer." Even "minority writing" today is such a tradition, and minorities themselves are always having to choose (or not) to write like particular minorities. Native American writers today, for example, must always decide whether or not "to write like Native Americans," which also presupposes choosing to have certain group memories, common experiences, family relationships, commonplace addictions, and so on. In this sense the subjective conditions of enunciation are, in part, bound up with the formal and linguistic possibilities that define historically the particular tradition that the writer inherits, which is to say that they are not reducible to individual conditions of experience and memory but already appear in an essentially fictionalized and impersonal form of collective enunciation (i.e., *a* literature).

Of course, the situation just described was no different for Kafka's own situation, and Deleuze and Guattari are very careful to provide an accurate accounting of the objective determinations of literary enunciation that define the various possibilities that Kafka, the writer and the Jewish minority living in Prague at the end of the Hapsburg monarchy, could choose from. Immediately, there was tradition formed by the members of the Prague School (Leppen, Meyrenk, Kisch, Werfel, Brod, Hasvek, and the younger Rilke), but also the German of Goethe and Kleist; the emergent Czech popular and nationalist literatures; the Yiddish folk literature and the popular Yiddish theatre of Lowy. As in the case of every writer, there is also the presence of other writers (who might serve as models or influences) who do not immediately belong to his context and situation in Prague. For example, he admires Dickens and takes him as a model for his first novel, *Amerika;* although Deleuze and Guattari will argue that only Kleist can be regarded as a Master who deeply influenced Kafka.

> He didn't want to create a genealogy, even if it is a social one, à la Balzac; he didn't want to erect an ivory tower, à la Flaubert; he doesn't want "blocks," à la Dickens. The only one he will take as his master is Kleist, and Kleist also detested masters; but Kleist is a different matter even in the deep influence he had on Kafka. We have to speak differently about this influence.[20]

At this point we might return to Jameson's argument that Kafka's "exceptionalism" and originality as a classical modernist writer were due to the lack of any previous model, in order to argue that, upon a finer-grain analysis of the literary culture of Prague in Kafka's own time, this was certainly not the case. (Rather, it only appears to be the case from the perspective of an essentially ahistorical, Universal, or "Singular Modernity.") In fact, the specific problem that Kafka faced was the existence of too many models, all of which Kafka rejected in favor of constructing what Deleuze and Guattari call "a bachelor machine" *(machine célibataire).*

I return now to my original question: What or who is a "Bachelor"? In some ways, Deleuze and Guattari's introduction of the notion of "the Bachelor" *(L'Homme Célibataire)* in naming "the expression of an artistic singularity" is an unfortunate choice of terms, because it has yielded too many immediate objections by feminist critics for its overtly masculinist and sexist character. What's worse, understood in this manner, it seems as if the above proposition could be reformulated to mean that Deleuze and Guattari were implying that heretofore all literature has only been produced by men! The linguistic possibility that the French term can also be applied to a solitary woman *(La Femme Célibataire)* does not assist us much in this controversy, as much as it is simply one more in the litany of problematic, ill-chosen, and "politically incorrect" phrases that belong to Deleuze and Guattari's works ("schizophrenic" or "schizoid desire," first of all, but also "Becoming Woman," "the Nomad," "The War Machine"). As I have argued elsewhere, we cannot imagine that they were so unconscious in their choices, especially with regard to the social and political ramifications, that the ensuing controversy surrounding the terms themselves was not already foreseen and thus part of their overall intentionality. Just as in the case of the phrase "Becoming-Woman," the choice of the term "bachelor," *including its potentially exclusionary and "sexist" associations,* is intended to underscore the reality of what they define in *A Thousand Plateaus* as "order words" *(mots d'ordre),* that is, the power function of certain phrases and statements that are taken up as expressions of concrete social assemblages.[21]

In Kafka's case, however, we must admit that there is something very specific and stubbornly truthful about naming the condition of being a bachelor as essentially bound up with the subjective determination of the literary enunciation. As we know from Elias Canetti's commentary on the letters to Felice Bauer, *Kafka's Other Trial,* the desire to remain a bachelor was so intimately bound up with his own specific understanding of the social vocation of the writer that the two desires became almost indistinguishable.[22] Eventually the subjective conditions of the desire to be a writer actually refer to the objective conditions of a real social process: that of "becoming-a-bachelor," an ongoing and unlimited *process* of extricating himself from every familial and conjugal demand, of politely refusing—always politely!—any expression of proximity or intimacy that does not serve the act of writing. In other words, Kafka established an unapproachable distance that is also a fundamental trait of Kafka's stories and the letters especially; at the same time, Kafka eschews most "normal social relationships" with women, unless they also serve as his copyists, his translators, or his private literary agents, as if creating a strange bureau of women that served as the bureaucrats and functionaries of his own writing machine. Deleuze and Guattari themselves constantly underline this characteristic in Kafka's diaries, which they define as the very milieu or environment of the total writing machine, and especially in his letters to Felice, which they define in unambiguously moral terms as vampirism. Hence, Kafka is a Dracula who determines women as both victims and accomplices; first seducing them through writing, then exchanging letters in mutual acts of tenderness and blood-letting, until they are finally drained by the Eros of distance that Kafka maintains throughout the relationship.

Here, we are also reminded that earlier on Deleuze described Proust in similar terms as a spider, the animal-*logos* who spins his vast and intricate web in order to capture signs and impressions and drink their blood, and Marcel the spider captures Albertine and holds her captive in order to drain her of all of her possible intensities until she is completely desiccated and the narrator has no more use for her. In asking what is the species of the animal-*logos* that exists at the center of the burrow, or Kafka's writing machine, we find Kafka is depicted as a Dracula who sends his letters as bats to both seduce Felice with his absence and then suck the blood from each letter she sends back expressing her desire to be with him sexually. As an example, I will quote from the letter that Kafka sends from Berlin, which displays the "typical" seduction by impossible distance:

(17 March, 1913)

Just a few words, dearest. First, my special thanks for your letter;
it arrived just in time to bring a person, who was heart and soul
in Berlin, a little nearer to his senses again. But secondly, something unpleasant, but typical of me. I don't know that I shall be
able to come. It is still uncertain today, tomorrow it may be definite.
I don't want to discuss the reason until it has been decided.
By Wednesday at ten o'clock you shall know for certain. But it is
definitely nothing serious; we shall see. But go on loving me despite
this dithering.[23]

In other letters, there are even the characteristic moments of Kafkaesque comedy often found in the stories, as when Kafka sends a letter at 1:30 a.m. explaining the multiple reasons why he cannot meet the next day at the appointed time, probably for a sexual interlude, and then five more letters by the afternoon scolding Felice for being so cruel as to not write him back, refusing her "intimate tenderness."[24] Thus, in the case of Kafka, the desire to remain a bachelor certainly provides the subjective determination of enunciation, especially in the letters, which Deleuze and Guattari define as the very milieu of the writing machine: it is the social desire of the bachelor that is directly linked to the process of writing, even serving as its motor. Here, the writing machine *is* a bachelor machine. This is not a metaphor, but a literal equivalence in Kafka's singular case.

Nevertheless, despite this singularity, Deleuze and Guattari also seek to give it a much larger social meaning, one that will not be restricted to Kafka's "private and individualistic concern," but will serve to provide an objectively determined and social meaning as well, which both Sartre and Jameson were attempting to postulate for the modernist writer: namely, a *unique model.* Certainly one of the most general features of the nature of the social desire that informs the concept of the bachelor and of the so-called modern writer is what Deleuze and Guattari call "a creative line of flight," partly defined as a movement of withdrawal from the world of others, or from the subjective situation of being determined as a subject for others; and by qualities that refer to the conditions of being alone that determine each social identity, even though these conditions are different in each case. Solitude is not a condition, much less a guarantee, of creativity in either sense, only an objective determination of time; moreover, withdrawal to a state of being alone does not necessarily lead to a process of creation in the case of the writer, and creativity does not naturally seem to belong to the condition of being a bachelor. That is, not all bachelors are creative, and not all writers are bachelors. After all, one can simply withdraw out of depression and not choose to write, just as one can find oneself in the state of being alone in the most intimate of relationships. Prior to becoming an abstraction or cliché, such as that of an "essential solitude" (à la Blanchot), the subjective determination of the writer would need to be understood formally as a withdrawal from concrete social determinations of being a subject for others that can be effected only by a process of writing (or perhaps also madness), a withdrawal that is invested with the desire to write in the first place (rather than to do something else, like fly airplanes), and this involves a very particular form of individuation between the living subject who writes and the conditions of subjective enunciation in literary writing. It may be true that writing indicates a movement of withdrawal from the world and also a kind of madness and obsession, but these are only vague motives that no one has any real idea about—only myth and speculation! Moreover, a writer's withdrawal is a condition that seems more frequently associated with a depressive position of certain modernist writers, especially Kafka, which forms one of the greatest clichés of the subjective determination of the artist in bourgeois society: the writer as foreigner, as stranger, as criminal, as outcast or class-traitor, as sexual deviant or pervert; but also, the writer as shaman, as trickster, as confidence man, as clown. For example, it is almost comical to think that Shakespeare was depressed, or sought to withdraw from the world; whereas, in the cases of Kafka and Proust, this not only becomes plausible but is the condition of their artwork. After all, can one even imagine a Kafka who is not depressed, or a Proust who is not estranged?

These questions again underscore the difference between Sartre's time and our own with regard to the question of writing or literature in general. The problem today is that both the objective determination of literature and the subjective determination of the writer are already overdetermined, bloated by too much interpretation, exaggerated to an extreme degree, and even Oedipalized in a way that is very different from the problem of the petty bourgeois writer that Sartre was addressing in his own time. It is here we must return to directly connect the concept of the bachelor to the modernist myth of the writer in a very particular way, keeping in mind all the while that Kafka is exemplary because he has been employed historically to establish the myth of the modernist writer in the first place, both as a form of enunciation and as a social form of desire. In other words, as a function of the modernist myth (as a signification within the framework of an ideology), the proper name Kafka belongs to a collective assemblage of enunciation that has produced the objective and subjective conditions of the modern writers that follow. This collective assemblage of enunciation is called, for the lack of a better term, "modern literature." It is perhaps for this very reason that Deleuze and Guattari select Kafka as the writer they will employ to counter this same myth, even by creating another Kafka, an "anti-Kafka," the Kafka of a bastard tradition of minor literature. Certainly, Deleuze and Guattari can be accused of participating in the modernist myth of the writer as a stranger or foreigner, and of a people who are missing or still to come, but as they also say, the thoroughly modernist myths of the writer and of a people "must be understood in a completely different way."[25]

If any political value is going to be attached to the situation of the writer today, regardless of his or her social identity, we must first do away with many of the major clichés that have obscured the nature of the desire that first responds to the question "Why write?" To echo

Sartre, the decision to write must actually be possible as an elective form of freedom, among other freedoms that are socially and politically defined, before the question of its specific value is even raised. Moreover, precisely because there is no external command that causes the activity, there is a peculiar subjective form of demand that is erected in place of objective social desire. *After all, no one is forced to write, or to become a writer!* The decision to write may very well be in the form of an elected freedom, but the writer is often a being who turns this freedom into a form of bondage, to become chained to one's own desk like a dog and eschew the desire to go outside for walks and a breath of fresh air (as Kafka often complains of his own particular habits), to smell of stale odors of cigarettes, coffee, or alcohol (not that all writers smoke or are alcoholic, but rather that all writers smell bad); moreover, to forgo the proximity of others (even if for periodic intervals), to build a vast and intricate burrow, to withdraw into the burrow and to live part of one's life there, alone, *or almost alone!* In fact, given the miserable and even grotesque state of the writer as an animal living in a burrow, it is quite amazing that society has come to hold writers in such high regard as angels of Humanity. Of course, this praise is possible only on the basis of a foreclosure of their reality, which then functions as a "dirty little secret" to be discovered later by generations of critics and readers. "Look!" they say: "How disgusting! He was really a pervert, a criminal, or a sexist!" "Look! He was secretly a fascist, or a poor little socialist." "Look," in the end, they say, "he was really nothing to admire after all."

Returning to our discussion of the subjective determination of the writing machine, there is a strangely obsessive and impersonal force that binds the subject of writing to his or her daily routines and particular habits, as if the writer is someone who, in the absence of an external law, must invent a law that can be applied only to his or her case. Kafka's particular obsession was to construct a writing machine that would complement the writing machine that existed in the office, which had its own bureaucrats and bosses who would enforce its laws and its daily routines; in this sense, I would interpret Kafka's bachelor desire by the measure of its severity and by the sacrifices it demanded in enforcing commitment to writing. In other words, the nature of the desire that informs an artistic singularity must first be understood positively as a "unique idea" that is formed to express a real social desire and not simply as a fantasy or merely as an aesthetic and dreamy escapism. Only when viewed in this way, as a specific desire that also informs a social form of individuation, can the myth of the modernist writer again be justified as describing both the subjective and the objective determinations belonging to a real process, "or as Kleist would say, a life-plan, a discipline, a method, not at all a phantasm."[26] The problem is that most critics of modern literature are not writers, even if they happen to write books and articles, which is why they often get it wrong. They simply do not understand the process.

As a real form of social desire, the writer engages in a process that "produces intensive quantities directly on the social body" and, moreover, "is plugged all the more into a social field with multiple connections."[27] The desire of "becoming a writer" exists alongside or "mixed in" with other social desires; it is collective before becoming an individual form of expression. But this is because there is no such thing as individual desire. All desire *qua* desire is already collective, which is to say, fundamentally social. Consequently, even the most solitary and solipsistic of desires already belong to a collective assemblage of enunciation of which the desire of the solitary writer is only one possibility; therefore, one does not "become a writer," any more than one becomes either a masochist or a political activist, by inventing a singular form of desire. Rather, according to Deleuze and Guattari, one enters into a state of becoming that is already subjectively determined by a collective assemblage of enunciation and objectively determined by other "social assemblages of desire."

In the case of the writing assemblage, the only condition of uniqueness or novelty occurs when a new statement is invented to be inserted into these other collective assemblages of enunciation, designating a new possibility for other kinds of becoming, which are defined as "new intensive quantities."

> Production of intensive quantities in the social body, proliferation and precipitation of series, polyvalent and collective connections brought about by the bachelor agent—there is no other definition possible for a minor literature.[28]

Therefore, even in its most private or subjective determination, fantasy still remains part of a collective assemblage of enunciation; likewise, "the most individual enunciation is a particular case of collective enunciation."[29] The process of becoming a writer exists only in relation to other kinds of becoming within the social field itself, becoming that the writer often takes up to fill with new contents and new statements. Likewise, the "becoming bachelor" of the writer exists only in relation to other bachelor desires, and to other real social bachelors, and here we might imagine other sexual bachelors, political bachelors, and minority bachelors as well (and even, as Deleuze and Guattari argue later in *A Thousand Plateaus,* that "Becoming Woman" is the first of all bachelor desires). We could also further extend the notion of the bachelor to occupy a point of collective enunciation that, at its furthest limit, also necessarily addresses the situation of a people. What is "becoming a people," after all, but a specifically collective expression of "becoming a bachelor"?

Nevertheless, I must immediately qualify this last statement concerning the concept of the bachelor machine, which is still in danger of remaining too abstract, or of falling back into the most commonplace of myths concerning the solitary writer as a purely impersonal and creative being, and writing (or literature) as the only privileged medium for the creation of a people. As Deleuze and Guattari often remark, *this would be a science fiction!* In fact, these are the two abstractions that we must chase away, just as K. often chases away his Assistants, even if only to have them return back through the window. (And the myths I am referring to are very much like K.'s Assistants, and it is almost impossible to chase them away completely because they are already in our heads.) The first myth I have already addressed is that of the bachelor desire in its modernist formulation: the writer as an aspecific, non-relational, and too singular form of individuation that includes all other singularities and is immediately capable of expressing them out of its own substance. This would be more approximate to the Joycean formulation—for instance, "Stephen Dedalus forged the consciousness of a people out of the smithy of his own soul." Here, of course, we need to remember that these are myths first invented by critics and not by writers themselves, except in the case of Joyce, who was not a bachelor.[30]

The second myth concerns the social position of the writer often defined as "a leading or cutting edge of deterritorialization," as if the bachelor and the writer are beings who always appear on the edge of any family or group, always at the margins, as if only to exist in "a world without others," and whose very being is defined as being the very embodiment of an absolute boundary into the social field itself, either approaching from the outside or seeking to become a completely different nature. In the end, a pure being of writing and the specific silence born of a writing that actively silences all other voices in a singular expression of one collective substance. As a result of its most general and mythic signification within the framework of a modernist ideology, this second myth has functioned especially to distort the position of the writer in minority expression and in the postcolonial field of literature (i.e., the writer as stranger, or foreigner, even in relation to his or her own people or race). In many cases, this has led to predetermination of the position of the minority and postcolonial writer—and of any minority expression, for that matter—as having an immanent relation to the politics of the group without any prior determination of its content, a prejudice that sooner or later leads to the discovery of contradictions, either implicit or explicit betrayals, and a entire range of "unfortunate complications."

Returning to the comments made in the beginning of this chapter, we can certainly say that there are no "literary people," no people who exist somewhere in literature, hiding somewhere in the text, lurking around the next phrase or passage, ready to leap out and materialize on the next page. Again, I want to emphasize Deleuze and Guattari's earlier point that this would turn the collective conditions of enunciation in literature into a common vehicle of science fiction:

> The most individual enunciation is a particular case of collective enunciation. This is even a definition: a statement is literary when it is "taken up" by a bachelor who precedes the collective conditions of enunciation. This is not to say that this collectivity that is not yet constituted (for better or worse) will become the true subject of enunciation or even that it will become the subject that one speaks about in the statement: in either case, that would fall into a sort of science fiction.[31]

To avoid falling into this trap, Deleuze and Guattari argue that the actual bachelor and the virtual community are, indeed, effectively real, but both must be understood as expressions of a collective assemblage. Accordingly, although the process of becoming a writer always refers to singular agents *(agents)*, literature is a collective assemblage *(agencement)* of enunciation. Thus, it is only in relation to a specific collective assemblage *(agencement)* that a statement is literary when it is taken up or expressed by a bachelor who precedes the collective conditions of enunciation. These conditions, however, must not be understood immediately as expressing the political conditions of a particular group, but refer only to the enunciations that are found to be missing an objective determination. If this process is described in the most technical or formalist terms, at first, it is only from the viewpoint that the most formalist of enunciation also constitutes the future points for "subjectivization proceedings," as well as assignations of individuality and their shifting distributions within discourse.

Yes, we might say, the writer hallucinates a direct relation to a people, and in some manner this becomes a hallucinated presence in a people in certain minor literatures; however, in perceiving this presence, that is, in feeling the intensity of a desire that provides it with an object or an image, the reader participates in the writer's hallucination as well. And yet the quasi-hallucinatory status of the perceived object does not deny the reality of both experiences. Deleuze writes later in *The Fold*, "Every perception is hallucinatory because perception has no object."[32] Here Deleuze is summarizing a proposition of Leibniz concerning the nature of perception in the monads, which he calls microscopic or minuscule; therefore, in the monads, perception (though *prehension* would be a more precise term) does not resemble the representation of an object of conscious or empirical perception. In fact, conscious perception is made up from all the microscopic perceptions that condition the appearance of an object, but what causes the object to appear in consciousness very much approximates the production of all the microscopic perceptions in the form of a hallucinatory apprehension of something that is present. Deleuze goes on to qualify this statement, however, in the following way: "Leibniz is not stating that the perception resembles an object, but that it evokes a vibration that is gathered by the receptive organ," thus every perception is hallucinatory, meaning that the object perceived is not the cause, but rather is an "unconscious psychic mechanism that engenders the perceived in consciousness."[33] For example, when I see the color white, it is because the perception of color is "projected" onto a vibratory matter by an unconscious mechanism. Although Deleuze was not referring to the perception of so-called objects in writing at this point, the same principle could be applied. How, after all, is perception produced in reading, except in a manner that closely approximates hallucination? In other words, what I perceive does not resemble an object of conscious perception, but instead results from a partly unconscious psychic mechanism of projection because it first occurs at the level of signs, but then also includes unconscious perceptions and intensive feelings as well.

Finally, because certain deliria and "states closely approximating hallucination" are real and constitute intensive moments of social experience, this is what Deleuze and Guattari mean when they say that writers produce real intensities directly on the social body, intensities that are communicable with other social subjectivities, inasmuch as readers can prehend the intensity in their own experience and in some sense can share the same hallucinatory reality. What is literary experience, after all? In point of fact, many writers do believe that their characters are real, and that writers do not as much invent their characters as the characters themselves dictate their own narratives and statements to the writer, who serves as a pure medium or as intercessor. It is in this last sense that Deleuze and Guattari might have a much better understanding of writers as strange animals who dwell in burrows, because they allow certain expressions of delirium to exist in literature, whereas critics often want to reduce the literary process to a rational form of communication between professionals, in which there is not the least hint of intensity or desire. What is "a people," after all, but the name of a very special delirium that has obsessed many modern writers, and the nearly hallucinatory presence of a people in many modern contemporary works can even attest to the existence of this kind of delirium. Modern literature may indeed be a delirium, or may include certain kinds of deliria that are shared between the writer and his or her community, but then we must understand that, according to Deleuze and Guattari, "all delirium is world historical."[34] In other words, like the positive status of bachelor desire I spoke of earlier, we would need to define the people as a specific form of delirium that thus has a hallucinatory quality of collective enunciation in certain minor literatures. The quasi-hallucinatory quality of perception that is found in both writing and reading is invoked in the introduction to *Essays Critical and Clinical,* where Deleuze defines literary production by the qualities of hallucination that determine everything that is perceived or heard in writing. By the means of writing, he says, the writer produces visions and auditions, which might be best defined as specific kinds of hallucinations that have lost their pathologically determined character, much like the writers discussed earlier produce a falsification of their particular situation as subject in a manner that cannot be morally or juridically determined as lying. Consequently, "there is no literature without fabulation, but as Bergson also saw, fabulation—the fabulating function—does not consist in imagining or projecting an ego."[35] This is because, finally, "to write is always to engage in a movement to become something other than a writer."[36] The writer does not speak about it, but is always concerned with something else. In other words, it is often from a critical perspective that the following questions are issued: "What is writing?" "Why write?" "For whom does one write?" and finally, "What is literature?" Even in moments of quiet reflection, writers can be heard to pose these questions concerning the process as well. But that is not important. What is important is that in engaging the process of writing, the writer has always sought to become something other than merely a writer. Who is to say, in the end, that becoming a people is also not a secret concern of the so-called minority writer today? But most importantly, who would forbid it?

5

A QUESTION OF STYLE IN THE PHILOSOPHY OF DIFFERENCE: "THE BARTLEBY FORMULA" (CA. 1989)

- Style as a Special Kind of Delirium
- The Exemplary Case of Antonin Artaud
- "The Bartleby Formula"
- The Political Economy of Style

Continuing our question, how does one begin to define the subject of the writer without already assuming the predicates of the individual, the person, the national, ethnic or racial subject? As I have already argued, Deleuze and Guattari's earlier solution begins with a discovery of the strange consciousness that they found operating in writers like Kafka and Proust: the subject of writing is more like a plant or an animal than a human being. However, this is not quite right either, because here it is a question not of resemblance or homology but instead of becoming, which must be defined through the literary process and in a manner that is immanently machinic. The writer may be described in terms of a process of "becoming animal," or "becoming flower," or even as I argued in chapter 4, "a becoming people"; however, these terms themselves do not exist naturally and must be produced as an aspect belonging to the total process specifically produced by the writing machine. For lack of a better term, I will simply call this aspect *a style*. The question of style in certain kinds of writing cannot be formally reduced to a manner of speaking or to the peculiarity of certain kinds of statements; rather, it is an aspect of becoming expressed by the writing machine—an expression in language that is also a real form of social desire that sometimes threatens to carry along the reader into a state that closely approximates a kind of delirium. ("Identification" is not a good term for naming the cause of this desire, even though the psycho-analytic theory of transference can be partially employed to understand its mechanism.)[1] Therefore, let us postulate the following chain of equivalence that will be the basis for discussing this aspect: *becoming = delirium = style.*

In both modern literature and philosophy, this equivalence has generally circulated around the themes of writing and madness. Concerning the first theme, I must begin by stating a truism: Today, *the philosopher is also a writer.* In other words, can we today any longer imagine a philosopher who does not entertain an essential relationship to the question of style? Can we imagine a philosopher who did not write? Of course, one can say that Hegel wrote, or that Kant conceived of his system in writing, that both were great composers of written works. But is this the same thing as the philosopher as writer? Hence, the question of writing must be understood to be both more general and more particular (one could say "historical") than the philosophical problem of representation as such, because the contemporary philosopher (that is, the one who professes to "do philosophy" in its current form and its academic setting, because there are very few "free thinkers" today à la Emerson and Nietzsche) is someone who must reflect on the formal, but also the material and institutional, conditions of his or her philosophical project as also a project of writing. The question of writing has even engaged some philosophers in an anxious reflection that sometimes threatens to reduce the philosopher's *logos* to a madness (or delirium) borne only by writing, thus threatening the former subjective determinations of the philosopher (an upright nature of thought and the good-will of the thinker) by turning its pretension for truth into the effect produced by the "insane game of writing" (Mallarmé). Simply the fact that this anxiety was first expressed by modern writers, or becomes an obsessive concern of certain modern literary works, does not make this peculiar kind of delirium any less a concern for the contemporary philosopher, who, whether or not he or she chooses to acknowledge it, is also implicated in the question of writing.[2]

The above statements can be readily supported in the opening pages of the early, perhaps most systematic, reflections on the relationship between philosophy and writing, Derrida's *Of Grammatology* (1967) and, of course, Deleuze's *Difference and Repetition* (1968). In the preface, Deleuze writes: "Perhaps writing has a relation to silence altogether more threatening than that which it is supposed to entertain with death."[3] A year before, Derrida wrote:

> Perhaps patient meditation and painstaking investigation on and around what is still provisionally called writing, far from falling short of a science of writing or of hastily dismissing it by some obscurantist reaction, letting it rather develop its positivity as far as possible, are the wanderings of a way of thinking that is faithful and attentive to the ineluctable world of the future which proclaims itself at present, beyond the closure of knowledge. The future can only be anticipated in the form of an absolute danger.[4]

In both passages, written at the very beginning of their respective "philosophies of difference," each philosopher seems to express a certain foreboding around the question of writing, which appears to one as an "altogether threatening silence" and to the other as an "absolute danger." For each, the limit (or horizon) of all philosophy will henceforth bear an ineluctable relationship to "the experience of writing," which is to say, to the particular *experience* effected in philosophy by modern literary machines.

Concerning the second thematic, recalling the arguments in the Introduction, by taking up the literary machine into its apparatus the philosopher's discourse has been exposed to the most essential confusion, one that is often addressed under the general themes of madness or schizophrenia. Here I would simply point out that the image of thought presupposed by certain philosophies, particularly those of Deleuze and Derrida, most closely approximates an expression that is brought into proximity with the experience of madness, in such a way that madness poses the situation of an alternative between thinking and the nature of "that which refuses or resists the form of thought" (to again recall Foucault's diagnosis of the modern *cogito*).[5] Given the importance of this question in both philosophers' respective works, it is fairly evident that while Derrida has the tendency to draw both themes, writing and madness, into relation to the form of Law (e.g., *"plus de littérature, plus de loi"*), Deleuze constantly attempts to place them in contact with the nature of Life, for whom writing is defined as "a passage that traverses both the livable and the lived experience."[6] The significance of this difference in tendencies (or inclinations) will be my primary subject in this chapter; to illustrate the sense of this difference, I have chosen two figures, Antonin Artaud and Melville's Bartleby, who already constitute perhaps the most enigmatic examples in modern literature of these opposing tendencies between life and law. I will suggest that between these two figures there is a more fundamental problem that is shared between Derrida and Deleuze, one that concerns precisely the question of style (i.e., the function of the literary machine) in the production of a philosophy of difference. For me, the question will be as follows: How can one not reduce the concept of difference to the question of style? That is, how is the conceptual image of difference different in each case in each philosophy of difference? Earlier on, I claimed that "difference" (as a presupposition) has become a dogmatic image of thought, in the sense that several postmodern philosophers, following Heidegger, can be united by the common presupposition of "difference" as the problem that determines the nature of their thought. To establish the uniqueness of their own projects, all philosophers must speak differently about difference. Nevertheless, as I said in the beginning, because philosophers do not speak today—having "no mouth, no teeth, no larynx"—the expression of difference can be said to make its mark only in writing, and this opens the fundamental relation between philosophy and writing, or more specifically, between a particular philosopher and a limited number of writing machines. This underlies the importance of only certain writing machines (especially, of a small and overdetermined group of writers and particular literary works) in the creation of a philosophy of difference.

Concerning the "exemplary case of Antonin Artaud" (Derrida), we might expect that the question of writing with regard to both regions of the law and life must be employed in a rigorous way to understand why

Artaud becomes exemplary within each philosophy of difference. Of course, it is well known that Artaud is a writer who suffered the questions of style and of madness in the most personal and idiosyncratic way, seeking in all cases to make both the unique expressions of "an enigmatic life named Antonin Artaud."[7] As to what this demand might signify for each philosopher, or more systematically within each philosophy of difference, we must take a few precautions. Again, just as the discussion of difference was not unique to either philosopher, neither was the name of Artaud. For example, we can postulate that perhaps to the milieu and the cultural limitations that conditioned each respective work, the figure of Artaud is not that unusual for French intellectuals of "this generation," no more than Kafka or Proust, as I argued earlier, and so we must be careful not to *essentialize* the appearance of the figure of Artaud as a common factor that, in itself or in himself, determines the relationship between the two works. In many ways, as I also argued, this can be reduced to an environmental factor, as they say in scientific case studies, no more important than the fact that Derrida and Deleuze both "shared" the same water in Paris at a particular historical moment.

Part of this environment that Deleuze and Derrida shared in common was the series of writings on the figure of the poet in several psychoanalytic and philosophical works published in the 1950s and early 1960s by Maurice Blanchot, Michel Foucault, and Jean Laplanche on the general theme of "madness and the work," and, in particular, around the poetry of Hölderlin and the writings of Artaud, who appear in the works of several critics, especially in the writings of Maurice Blanchot, who is frequently cited by both Deleuze and Derrida during this period as well.[8] In 1965, Derrida publishes in the journal *Tel Quel* the famous article "La parole soufflée," which later appears in *L'Écriture et différence* (1967). In this article, Derrida addresses the problematic conjunction, even confusion, of the two discourses, "the critical and the clinical," concerning the figures of Hölderlin and Artaud in particular. Derrida writes, "Although they are radically opposed for good reasons, the psychoanalytic reduction [performed by Laplanche] and the Eidetic reduction [exhibited in the writings of Foucault and Blanchot, particularly in *Livre à venir,* where Artaud's entire journey becomes exemplary] function in the same way when confronted by the problem of madness or of the work, and unwittingly pursue the same end."[9] That is to say, even by an opposite path, both come to the same result: the creation of an example, in critical discourse, or a case, in the clinical. Derrida initially questions this reduction, however inevitable to both discourses, but especially in the case of Artaud, who would never accept the scandal of "his thought separated from life."[10]

As the title of Derrida's essay indicates, at first glance and in light of Artaud's own protests, such a reduction would amount to an act of "theft," the "stealing of property" (and the experience of the body first of all, which was stolen before his birth). Thus, Derrida's commentary highlights this aspect of appropriation or theft in order to question the manner in which Artaud's body has been separated from his own experience by being divided between the clinical and the critical discourses. Here, Derrida appears in the guise of an attorney—and thus the question is clearly situated "before the law" *(devant la loi)*—in order to prosecute the case of "poor Antonin Artaud," and not as a particular case of "the poet," but rather Artaud himself, as *the self-present, unique or singular.*

> If Artaud absolutely resists—we believe, in a manner that was never done before—critical and clinical exegesis, he does so by virtue of that part of his adventure (and with this word we are designating the totality anterior to the separation of the life and the work) which is the very protest against exemplification itself. The critic and the doctor [and to this list we might also add the lawyer as well] are without resources when confronted by an existence that refuses to signify, or by an art without works, a language without trace. That is to say, without difference.[11]

In other words, Derrida pursues the critical issues posed by the experience of Artaud as a legal question of the "restitution" of stolen property (i.e., Artaud's body proper, meaning his singular body, which can belong to nobody else), foregrounding the failure of his singularity before the law. By so doing, Derrida reveals an irreducible gap or void in the discourse of knowledge whereby the singular is extinguished in favor of the example, the exemplary, and the case (all of which reduce the singular to a species of the particular). It would seem natural to conclude from the above discussion that if properly represented according to the poet's own prescription, Artaud would not become an example of the thetic construction of "madness and the work." In other words, he would not become "a particular case," spirited or stolen away from his own experience in order to become a signifier for other cases, or as Derrida remarks, "the index of a transcendental structure."[12] I will return to address this below, because this is not at all the real issue that underlies Derrida's argument. In fact, Derrida's critique runs in the opposite direction: *to attack the very silence of life by analyzing it and decomposing it even further in order, finally, to discover or exhume the historical and common ground in which both the critical and clinical discourses are imbedded.*

During the same period that Derrida is making this argument, Deleuze also addresses—not for the last time, of course—the critical and clinical representation of the writer, and also around the figure of Artaud, whom he remarks as being "alone" (i.e., singular, unique). In *Logique du sens* (1969) Deleuze writes, in terms almost identical with Derrida's earlier comments, that both "the clinical psychiatric aspect and literary critical aspect are botched simultaneously": first, "by believing to have discovered identical materials that one can inevitably find everywhere; second, by believing to have discovered analogous forms which create false differences."[13] In this context, we should also recall an earlier example that Deleuze himself uses to interrogate the relationship between critical and clinical: the example of Sacher-Masoch. First addressing the question of the clinical determination of literary work in *Présentation de Sacher-Masoch* (1967), Deleuze discerns that the extraction of the "clinical entities" of sadism and masochism from the work of Sade and Masoch results in an evacuation of the descriptions offered by these works themselves. There is a reduction of the language that was specific to Sade and Masoch in which symptoms later associated with the psychoanalytic terms that bear their names were first arranged together and displayed upon a critical tableau indistinguishable from the art of Sade and of Masoch. On the other hand, if we are to regard Sade and Masoch following Deleuze's argument as the "true artists and 'symptomatologists,'" something curious happens when psychoanalysis appropriates their clinical discoveries: the critical is obscured by the clinical in the same way that Sade and Masoch are separated from their own writing machines. This is why Deleuze writes that, in the case of the psycho-analytic appropriation of Masoch and Sade, because the clinical judgment is too full of prejudices, "it is now necessary to begin again with an approach situated outside the clinic, a literary approach, from which these perversions originally received their names."[14] Deleuze's early work, therefore, functions as both a critical introduction to and a clinical recovery of Masoch's own language, because the text is accompanied by a new edition of the novel *Venus in Furs* (i.e., in Masoch's own words). In the title under which this work appears in French, *Présentation de Sacher-Masoch*, the term *présentation* assumes the precise sense of a legal "discovery," the stage in which evidence is gathered from an opposing party in the initial phase of a trial. Deleuze's critique of the clinical appropriation of Masoch can be understood precisely as pleading for the defense in a proceeding against psychoanalysis, a proceeding that would finally be brought to trial later in *Anti-Oedipus* (1972).

Even in light of the above similarities in their approach to the problem of the critical and the clinical, we might nonetheless expect that Derrida does not share Deleuze's strategy concerning the overturning of the conjunction between work and madness in exactly the same manner. The following passage from Derrida's argument in "La parole soufflée" may shed some light on the division in their approaches to the theme of madness. This passage concerns the figure of the poet Hölderlin in Laplanche's reading, but can also be extended to address the issue under discussion with regard to the general notion of schizophrenia, and in some ways can also be applied to Deleuze and Guattari's "reappropriation" of the psychoanalytic category in *Anti-Oedipus*. According to a thesis that Derrida ascribes to a certain philosophical treatment that follows the disappearance of both psychological and structuralist styles, the question of schizophrenia that was reopened by Hölderlin and Artaud is "a universal problem."

> [It is a] universal and not only human problem, not primarily a
> human problem because a true anthropology could be constituted
> upon the possibility of schizophrenia—which does not mean that the
> possibility of schizophrenia can in fact be encountered in beings
> other than man. . . . Just as "in certain societies, the accession to the

Law, to the Symbolic has fallen to other institutions than the Father"
[Laplanche] . . . similarly, analogically, schizophrenia is not one
among other dimensions or possibilities of the existent called man,
but indeed the structure that opens the truth of man.[15]

What is remarkable in this description is the fact that Derrida is already
forecasting, seven years prior to the publication in French of *Anti-
Oedipus* in 1972, the space of a problem that Deleuze and Guattari will
baptize as the discourse of "schizoanalysis," the original and creative
conjunction and overturning of the two dominant representatives of
the clinical and the critical, psychoanalysis and Marxism. Hence, in this
passage we find a certain number of assertions that would find implicit
support in this later work:

1. That the only "true anthropology" can be constituted on the
basis of the actual existence of schizophrenia.
2. That there are other organizations of sexuality, accessions to
the symbolic and the law, that have not fallen to the institution of the
Father (i.e., to Oedipus).
3. That the external limit of schizophrenia within psychoanalytic
discourse opens the possibility of accession to these other dimensions, which are like the future societies that exist either before or
beyond the paternal function.

With regard to the third thesis, Deleuze will later take up this
possibility again in reference to Bartleby and Ahab, concerning America
as precisely the loss of the paternal function as the psychic glue of social
institutions. Deleuze describes this possibility earlier in *Difference and
Repetition*:

It is not a question of opposing to a dogmatic image of thought
another image borrowed, for example, from schizophrenia, but
rather of remembering that schizophrenia is not only a human fact
but also a possibility of thought—one, moreover, that can only be
revealed as such through the abolition of that image.[16]

Nevertheless, Derrida suggests, at a crucial point of his own argument,
that there remains a possibility still of establishing the "unity" of

madness and the work of art on the basis of a certain "historicity," that is, at the moment when "the deciphering of structures has commenced its reign and determined the position of the question," a moment "even more absent from our memory in that it is not within history."[17] Therefore, Derrida argues, what authorizes the disappearance or the loss of the unique itself is precisely "the conception of the unique or the unicity of the unique—here, the unity of madness and the work—as *conjunction, composition,* or *'combination.'*"[18] Here Derrida is explicitly stating that the condition of madness and the work is the historical appearance of a certain notion of structure that demands both phenomena as its internal precondition and extreme limit as two forms of "non-sense": on one side, the non-sense expressed by madness as the deviation or the absence of the structure, and on the other side, the non-sense of an automatism, or the purely mechanical repetition of the structure in all its contingent parts. In other words, here we have the necessary conjunction between what lies outside "Structure," in both senses, and the concepts of difference *and* repetition. These states express the internal and external preconditions and the limitations in the notion of structure itself: its absence (for example, the foreclosure of structure in the experience of schizophrenia) and, at the same time, the emission of non-sense elements and particles that are like the genetic actualization of the structure's purely formal repetition (for example, esoteric and portmanteau words, or Artaud's screams).

It is for this reason that Antonin Artaud, or "the universal schizophrenic man," can become an exemplary case, because his experience expresses the condition of the closure of a metaphysics of presence, or at least represents an extreme limit case. Deleuze, in fact, will find the same condition in *Difference and Repetition* when he defines a "structure" as two coexistent series (for example, a psychic series and a linguistic series) "and *neither of these series can any longer be designated as the original or the derived.*"[19] Consequently, the relationship between madness and the work, the clinical and the critical, is the result of the "displacement" or of the "disguising" of one series within another. Whatever resemblance or identity is discovered to operate the unity between these two regions of experience, madness and the work, even the appearance of one as the implicit "truth" of the other, is the result, not of their eternal presupposition or the universality of their conjunction, but of the pure effects of a certain "dark precursor," whose function could perhaps be defined along the same lines as Derrida's description of the moment that lies outside every structure, that "conjoins the two senses of non-sense in a unicity" (for example, the historical univocity of madness and the work). Given this common intuition, however, it is interesting to note that Derrida does not choose to follow this intuition to its final conclusion, as Deleuze does later on in his work with Guattari. That is to say he does not choose to bestow some revolutionary potential or vitally productive force on the historical closure of schizophrenia, which is thus defined as the "negative" of structure, the secret essence, or the truth of structure—that is, the truth of capitalism, for instance, in the major thesis of *Anti-Oedipus* that schizophrenia is the negative of the capitalist formation.

Derrida's decision is to remain willfully naive concerning this potential, and perhaps this is because, as Derrida writes in the conclusion, "this obeys a law too"[20]—that *a life* named Antonin Artaud, who desired himself absolutely and lawlessly, must risk becoming, in the act of cruelty that authorizes all transgression, *yet another law*. In other words, for Derrida the image of closure that Artaud announces already belongs to the history of the Same. Here again, we must recall the convergence between the clinical and critical around the themes of madness and the work; both concern the supposed access to "a place beyond"— symbolic access to another law than the one that falls to the Father, or to another language, "a foreign language within language."[21] Before all these possibilities, Derrida chooses to remain naive. *He prefers not to* see this difference "in-itself" as productive and critical; rather, he prefers to see this conception of difference as naive and uncritical of its own duplicity—perhaps even complicity—with the metaphysical presuppositions of the text that it inhabits and seeks to demolish. "The duplicity of Artaud's text," Derrida writes,

> simultaneously more or less than a stratagem, has unceasingly
> obliged us to pass over to the other side of the limit, and therefore to

demonstrate the closure of the presence in which he had to enclose himself [an enclosure that Derrida earlier compares to a tomb or sarcophagus] in order to denounce the naïve implications within difference. At this point, different things ceaselessly and rapidly pass into each other, and the critical experience of difference resembles the naïve and metaphysical implications within difference, such that to an inexpert scrutiny, we could appear to be criticizing Artaud's metaphysics from the standpoint of metaphysics itself, when we are actually delimiting a fatal complicity.[22]

By analogy, we could easily apply many of the above criticisms to the early text of Deleuze and Guattari. For example, concerning the desire for abolition or demolition of a certain structure, I recall these lines from *Anti-Oedipus*: "Destroy, destroy. The task of schizoanalysis goes by way of destruction—a whole scouring of the unconscious, a complete curettage. Destroy Oedipus, the illusion of the ego, the puppet of the superego, guilt, the law, castration."[23] In addition, we might take up Derrida's remarks to reopen any one of the great themes that occur in *Anti-Oedipus* concerning, for example, schizophrenia as the "internal limit of capitalism," as "the truth of desiring production," or the schizo as a "revolutionary alternative to paranoid or fascist desire." Finally, we might even choose to question other presuppositions in this work, or elsewhere in the works of Deleuze and Guattari, such as how the schizophrenic as a clinical entity is related to the concept of the body without organs, or to the figure of Artaud himself, who is identified with the "universal cry of schizophrenic man."[24] Anyone who has taught these works would immediately agree that one of the primary obstacles one encounters is precisely the objection concerning the univocity of "suffering" and a certain pathos with which there is a need to preserve this madness of "the Other as Other." The frequency of these moral and ethical objections appear on first glance to confirm Derrida's argument that "the schizophrenic" has been used to create a contemporary myth from the reality of madness— one that only neurotics really believe in! In his essay "Louis Wolfson; or, The Procedure," however, Deleuze himself is careful to distinguish the real language of madness, which is more like an inarticulate block

of expression, a void that links directly to itself, or to its own lived experience, and that never refers outside of itself.[25] This note of caution
concerning the possibility of representing madness "in-itself" seems to
agree with a statement made by Derrida (in the same essay, but also repeated in his seminal essay "The Cogito and the History of Madness")
"that there is no such thing as an art without works, a language without
trace or difference."[26] Likewise, according to Deleuze, what the language
of madness is lacking (that is, if it can truly be called a language at all,
rather than simply what Deleuze calls a "linguistic procedure or pro-
tocol") is a "vital process that is capable of producing vision."[27]

These potential criticisms might be severe except for that fact that,
by his own words repeated several times throughout the essay, Derrida's
own approach to this question remains "overtly naive." What does this
mean? The essay begins with the following declaration: "*Naiveté* of the
discourse we open here, speaking in the direction of Antonin Artaud.
To reduce this *naiveté,* we would have to wait a long time—in truth,
until a dialogue between the critical and the clinical was inaugurated."[28]
(In response, it could be said that Deleuze inaugurates this dialogue two
years later in his preface to Sacher-Masoch, which I will return to below.)
However, at this point Derrida already resolves his own position and announces his strategy concerning where he himself is speaking from, because to speak with knowledge or expertise concerning the experience
or the work of madness would be to assume the position of either the
critic or the doctor, either the critical or the clinical. Unable, or rather
unwilling, to choose either discursive position, Derrida's only alternative is to remain stubbornly naive; therefore, "our initial stipulation of
naiveté was not a stipulation of style."[29]

For Deleuze, on the other hand, naiveté is not a very good method.
A better method would be provided by the image of "stupidity," as I have
already discussed, which Deleuze describes elsewhere as "the highest
finality of thought."[30] Thus, Deleuze's implicit response to Derrida's
strategy might be that it is preferable to be stupid than willfully naive,
since naiveté still retains an image of the "beautiful soul" who seeks to
protect itself from an encounter with error. To mistake madness for the
work, or the work for madness—this is a trap that Derrida attempts to

avoid by remaining forcefully naive, and by refusing the risk of "transgression," which might also become a new form of error, even an error *in principle*, that is, the repetition of an error that grounds the history of metaphysics itself. He writes: "The transgression of metaphysics through the 'thought' which, Artaud tells us, has not yet begun, always risks returning to metaphysics."[31] In some sense Derrida is *also* guilty of reducing the entire experience of Artaud to the single possibility of error, which is to say he reduces this thought to the circular error of metaphysics. In defending himself against the possibility of error, he circumnavigates Artaud's thought, "in the sense in which one poses a net, surrounding the limit of an entire textual network," but ultimately in a manner that seeks to contain this thought "in-itself" and to maintain its position outside this history as singular, self-present, and unique.[32] For Deleuze, on the other hand, the possibility of error proves nothing concerning the positivity of this thought, because error can no longer be taken as the sole "negative" of thought.[33] Moreover, "as for the true transcendental structures of thought and the 'negative' in which these are enveloped [for which 'schizophrenia' remains one possible name], perhaps these must be sought elsewhere, and in figures other than those of error."[34] From these observations concerning the case of Artaud, we might conclude that although they share the same criticism of the historically determined discourses of the critic and of psychoanalysis, we might see here why they do not share the same strategy of occupying the interval between life and the law. Derrida, here and at all times, remains cautious and resolutely naive *before the law* in encountering the singular possibility of a life named Antonin Artaud; Deleuze, on the other hand, runs on ahead somewhat precipitously, even blindly, seeking an encounter with the immanence of "a life" that at all times refuses to be reduced to the event of error. As for Artaud himself, who exists somewhere between Deleuze and Derrida, his experience nonetheless remains inscrutable to each philosopher: as the enigma of "a life that wanted properly to be named Antonin Artaud."[35]

Turning now to the specific case of Melville's character, let's recall that "Bartleby, the Scrivener" is the story of a copyist on Wall Street who one day appears in the office of the narrator, a lawyer, and is hired under a special and secret arrangement to supplement the copying service of

the other two clerks, who are almost Kafkaesque in their comic inept-
ness. I will return to question this arrangement below, because it will
become particularly important in Deleuze's commentary. "Is there a relation of identification between the attorney and Bartleby?" Deleuze
asks in his commentary. "But what is this relation?" "In what direction
does it move?"[36] Whatever direction or sense this identification will
take, its movement will be traced through the strange or enigmatic
formula that Bartleby enunciates in response to every one of the lawyer's requests: "I would prefer not to." In commenting on this formula,
Deleuze first of all underlines its essential agrammatical character. Although technically correct, even a common expression of the American
spoken idiom, Deleuze underlines its "queer use" of the word "prefer"
and abrupt termination, NOT TO, which leaves what it rejects undetermined and, therefore, allows an infinite play of substitutions to complete the infinitive. According to Deleuze's formulaic reading of the
statement, because it stands at the limit of several proper variables, it has
this limit function of an expression that falls to an almost degree-zero of
a speech event between a stereotypic utterance and highly poetic expression and, at the same time, would be neither one nor the other. In
other words, although in the story its enunciation has the character of the
former, being "bare, mechanical speech," it is singular to Bartleby and
forebodes, as Deleuze says, a kind of "foreign language introduced into
Standard English" that exhibits a poetic character of repetition not typical
of clichés.

Concerning what the formula "negates," or "refuses" (even though
the formula neither affirms nor denies anything determinate), Deleuze
underlines the fact that every instance of this response is directed at all
the activities performed by a subject whose assigned role or job title
is indicated in the title next to Bartleby's name, "scrivener" (collating,
copying, running errands, filing, proofreading, etc.). This is why the
formula does not seem to refer to this or that particular assignment, or
action, but threatens "to subsist once and for all and in all cases."[37] In
short, in every case Bartleby's formula inserts a space or interval between the requested action that is expected of his position (a scrivener, a
"legal writer" or "copyist") and his "response," even his "respons-ibility."
Thus, the formula strikes against this very identification of Bartleby as

subject, as a subject to the duties that arise naturally from the duty of identification with his position in the lawyer's office, or his position in society, with his vocation (or "calling"). And yet Bartleby never rejects these subjacent identifications; one could easily temporalize the formula by adding the word "now," I would prefer not to right now, at this moment, at this time, which leaves open the possibility that he will perform these assignments later, at some other moment, perhaps of his own choosing, even though this is not likely. It is precisely because of this that Bartleby becomes uncanny, he remains a copyist, but one who would *prefer not to* copy.

Reading Deleuze's commentary on the figure of Bartleby, there is a certain uncanny resemblance to Derrida's formula of "deconstruction" (which I remind the reader is neither a word, nor a concept, but is presented as a strategy of repetition, that is, of a certain formulaic procedure of the copy itself). Was this Deleuze's intention? To secretly, as if by some enigmatic joke or sense of irony, place the philosophy of deconstruction under the sign of Bartleby (in America)? At first glance this comparison may seem a little too mechanical and forced, and one could suspect that the effects of Derrida's constant refusal to define the term have engendered this association. But then, I would argue this would be the first trait that the two formulas share in common, a certain proliferation within a major language, like a void introduced into a standard language that threatens to carry it off, to stutter, to defer its own sense. Thus, the first trait of my comparison is precisely this propagation, which in the case of Derrida is literally that of a foreign language (at least its copy or translation) in a standard or major language. We might ask, concerning this secret affiliation between Bartleby's formula and the formula of deconstruction: like the effect of Bartleby's formula on the lawyer, *hasn't Derrida's formula caused at least some readers to go a little bit mad?* Moreover, the resemblance does not stop at the surface of the effects that both of these formulas have engendered in language, or more specifically, the means by which both formulas inhabit and reproduce or propagate themselves in a common language. Rather, I would argue, they share the same sense of responsibility, or the same strategy of the response, not one of "non-response" (refusal or ethical naivete of the beautiful soul), but rather a tactic or strategy of a "deferred response" (an ethics of responsibility that never assumes the power or position to respond to and for the Other). In other words, they enact the same gesture with regard to the social situation of speech, and even say the same thing, according to different formulas and procedures.

Commenting directly on Bartleby's formula in *The Gift of Death* (1995), Derrida writes:

> Bartleby's "I would prefer not to" takes on the responsibility of a response without response. It evokes a future without either pre- dicting or promising; it utters nothing fixed, determinable, positive, or negative. The modality of this repeated utterance that says nothing, promises nothing, neither refuses nor accepts anything, the tense of this singularly insignificant statement reminds one of non-language or a secret language. . . . But in saying nothing general or determinable, Bartleby doesn't say absolutely nothing. I would prefer not to looks like an incomplete sentence. Its indeterminacy creates tension: it opens onto a sort of reserve of incompleteness; it announces a temporary or provisional reserve, one involving a provision. . . . We don't know what he wants or means to say, or what he doesn't want to do or say, but we are given to understand quite clearly that he would prefer not to. The silhouette of content haunts this response.[38]

Given the silhouette already outlined in the above passage, it is not without precedent that we might read Derrida's formula together with Bartleby's, or to read Derrida under the *sign* of Bartleby. But why not? Bartleby is a copyist who prefers not to be "a copyist"; Derrida is a phi- losopher who prefers not to be "a philosopher." Moreover, we could easily supplement Bartleby's formula with any number of Derrida's for- mulaic utterances:

- I would prefer not to . . . merely copy the text of metaphysics.
- I would prefer not to . . . transgress.
- I would prefer not to . . . answer your question.
- I would prefer not to . . . respond, that is, according to your own terms.
- I would prefer not to . . . speak clearly, that is, according to some social obligation whose origin is unknown, ineffable, and probably dangerous.

There is, of course, an endless almost infinite number of permutations and possible applications of Bartleby's formula to Derrida's own remarks in this or that text, interview, or public occasion. Reading any one of his interviews would be evidence enough of the necessary and undeniable link between Bartleby's strategy and the strategies of "deconstruction." Moreover, there is a third trait of comparison, which is that of "politeness" (politesse). It is what makes the enunciation of the formula so strange in Melville's story, because this aspect of politeness in the act of declining, or resisting, provides the mask or simulation of observing the social ritual of response even in the face of absolute resistance to social imperative or command, of "non-response." This again addresses a certain silence at the basis of the statement, a silence that is more performative gesture than speech. "Because there is an art to non-response, or the deferred response which is a rhetoric of war, a polemical ruse." Derrida writes,

> Polite silence can become the most insolent weapon and the most deadly irony, but then this non-response is still a response, the most polite, the most vigilant, the most respectful—both of the other and the truth. This non-response would again be a respectable form of politeness and respect, a responsible form of the vigilant exercise of responsibility. In any case, this would confirm that one cannot or that one ought not to fail to respond.[39]

Returning now to Deleuze's own reading, it is clear that the situation that is being addressed is what Althusser called the "interpellation of the subject." It is not by accident that Bartleby's formulaic utterance takes place within the apparatus of the law, in a lawyer's office, or that the character of Bartleby emerges in Melville's universe as a kind of limit case of a society of laws, and of the very possibility of a strange being that seems to belong to the same condition as the law itself. Bartleby's statement announces or hails from a region that must be placed beyond the name of the Father. Moreover, it is because Bartleby prefers not to be . . . a particular subject that he is described as a kind of "void" in the social relationships that govern language as a social institution, creating a vacuum within language *(langage)*. For this reason, according to Deleuze, Bartleby becomes "a zone of indetermination," a silence that does not respond to or has no correspondence with the implicit and subjective conventions of all speech acts, making him a pure outsider *(exclu)* to whom no social position can be attributed.[40] If Bartleby appears to be enigmatic, moreover, it is not from some hidden principle of his character—Bartleby often exclaims that "there is nothing particular about him"—but from the character of his silence concerning his proper role and from the alterity that this silence announces. It is the silence around the question of "duty" that is most critical and ends up becoming a crisis for the lawyer, who, as the law's agent, must dispel all secrets in order to reveal the motive behind them, which is why all secrets have a tinge of furtiveness and criminality, or scandal, about them like an aura of an evil or narcissistic, essentially antisocial motive. Derrida observes in another context, "It is precisely in the sense of respect for duty that Kant often evokes the necessity of penetrating behind secret motives to see if there might not be a secret impulse of self-love behind the greatest or most moral sense of duty."[41] This could also be the sense in which Bartleby's formula could be justified as the strictest observance of the duty to oneself, "be true to oneself." It is for this reason, as well, that the lawyer's response to Bartleby's statement gradually becomes more delirious—as the law's representative, he is at the same time confronted with the presence of a being such as this, without particularity, and yet who continues to occupy a space very near him, and who even sits at his own desk.

Let us now return to the question of whether Deleuze was in fact commenting on Derrida's formula in the guise of Bartleby, as if he was secretly *signing* "Derrida" or "deconstruction" under the *sign* of Bartleby, who is also defined as the scrivener (the writer). There are many hints in Deleuze's essay that would seem to support this interpretation. Certainly, Derrida is a philosopher who can also be defined as a "copyist" à la Bartleby. However, the most obvious identification is contained in the oblique reference to the central scene of *La Carte postale* (1980), in which the figure of the lawyer who assumes Bartleby's position repeats exactly the portrait of Socrates (the philosopher), sitting at the writing desk taking dictation from Plato (the writer). To give my reading some semblance of credibility, I will turn to one of those rare occasions when Derrida chooses to respond and to address himself directly to Deleuze's interpretation of Bartleby, in his seminar of "Questions of Responsibility" conducted at the University of California, Irvine, in 1996.[42] As if by some secret telepathy, on this occasion Derrida could not help but speak on the figure of Bartleby from his own position, that is, as someone who, like Bartleby, has chosen a certain logic of "non-response" and as a result has experienced a certain madness of the law in response to his own formula. Thus, at a crucial juncture of his lecture on Deleuze's own commentary, Derrida intervenes to turn the tables on Deleuze, so to speak, in order to appropriate the Bartleby as his own figure or "proper representative" (or what Deleuze will later on call a "conceptual persona").

Of course, the intervention will take place around a particular passage, even around a certain word translated from Melville's story. Deleuze writes at a certain point: "Bartleby stops copying altogether and remains on the premises, a fixture [*impavide*]."[43] The statement refers to the point in the story where Bartleby stops copying altogether and thus loses all relation to his supposed function, but rather becomes a dead and external thing, an object or useless fixture. Of course, this scene repeats in an original manner the traumatic scene of the division between speech and writing: the event at the origin where writing diverges from speech, where it prefers not to copy, where its external and arbitrary relation to speech suddenly appears as a point of crisis, but rather inaugurates the dialectic of mastery over the "property" of writing that defines the history of metaphysics, a dialectic that one might define as the primary or original masochistic contract. In short, Derrida reads Bartleby's silence as already a displaced representative of the silence of nonresponse, noncorrespondence, the concept of *différance* that "speaks everywhere throughout language" even though "it remains silent, secret and discrete as a tomb."[44] This is the critical point in Derrida's commentary on Deleuze's reading of Melville's story. It seems obvious, so evident and plain to see, that the crucial trait that determines Bartleby's character is this displaced representative of *différance*. Thus, as Deleuze writes in the beginning of his commentary, "Bartleby is not a metaphor of the writer."[45] "Yes," Derrida responds, "he is writing itself, and the possibility of the formula 'I would prefer not to' is always already conditioned by the possibility that writing engenders in the contract of speech, the original possibility of its noncopy, of noncorrespondence, where it comes free."[46]

To reinforce this appropriation in his lectures, Derrida adds a word that is nowhere in either Melville's story or Deleuze's own reading; the word is *secretaire* and refers to Bartleby's supposed position in the lawyer's office, but also means a bureau, a cabinet for filing papers, provided with a surface for writing. Of course, other significations flow from this word as well, all of which seem to unlock the predicates of Melville's character of Bartleby: *secretum* (or secret), *confidential* (or confidant). All of these significations can be understood to refer to the nature of the secret pact between Bartleby and the lawyer, who at one point in the pitch of delirium over Bartleby's presence declares, "Yes, Bartleby, I never feel so private as when you are here . . . I penetrate to the predestined purpose of my life."[47] Around this proximity Deleuze, in his commentary, again raises the possibility of a strange and secret pact between Bartleby and the lawyer, as if the lawyer's actions and delirious protests against the figure of Bartleby betray a secret guilt, or sexual responsibility. We might locate the nature of this pact in the unconscious or some ideological contradiction that the lawyer becomes acutely sensitive to; as a representative of the law, the subject of law, Bartleby, would be, according to this interpretation, the law's own double or underside. In other words, if every subject is a subject of interpellation, then we must consider the difference of the condition of a being who is outside interpellation, who resists identification absolutely. Such a subject could not be a subject in Althusser's sense, that is, "a subject of ideology," because ideological interpellation demands that there be a subject who is, in every instance, (a) "particular." Therefore, it is clear that where there is no interpellation, there will be no subject either.

For both Derrida and Deleuze, such a being goes by the name of literature, which very much appears as the law's double or simulacrum in "our era." Derrida says this quite clearly at several points: no law without literature, no literature without law *("plus de littérature, plus de loi")*; or "no democracy without literature, no literature without democracy."[48] (Of course, for both phrases we could substitute a positive declaration, which the French allows: "the more democracy, the more literature; the more law, the more literature.") Derrida's expansion on the subject of literature will allow us to profile in a more summary manner what he shares in common with Deleuze around the question of literature:

> Literature is a modern invention, inscribed in the conventions and institutions which, to hold on to just this trait, secures in principle the right to say everything. . . . This authorization to say everything (which, moreover, together with democracy, as the apparent "hyper-responsibility" of the subject) also acknowledges a right to absolute non-response, just where there is no question of responding, of being able to or having to respond. This non-response is more original and more secret than the modalities of power and duty because it is fundamentally heterogeneous. We find here the hyperbolic condition of democracy which seems to contradict a certain determined and historically limited concept of democracy, a concept which links it to the concept of a subject that is calculated, accountable, imputable and responsible, one that "must respond" and "must tell the truth, the whole truth, and nothing but the truth." Of having to confess, to reveal all their secrets, with the exception of certain situations that are determined and regulated by law.[49]

At this point, several remarks could be drawn from this passage concerning the positive affirmations that Deleuze and Derrida share *(partage)* concerning the question of literature (or "the literary machine"). Both thinkers identify literature with a certain absolute nonresponse, which could be understood that the subject who "speaks" in literature speaks in an absolutely original manner, which does not copy or reproduce or respond to the subject in social space, inscribed in its rituals and conventions, in its ideological apparatus. This allows us to understand the special nature of literary enunciation, which does not directly represent social enunciation or other kinds of statements, but allows the possibility for new statements and thus new subjects of enunciation (like Bartleby, for example, who is a pure fiction). This very possibility is something that Deleuze has determined as the condition of being "a bachelor," that is, of a subject who establishes the virtual link of the literary statement to collective enunciation. Second, the "heterogeneity" between the subject in literature and the subjects of moral duty and respect functions as the second meaning of "nonresponse," because the literary subject exceeds both of these regimes and does not arise from interpellation, but absolutely eludes this ideological mechanism (perhaps even contrary to the function of criticism in the modern period, which can be said to be one of binding literary statements to interpellated subjects and known identities). The figure of Bartleby has prefigured this for us in a striking manner. My third remark concerns what Derrida calls "the hyperbolic condition" of the subject (of enunciation): That the literary subject exceeds or emerges outside the "calculated" identity of the moral or civil subject (and I have used the word "interpellation" to substitute for this calculating regime that belongs to modern disciplinary societies) creates the possible identification of the space of literature as the space of *différance (that is, a spacing defined as both displacement and temporal delay)* between the closed, relatively determined, or calculated democracy and what Derrida calls the "democracy to come." This might also address what Deleuze defines as "a place where Bartleby can finally take his walks" and is something that Deleuze would affirm as well, concerning the possibility of certain statements in modern literature as the seeds of collective enunciation of a missing people, or "a people to come."

Finally, if there is a duplication of Derrida's logic inscribed in the relation between Bartleby and the lawyer, does this association imply that we may read Derrida's formula under the sign of "masochism," particularly as a certain manner of creating contracts that are made in the absence of the Name of the Father or, in Derrida's words, that do not "fall to the Father" or to the principle of Law (the Symbolic)? We recall Derrida's statements above concerning the case of Artaud, but also the statements in Deleuze's commentary on Bartleby concerning the different figures in Melville who all live in the realm devoid of the Father, in an OUTLANDISH or deterritorialized realm, which he calls "America": confidence men, raving psychotics, monomaniacal demons like Ahab who also bear a kind of "secret and evil pact" with a primary nature that exceeds the secondary order of the Law, and others like Bartleby, whom Deleuze describes as "orphans," whose relation to the Father occurs by "unnatural alliance." For both Derrida and Deleuze, the problematic is always the power of these states of exception, perhaps even exemplary cases, in revealing or interrogating the nature of the primary contract, the one that runs prior to and stands at the condition of even the "linguistic contract."

However, we have to be more precise concerning the event of the contract in question, which also engages at a fundamental level the question of literature. This is the creative possibility that Deleuze finds in the literary process; it is the capacity to "invent" new contracts, the capacity that belongs to what Deleuze calls a "nonorganic life" that can be found in the written line, in the curvature of the sentence, to invent new percepts and affects, new "signs" that imply ways of living, possibilities of existence, new forms of resistance—most of all, to free life from the forms that imprison it. Again, as Deleuze said later: "Creating isn't communicating but resisting."[50] For Derrida, on the other hand, there is more than a difference of style concerning how to pursue this question. First of all, he has always stressed an absolutely nonoriginal and, let us say, absolutely unimaginative relation to the event of difference. Most of all, he has strenuously objected, on several occasions, to the term "creative" as a way of describing his procedure. "This implies that the subject . . . becomes a speaking subject only by making its speech conform—even in so-called 'creation,' or in so-called 'transgression'—to a system of the rules of language as a system of differences, or at the very least conforming to the general law of *différance*."[51] Therefore, if "masochism" is perhaps a good way of characterizing Derrida's procedure by way of analogy, it is not because it is an exemplary means of "transgression," in the creation or invention of new contracts, since it already owes this particular trait to the primary contract between speech and writing, which, as Derrida has shown throughout his entire body of work, is already showing signs of being strained, arbitrary, differential. "Arbitrary and differential," as Saussure says, "are two correlative characteristics."[52] Thus, for Derrida the question of creation in literature would have to be something more akin to a theory of "masochism" without transgression, more akin to the event of something "that 'produces'—by means of something that is simply not an activity—these differences, these effects of difference."[53] This is why we can describe his procedure as one of "tracing" the movement of an original default, or nonreproductive instance that belongs to this primary contract, or of extending and deploying it throughout every other region it informs, and the procedure itself is only an effect and a "kind of intensification of its play."[54] This would be a particularly compelling way to read both the clinical and the critical dimension of his work concerning a default at the heart of the symbolic order, a default that is nothing more or less than the possibility of a grammatical error. He does so, he says so explicitly, by tracing this movement, by inserting a chain of nonsynonymous substitutions precisely in the place of this simple grammatical substitution, "this silent lapse of spelling," because *différance* makes the movement of signification possible.

Do the above statements also imply that writing has replaced death as the absolute border of silence (nonbeing) and finitude? If so, what is its specific threat or danger—a harmless supplement, a secondary appendage to speech, a mere automaton? After *Of Grammatology*, at least, no one can so easily dismiss the question of writing as that point where its all-too-self-evident meaning dissolves in favor of movement that necessarily exceeds consciousness, thereby dislocating the unity of the work with regard to its former end, goal, or *telos*. As a consequence of Derrida's interrogation, no one today can (or rather should) approach the question of writing innocently. Its sign, as Derrida announces very early on, is always presented as a sort of "monstrosity," as "an absolute danger," as I quoted earlier. This is a sign not merely of the times, according to Derrida, but of the "inflation of the sign itself, absolute inflation, inflation itself."[55] Today, in fact, we can still perceive all the symptoms of this inflation (of language, of writing) in the manner by which the subject—including every aspect of this subject's "life-world" (*Lebenswelt*), such as its culture, politics, knowledge, economy—is absolutely comprehended by an order of signs, one might even say precomprehended, in a manner that necessarily exceeds consciousness. Thus, the weight and measure of the subject's own activity and experience has disappeared under the gravity of another measure that takes the form of a shadowy writing that the subject barely discerns, even though it already animates every perception, action, feeling, or thought.

> There is not a single signified that escapes, even if recaptured, the play of signifying references that constitute language. The advent of writing is the advent of this play; today such a play is coming into its own, effacing the limit starting from which one had thought to regulate the circulation of signs, drawing along with it all the reassuring signifieds, reducing all strongholds, all the out-of-bounds shelters that watched over the field of language. This, strictly speaking, amounts to destroying the concept of the "sign" and its entire logic.[56]

If one does not enter lightly into this dangerous and insane game of writing today, this is because the border that separates our knowledge from our naivete or simple ignorance has been eclipsed. Deleuze remarks, "We write only at the frontiers of our knowledge, at the border which separates our knowledge from our ignorance and transforms one into the other. Only in this manner are we resolved to write."[57] All the old reference points are gone (or at least strangely dislocated); once we enter the game, there are no more "time-outs," and what's worse, we only come to discover that we were always already playing and being played. Given the gravity of this "new" situation, therefore, it would seem plausible that one could (even should) simply choose not to enter into the game, to continue speaking of and from that former limit, to hold onto all the old reassuring signifieds, to cling to a concept of the "sign" as spoken, intentional, ordered, and most of all, "logical." However, if the future introduced by the advent of writing exposes one to the measure of a certain insanity (one that necessarily exceeds Hegelian "bad infinity"), then the avoidance or reduction (perhaps even the "foreclosure") of this moment only exposes one to another, potentially more dangerous and violent, form of madness.

My last statement can be readily illustrated by the following observation: if, as suggested above, the boundary- or limit-concept of knowledge has been transmuted from death into "writing," then the reduction of the question of writing (again) to a former position of "secondariness" would be comparable to reducing the question of finitude (again) to the status of mortality of the "creature" *(ens creatum)*. But I think this reduction has also happened quite recently in philosophy and the "return of religion." It is not by chance that we see in this response the nostalgic reassertion of a certain theological solution, since, as Derrida has remarked many times, the production of theology (in the West) has always taken place by means of a certain repression of the limit first introduced by writing (although one could also say, in this context, by a certain history of writing, or even the repression of history as such, which can be defined as "the total movement of the trace"). Thus, Derrida writes, "in its origin, to be sure, one can already suspect that an origin whose structure can be exposed as 'signifier of the signifier' conceals and erases itself in its own production."[58]

In addressing the question of style in the two major philosophies of difference "in our era," I have attempted only to demonstrate what, upon first glance, might seem all too obvious: Derrida and Deleuze are philosophers who write. It is difficult to judge which activity grounds the other, in the sense of which provides the necessary conditions for the other activity to take place—philosophizing or writing? Does it even make sense any longer to pose this distinction? Certainly one factor would be the evolution in the systems of writing, publication, archiving, or more generally, the dispersion of the public functions of discourse (especially written discourse), including all the civil and legal codes—here one might recall Foucault's descriptive genealogy of the author as a discursive function—that determine the circulation of written works and their relationship to proper, identifiable individuals. This has certainly become a constant, even obsessive, theme in Derrida's later writings concerning the signature, the proper name, the enunciating dimension of the speech act or performative statement (such as the promise or oath). One cannot account for this series of themes except to say that they mark the limits and the tertiary borders of a properly philosophical (demonstrative) discourse. They form the outside of philosophical representation, an outside that reappears as the very condition of philosophy in its contemporary mode—the wildly different appropriations of the term "deconstruction" already attest to this—and thus become occasions for

Derrida's own interrogation concerning the various convergences and, more often, the *"destinerrance"* of his body of work. Therefore, a second factor for understanding the emergence of the question of writing in philosophy is a certain "contamination" that has taken place between the genres of philosophical and literary discourse in the modern period, after Nietzsche in particular. One might argue that this has always been the case (for example, Plato's dialogues, or Hegel's "philosophical *Bildungsroman*"), but there is something distinctly modern in the emergence of "literature," and in the concept of writing that accompanies it, as distinguished from the earlier forms of rhetoric, poetry, or *"belles lettres."* It is around this development that the question of writing is especially marked and around this question, I would argue, that the most dizzying and contracted dialogue between "the philosopher" and "the writer" has ensued in the contemporary period. At a moment of near identification, we can locate many places in both Deleuze's and Derrida's work where the philosopher emerges to assert that what he is doing is not "merely literature." Derrida complains, and not only once, "Those who accuse me of reducing philosophy to literature or logic to rhetoric . . . have visibly and carefully avoided reading me."[59]

Yet, it is precisely this confrontation and even struggle around the question of writing that for both Derrida and Deleuze the question of philosophy has recommenced in the postmodern period. In the 1995 interview "Is There a Philosophical Language?," Derrida addresses this "contamination" of a "properly philosophical language" and a "purely literary discourse":

> The explanation between "philosophy" and "literature" is not only a
> difficult problem that I try to elaborate as such, it is also that which
> takes the form of writing in my texts, a writing that, by being neither
> purely literary nor purely philosophical, attempts to sacrifice the
> attention to demonstration or to theses nor fictionality or poetics of
> language. In a word, . . . I don't believe that there is a "specifically
> philosophical writing," a sole philosophical writing whose purity is
> always the same and out of reach of all sorts of contaminations. And
> first of all for this overwhelming reason: philosophy is spoken and
> written in a natural language, not in an absolutely formalizable and

universal language. That said, within this natural language and its uses, certain modes have been forcibly imposed (and there is here a relation of force) as philosophical.[60]

Consequently, by means of the proliferation of many experiments on the level of genre (*Disseminations, Glas, The Post Card,* and *Circumfessions* are perhaps the most notable works in this mode), Derrida has constantly called into question the supposed naturalness of a certain mode of philosophical discourse. There is a politics of style, and by means of this experimentation, style becomes a political question, because "each time a philosophy has been opposed, it was also, although not only, by contesting the properly, authentically philosophical character of the other's discourse."[61] Moreover, there is a certain violence, at least the visibility of "force," that Derrida's writing causes to appear, precisely in not obeying the traditional and institutional norms that always command the reproduction of an entire historical apparatus (of authorities, protocols, linguistic and discursive norms, national differences, and so on). "A philosophical debate is also a combat in view of imposing discursive modes, demonstrative procedures, rhetorical and pedagogical techniques."[62] It is precisely this combat between force and signification, which was invisibly present in the tradition of philosophy (constituting its "white mythology"), that Derrida's style manifests as a phenomenon that must now be incorporated into its total signification.

As for Deleuze, it goes without saying that his work experiments with the normative conventions of a properly philosophical discourse, perhaps even to a hyperbolic degree in the case of the writing machines of *Anti-Oedipus* and *A Thousand Plateaus.* Even his "traditional" philosophical commentaries are extremely deceptive and no less experimental in terms of innovating the discursive form (as in the case of *The Fold*). Of course, this program or "style" of experimentation is already foreshadowed in the frequently quoted passage from the preface to *Difference and Repetition*:

The time is coming when it will be hardly possible to write a book of philosophy as it has been done for so long: "Ah, that old style. . . ." . . . It seems to us that the history of philosophy should play a role roughly to that of collage in painting. The history of philosophy is the reproduction of philosophy itself. In the history of philosophy, the commentary should act as a veritable double and bear the maximum modification appropriate to a double. (One imagines a philosophically bearded Hegel, a philosophically clean-shaven Marx, in the same way as a moustached Mona Lisa.)[63]

Given that the question of writing and a certain strategy of experimentation are fundamental traits in both philosophies of difference, I return to my initial question: Can the concept of difference be reduced to the question of "style" in writing? But again, this begs a more preliminary question: "What is style?" In response I will simply say that style is an image. But an image of what, exactly? As we saw in our reading of the final edition of *Proust and Signs,* Deleuze defines the function of style as the form of the communication of the whole within the work. Its function is to unify a multiplicity of viewpoints, even at the level of the sentence, without thereby submitting this unity to a closed totality. "But just what is this form, and how are the orders of production or truth, the machines organized within each other?" Deleuze asks. "None has the function of totalization."[64] In several places Deleuze even refers to style as an "essence," despite the inappropriateness some might ascribe to this word, since it allows a viewpoint to open up onto the work as a whole: "an individuating viewpoint superior to the individuals themselves, breaking with their chains of associations."[65] Thus, the essence of essence, of style as the essential viewpoint in the work, is "syntactic" or "conjunctive": "Essence appears alongside these chains, incarnated in a closed fragment, adjacent to what it overwhelms, contiguous to what it reveals."[66] *Alongside, adjacent,* and *contiguous*—style, nevertheless, expresses unity, the unity of this multiplicity of fragments, blocks, and parts. Thus, style must also be defined as the unifying trait that is produced after the work, at its end—one might say as the gesture of a final brushstroke or word—but that nevertheless continues to exist alongside the work. The fact that this unity continues to exist "alongside the work," contingently related, possibly undergoing further permutations, is what makes the image of a style an object of criticism. Each critic seeks to grasp in an image the unity of a work (of a given author) by discovering the most stylistic element that defines the work's genetic structure and its essential idea. The fact that most critics fail to discover this element of style, or that it is open to such intense disagreement and even conflict, is what makes the function of style so interesting, because it opens the question of the work's unity (its genetic or formal history) to a seemingly endless number of appropriations. It is by this trait that "style" actually functions like a foreign language discovered within the language of the work, as a second-level order of signification, or new convention by which the work is determined, even if this determination is only "contingently" fixed and can undergo further translation or repetition—almost infinitely.

Does this mean that style is external to the work? Is the translation of the work's meaning into another, so-called secondary and descriptive language, like a foreign language borne within the work, but abutting its external representation? Each work, according to Umberto Eco (who is cited by Deleuze in this context), "produces new linguistic conventions to which it submits, and itself becomes the key to its own code."[67] Later Deleuze will rename this "foreign language within language" or this "transversal dimension" (the very element of style) as, simply put, "the Outside." For example, the following passage from "He Stuttered" concerns this concept of style:

> When a language is so strained that it starts to stutter, or to murmur or to stammer . . . then language in its entirety reaches the limit that marks its outside and makes it confront silence. When language is strained in this way, language in its entirety is submitted to a pressure that makes it fall silent. Style—the foreign language in language—is made up of these two operations.[68]

Finally, according to Deleuze, it is through this "outside" or "transversal dimension" that the work is able to communicate with other works by the same writer, even those that do not yet exist, in addition to the works of other writers or artists.

> For if the work of art communicates with a public and even gives rise to that public, if it communicates with the other works of the

same artist and gives rise to them, if it communicates with the works of other artists and gives rise to works to come, it is always within a dimension of tranversality, in which unity and totality are established for themselves, without totalizing objects or subjects.[69]

Taking up the same issue of style (the definition of the work, of its manner of unifying itself, the existence of a unique idiom or style), Derrida also speaks to a certain "unity without totalization," a unity that exceeds the identity of the signature, or the individuating viewpoint of the writer (i.e., the limited chain of associations):

There is a legal copyright and a civil identity, texts signed by the same name, a law, a responsibility, a property, guarantees. All this interests me very much. But it is only one stratum of the thing or the singular adventure called a work, which I feel is at every moment in the process of undoing itself, expropriating itself, falling to pieces without ever collecting itself together in a signature. I would be tempted to retain from the old concept of work the value of singularity and not that of identity to itself or of collection. If anything repeats itself in me in an obsessive fashion, it is this paradox: there is singularity but it does not collect itself, it "consists" in not collecting itself. Perhaps you will say that there is a way of not collecting oneself that is consistently recognizable, what used to be called a "style."[70]

Perhaps echoing the passage by Deleuze quoted above, the condition of this singularity, the condition of the "recognition" of style—whether this is attributed to the work or to the writer, it is difficult to say—is *repetition* from the perspective of an other writing machine. One can never recognize one's own style, or rather, this occurs only when the writer is already located in the position of the other, which is to say, at a certain distance and according to a measure and technique that is highly determined. Following Derrida's comment concerning style, any such nomination or viewpoint always comes from the other, whose apprehension provides the very basis of the work's communication.

This can be perceived only by the other. The idiom, if there is any, that by which one recognizes a signature, does not reappropriate itself, as paradoxical as that may seem. It can only be apprehended by an other, given over to the other. Of course, I may think I recognize myself, identify my signature or my sentence, but on the basis of an experience and of an exercise which I have undertaken in which I will have been trained as other, the possibility of repetition and thus of imitation, simulacrum, being inscribed at the very origin of this singularity.[71]

It seems that we have located the essence of style in this event of expropriation of a singular and unique idiom, from the moment that this idiom is already handed over to the powers of repetition or imitation, revealing instead a discourse that is strangely divided from itself at its very origin. On the basis of this observation concerning the possibility of a singular or unique instance of "I," it is interesting to remark that even to speak of the works of "a Deleuze" and "a Derrida," we are speaking from a pure convention, a fiction that belongs more to the history of the signature, the proper name, the bounded determination of the work as a property that belongs to an attested civil identity. It is even from this viewpoint that Derrida or Deleuze could be said to imitate or repeat themselves from the moment that they begin writing, because they themselves are marked or limited by the same institutional conventions that determine their civil identities and that define the very conditions of written enunciation. One can see why the works written with Guattari, where the status of the signature and the proper name is constantly frustrated by a writing process that refuses to obey the normative conventions of authorial identity, continue to trouble most of Deleuze's commentators—and perhaps this constitutes Deleuze and Guattari's most radical experiment, one that transgresses not only philosophical conventions but the underlying conventions of written forms, which is to say the rules that determine the dominant conception of the writing machine.

Returning to the late essay "He Stuttered," in conclusion, Deleuze often speaks of "a non-style," which is made up from "the elements of a style to come, which does not yet exist."[72] In a certain sense, modern philosophy (after Nietzsche) has always concerned itself with the question of style as a variable that will "make difference" by means of a new species of repetition, one that assembles together all the elements of the "not yet" and the "to come." Nonstyle, therefore, can be defined as virtual, suspended between the tensors of the "to come" and the "not yet," scattered and fragmentary. On the other hand, Deleuze also defines style as essentially economical: "Style is the economy of language."[73] However, this sentence would be misunderstood if "economy" were conceived as an order in equilibrium and balance; instead, economy must now be redefined as the duration perched between boom and bust, as an order of profound disequilibrium.

> Can we make progress if we do not enter into regions far from equilibrium? Physics attests to this. Keynes made advances in political economy because he related it to a situation of a "boom," and no longer equilibrium. This is the only way to introduce desire into the corresponding field. Must language then be put into a state of boom, close to a crash?[74]

Likewise, we might think of Derrida's program along the same lines: to introduce the question of language into a region far from equilibrium. In this manner, Derrida poses as his fundamental gesture the question of writing as an essential disequilibrium within what he names as the logocentric tradition. He summarizes this strategy in the interview "A 'Madness' Must Watch Over Our Thinking": "The act of writing or rather, since it is perhaps not altogether an act, the experience of writing . . . gives one a way that is better than ever for thinking the present and the origin, death, life, or survival."[75] Finally, in this context, allow me to recall a very early passage by Derrida, almost nearly at the very beginning of his work. He speaks about a certain boom that will inevitably lead to the bust of language. He writes:

> The devaluation of the word "language" itself, and how, in the very hold it has upon us, it betrays a loose vocabulary, the temptation of

a cheap seduction, the passive yielding to fashion, the consciousness
of the avant-garde, in other words—ignorance—are evidences of this
effect.[76]

My emphasis on these passages from the works of both philosophers is
not merely to produce an analogy of themes based upon the repetition
of the economic metaphors of "boom" and "crash" (or "bust"), but rather
underscores the redefinition of an economy of difference and repetition
that no longer is related to the equilibrium of a certain return or recovery of the same (of metaphysics, identity, self-presence, and so on).
Thus, the economy of disequilibrium either is defined as the point where
the being of language cracks and shudders, and when language itself is
pushed to a state of boom, close to a crash, or is revealed as expressing
all the inflationary signs of a crash—perhaps even one that is "immemo-
rial." In turn, this raises the question of silence in the region of language.
There are actually two silences: one that is peaceful, marking a pause, a
breath, which is already made possible by the order of speech. In fact,
this is not silence at all, since it is already "impregnated" by the signifier
that speaks through it and replenishes its significance. The other silence,
one might say, can never be heard. Instead of peaceful, it is essentially
brutal; it marks, not a pause between two words, but the rupture of language with itself. In this second silence, no breath is possible, because it
is not made for the breath, but for the eye. It is this other silence that is
announced earlier on by Deleuze as "altogether more threatening" and
by Derrida as a "dangerous future," a silence that is introduced by a philosophy of difference and repetition.

Finally, there is also a divergence present here between the two
manners of reaching this point, and it is on this ridgeline or border that
we can sharply distinguish the philosophical projects of Derrida and
Deleuze. Whereas Derrida will trace the effects of this profound disequilibrium of a difference "that speaks everywhere throughout language," Deleuze will understand it as an act or activity of creation: to
place language in a situation of a boom, close to a crash. For the latter,
difference is essentially, and perhaps "supremely," created difference and
not the effect of some flaw or crack, some essential lapse, in the orders of

being and language. Here we might locate a difference in style between these two philosophers, or rather, between the style of these two major philosophies of difference today. To put it succinctly, I would simply say that Deleuze is a philosopher of the boom, whereas Derrida is the philosopher of the crash.

The "boom" can be demonstrated in several different senses: in language, to push syntax to its limit, to the point of stuttering; in desire, to crack desire itself up to the point of causing it to multiply its objects and states of becoming, beyond Oedipal familiarity; in politics, to break from the individual and the fascist collective organization alike, in order to cause the very phenomenon of collective assemblages to become more supple, molecular, and even experimental. All these mark the characteristic traits of a Deleuzian style of the critical (as the moment of turning, *krinein*, or crisis). Of course, the crisis of every boom is the risk of a crash. Thus, as Deleuze often warns, desire risks becoming trapped, or blocked; a schizoid process risks becoming schizophrenic; the body without organs risks becoming petrified, the vitriolic body of a junkie filled with refrigerator waves. As for language, there is the risk of it falling silent, and nonstyle can easily come to resemble all the trademarks of an all-too-familiar style. The point, it seems, is to keep on moving, that is, creating. The moment one stops, difference risks becoming uncreative, static, (non) Being.

For Derrida, on the other hand, one could say that the crash is itself the creative moment par excellence, and one does not approach it by dint of force, much less by exceptional or creative effort. One can find this axiom supported early on in "Force and Signification" (from *Writing and Difference*), where Derrida already announces the critical forces of this crash: "The force of our weakness," he writes, "is that impotence s*eparates, disengages,* and *emancipates.* Henceforth, the totality is more perceived, the panorama and the panoramagram are possible."[77] Moreover, the crash—of a certain metaphysical epoch, a logocentric tradition, a certain subject of representation, of a certain idea of science and writing—has already happened. This is already evident in a passage from the same essay where this approach or strategy is methodologically announced (what would later be baptized as a "deconstructive operation") in terms of a certain solicitude or solicitation of the Whole:

> Structure can be methodically threatened, in order to comprehend
> more clearly not only its supports but also that secret place in which
> it is neither construction nor ruin but labiality [one might say at its
> fringe, margin, or border—terms that Derrida will make much use
> of from this point onward, but already in *Of Grammatology*]. This
> operation is called (from the Latin) soliciting. In other words,
> shaking in a way related to the whole (from *sollus,* in archaic Latin,
> "the whole," and from *citare,* "to put in motion"). The Structuralist
> solicitude and solicitation give themselves only the illusion of
> technical liberty when they become methodological. In truth, they
> reproduce, in the register of method, a solicitude and solicitation of
> Being, a historical-metaphysical threatening of foundations. It is
> during the epochs of historical dislocation, when we are expelled
> from the site, that this structuralist passion, which is simultaneously
> a frenzy of experimentation and a proliferation of schematizations,
> develops for itself.[78]

In this passage one can already detect in the italicized terms all the earmarks of a Derridean style that would be methodologically deployed in subsequent works. More importantly, we might note the transformation midpassage where Derrida ascribes the structuralist moments, their "method" as well as their "passion" for form, to a more original cause. Thus, the structuralist gesture is not original, but already a reproduction or response to an ontological becoming that has resulted in the shaking of foundations of science and knowledge. In truth, "the structuralist activity," as Barthes once defined it, is here described as a supreme passivity, an openness and a vibration with a more original event having to do with "our historical dislocation." Today one is left only to demonstrate its "taking place," to allow its event to unfold throughout all its ramifications, a task of demonstration that requires an infinite patience of a Derridean style of radical critique.[79] Here, the character of the *krinein,* the crisis demonstrated by means of the critique, bears a negativity that speaks to a secret affiliation between the Derridean style of critique and Heideggerian *Lassenheit* (as a "letting be" or "opening to" the eventuality of the event of difference), but that also opens to the dimension of the "not yet" or the "to come," a patently *noncreative* dimension of *a nonstyle*.

Stepping back from this extremely shorthand sketch of a major distinction in these two philosophies of difference, one can now glimpse the reason behind Derrida's hesitation over the definition of philosophy as "the creation of concepts."[80] For Derrida, the task of philosophy is largely demonstrative, and although the creation of a new concept can serve to demonstrate a shift in or transformation of the old ground (or closure), it cannot become the highest definition of philosophical activity. In fact, this supreme act of creativity, "this frenzy of experimentation and proliferation of schematization" as Derrida would say, is only the effect of a more primordial dislocation, which becomes the condition of any subsequent "play" and "creation." Although the force of creativity is often characterized as a power (for example, as a power of imagination and affection), in fact it is the power of a fundamental passivity, weakness, impotence, disengagement—*critique and emancipation*. Consequently, deconstruction is not an act of creation, but rather the demonstration (monstration, or the bringing to manifestation) of a silent lapsus that insists in any order of signification, marking the very opening of this order to what exceeds it. In this way, *différance* can be better likened to the manifestation of the silent *lapsus calumi* that Freud discovered in *The Psychopathology of Everyday Life.* When a slip of the tongue or pen occurs, the literal meaning of the text is opened to another text, another production or logic of signification. The slip, the error, or lapse—all interrogate this order, which can never close upon itself finally to assign identity, or meaning. In a certain sense, one can say on the basis of the above that Derrida also believes with Deleuze that the nature of the unconscious is productive, although this production is not for that reason located in an "unconscious" as an agent of production and creativity. Rather, the unconscious is the name for the silent lapse that strikes against the being of language. What is the other name for this silence but writing? Thus, I return to my initial question. Can we imagine a philosopher today who did not write? In response, I would pose another question: Is there anything more pitiful than a writer? Anything more deluded, more helpless, more in error? The one who writes is not to be admired. He (or she, but what difference does this make, except the trait of a final anthropomorphism of the writing machine?) only suffers from a delirium, that is, from a lack of style. Style, then, can only represent a partial solution to the "altogether threatening silence" that strikes against the being of one who writes, "Unquestioning. I, say I. Unbelieving."[81]

6

THE IMAGE OF THOUGHT
IN MODERN CINEMA:
THE BRAIN MACHINE
(CA. 1985)

- Between Image and Opinion *(doxa)*
- On "Spiritual Automata"
- Modern Cinema and the Brain
- Between Virtual Instinct and the Brain World

The problem we have been preoccupied with concerns the renewal of the image of thought experienced by modern philosophy, given the new situation I described in the Introduction where the classical image of thought has either grown stale, or philosophy is no longer a machine for producing real intensive ideas coexisting with signs and impressions on a plane of immanence. However, this problem is not experienced by philosophy alone, but is also present in the development of modern cinema. In fact, the problem of renewal of the image has been the basis of the various renewals that have occurred in modern cinema, particularly in what is commonly referred to as "intellectual cinema," and is present from the very beginning of this modern industrial art form. For this reason, in the mid-1980s, immediately following the completion of the second volume with Guattari, Deleuze turned his attention to this corollary crisis around the "image of thought" in modern cinema, especially in what he calls "the cinema of the brain." The two volumes of the cinema studies, *Cinema 1: The Movement-Image* and *Cinema 2: The Time-Image,* should in no way be understood as "film theory"; rather, they are Deleuze's attempt to draw a map of the situation confronted by modern cinema concerning its own image that might provide philosophy with a new means of creating concepts that would replace its earlier universals. Concerning the relationship between cinema and thought, Deleuze writes in the conclusion to *Cinema 2*:

> Cinema is not a universal or primitive language system [*langue*], nor a language [*langage*]. It brings to light an intelligible content, *which is like a presupposition,* a condition, that is, a necessary correlate by which language constructs its own "objects" (signifying units and operations). But this correlate, though inseparable, is specific: it consists of movements and thought processes (prelinguistic images), and of points of view on these movements and processes (pre-signifying signs). It consists of a whole "psychomechanics," *the spiritual automaton.*[1]

Moreover, in *Cinema 2* we find another installment of our earlier chapters on "the image of thought" that we have discussed in relation to *Proust and Signs* and *Difference and Repetition,* this time in relation to what Deleuze calls "the cinema of the brain."

Once again, let's recall our guiding questions: What kind of image is to be deduced from thought? How can thinking be determined by the image, and where does image first acquire its power over thought—that is, to induce, to *provoke* what is called "thinking" to occur within the subject? In attempting to respond to these questions around the relationship between modern cinema and thought (or the brain), Deleuze recounts a story of modern cinema concerning a vague and nebulous interval where thinking is attached to an image, only later to go astray and to lose its way back through "the image" to the actualization of the interval in thought. As I have already discussed in chapter 1, cinema is immanently machinic (i.e., a machine for producing images of perception, language, emotion, and thought—a "brain machine," or what Deleuze calls a "spiritual automaton"), which is shown to succumb to repeated and frequent crashes in the modern period, either by getting trapped in reproducing a habitual automatic movement (clichés of perception and stock experience), or by being "stolen away" by other technical machines that transform its creative powers and cause it to serve their own ends in reproducing national or class interests, or simply in making money. Walter Benjamin had clearly perceived these dangers when he stated that modern cinema represents the technological synthesis of the goals of art with the goals of politics, which could produce nothing more than the very conditions necessary for the emergence of fascism. (Albert Speer's crystal palace of National Socialism prefigures Industrial Light and Magic by only half a century.) The fact that Benjamin's early assessment of the industrial art form has been surpassed by more difficult and finer analyses of the problems of mass art and mass politics in "an age of mechanical reproduction" does not make his argument any less accurate or thought provoking for us today.

On the second level, intimately bound up with the first, Deleuze locates the point of divergence in a veritable crisis around the "image of thought" that takes as its goal a "total provocation of the human brain" (i.e., the principle of "nooshock") as it is first defined by Sergei Eisenstein. For Eisenstein, the early lesson of the Kabuki offered a highly artificial and stylized set of conventions for the production of cinematographic representation while avoiding the trappings of "naturalism," or "vulgar realism."[2] Its contrapuntal method provides the example of an extreme formalism with regard to the possibilities of construction and, at the same time, an extremely free and indeterminate range of possible combinations with regard to the elements of expression. Consequently, there is a certain freedom sought in the ensemble of the elements of the spectacle, although this does not presuppose that they are uncoordinated. Rather, their assemblage bears the collective unity of a team working toward a common goal—"Kabuki is soccer"—and the "goal" is precisely the event that is defined above as the "total provocation of the brain."[3] In fact, the "goal" in soccer is a perfect illustration of the nature of the cinematographic event. Although the various components and elements that come together as its condition (the ball, the players, the grid or field of play, the rules of the game, etc.), they do not take the form of a direct causality, because the scoring shot is an *effect* that surpasses all of the former even though it presupposes their free and indeterminate coordination. Without this freedom and play between the various components, scoring a goal would simply be a matter of following a predetermined order or causal sequence like a physical process or a mathematical equation. Thus, it is by a strict adherence to technique that film becomes a process that can break open the already established forms of perception and thought and discover a fresh syntax before words, before images.

Eisenstein contrasts this technique with the function of "orthodox montage" in cinema, which operates by means of the "dominant" (a leading indicator or guiding shot). For example, taking the following sequence of montage images—a gray old man, a gray old woman, a white horse, a snow-covered roof—the meaning of the sequence will be determined, in orthodox montage, by the guiding shot, which "'christens' the whole sequence in one direction or another."[4] For example, we might add, preferably earlier on in the series, the whiteness of cataracts in a pupil, thereby producing the feeling of the hardening of old age, or a rheum of saliva forming at the corner of the mouth expressing its concomitant regression, or "becoming a child"; perhaps even a wide-angle shot of a winter field in which all distinguishable boundaries are erased by snowdrifts producing the impression of the fading of memory and the approach of death. These elements come together to produce the illusory effect of cinematic duration much in the same manner that cognitive science might account for the "illusion" of conscious duration by constructing the following sort of formula: a red light is followed by a green light, producing in the spectator's consciousness the "illusion" of continuous movement, or "red becoming green." This illusion, baptized as such by the presence of a subject who determines the separate components as synthetically real, is precisely the shadow traced by the movement-image across an interval made up of overtonal associations and undertonal depths. That is, "the central stimulus . . . is attended always by a whole complex of secondary stimuli" that are spatially inexpressible and constitute a dimension that is exterior to the image, but from which the image draws its components for expressing a feeling of lived duration, a duration that closely resembles "intuition," although this must be understood as overflowing a purely psychological determination.[5]

The goal of "thought montage" exemplifies a break with preestablished forms of visibility and sense in order to restore the immanence between thought and the brain: to give thought a sensible form, one of shock, which yields an emotional intelligence (one of conviction, or belief), and which, in turn, lays claim to the reality of what is perceived.

Taking up Deleuze's account of the character of "automatic thinking" that appears as a result of the early dominance of the movement-image, the image first acquires this power over thought because the industrial art of cinema already "makes movement the immediate given of the image" and it is only a small step between movement and thought in as much as "automatic movement gives rise to a spiritual automaton in us, which reacts in turn on movement."[6] In other words, cinema achieves by direct means what was only indirectly present (or even demanded) by the other arts where it is spirit (or mind) that causes movement to occur: for example, the eyes to trace the words across the page, to follow the curvature of the lines in painting or sculpture, or to apprehend the composition of bodies in dance or theatre, or the ears to discern the melody across a surface of notes. Within cinematic duration, on the contrary, "it is the image itself which moves in itself" (i.e., automatic-movement), no longer dependent "on a moving body or object which realizes, nor on a spirit which reconstitutes it."[7] The movement-image is primary and now occupies the position of the subject-that-moves or the subject that causes movement; the mind must react or respond to the movement that is immediately given, and this response is organically part of the image itself, marking an event that Deleuze will define by the concept of "nooshock." The cause of thinking and perceiving is no longer on the side of the subject, and so thinking is no longer a logical possibility that one can either take up or not, but instead becomes a physiological imperative, a "totally physiological sensation."[8] The mind of the spectator is forced to respond, to react, to think; and this, in turn, changes the shape and the sensibility of thought, which appears from a shadowy region that is outside the subject's own powers of auto-affection. Henceforth, it appears as if in this moment receptivity of the image assumes a command structure: LOOK! In other words, REACT!

We might take these remarks concerning Eisenstein's theory of intellectual montage as preliminary to a more general discussion of the relationship between cinema and thought, so long as we keep in mind that a battle is being waged over the territory of the human brain, which appears here as both the "spiritual automaton," the dummy of natural consciousness, and as its double, "the cinematographic I THINK." If the threat of "naturalism" is what Deleuze calls a certain "spiritual

automaton" that exists within each one of us, cinema solves this problem
by the artificial creation of another automaton that enters into conflict
with the first by causing it to react. The explosive shock, therefore, is
simply the registered effect of an opposition between two "spiritual au-
tomatons" on the brain, which is then mediated by the dialectic of intellectual montage. Deleuze describes this dialectic as follows:

> [Intellectual] montage is in thought, "the intellectual process itself,"
> or that which, under the effects of the shock, thinks the shock.
> Whether it is visual or aural, the image already has the harmonics
> which accompany the perceived dominant image, and enter in their
> own ways into super-sensory relations . . . : this is the shock-wave
> of the nervous vibration, which means that we can no longer say "I
> see," "I hear," but "I FEEL," "totally physiological sensation." And it
> is the set of harmonics acting out on the cortex which gives rise to
> thought, the cinematographic I THINK; the Whole as subject.[9]

Thus, as "the most notable of arts," the industrial art of cinema assumes
the pinnacle of the progression that Hegel had earlier established for
philosophy; Eisenstein himself had described the potential for cinema
to replace philosophy as the true and authentic expression of dialectical
materialism. If the "dialectic" can be understood as the movement-
image that causes thinking to occur in the subject, even as the unfolding
of thought itself in its relationship to perception and to language, then
the movement-image in cinema has a more direct means of causing
movement to occur and to make language and perception the material
of a brain machine; therefore, "the form of montage is a restoration of
the laws of the process of thought, which in turn restores moving reality
in the process of unfolding."[10] If Deleuze shares in this optimism, however, the experience has been modified by the direction taken by both
cinema and philosophy in the postwar period. If the event of thought
itself, which has been named by Heidegger and differently by Artaud, is
the moment when we are confronted by the fact *that we are not yet
thinking (impouvoir)*, then cinema shares in this event by establishing as
its highest goal that moment when we apprehend that we are not yet
perceiving or hearing "the world as it is."

Once again, in Deleuze's account the figure of Antonin Artaud occupies the pinnacle moment of this break where the "image of thought," instead of becoming identified with the power of a subject capable of externalizing itself in a series of images by which the Whole undergoes change, instead becomes fissured and more receptive to a fundamental powerlessness that testifies to "the impossibility of thinking that is thought" (Artaud). "It is indeed a matter, as it was for Eisenstein," Deleuze writes, "of bringing cinema together with the innermost reality of the brain," but this innermost reality is not the Whole, but on the contrary a fissure, or "crack."[11] In other words, thought does not accede to a form that belongs to a model of knowledge, or fall to the conditions of an action; rather, thought exposes its own image to an "outside" that hollows it out and returns it to an element of "formlessness." We might conceive of this event in terms of the notion of formlessness that we explicated earlier in relation to modern art or literature, except in this instance the relationship to the Whole undergoes an absolute break, which in the subject takes the form of a permanent and irreparable state of disbelief. Thus, the problem of ideology receives its most authentic expression from Artaud when he cries: *My body was stolen away from me before birth; my brain has been used by an Other who thinks in my place.* Artaud experienced and gave expression to this problem in its most extreme form, as if suffering from the memory of a physical, mental, and spiritual rape. However, "rape" is being employed here not as simple metaphor but instead as the most direct translation of Artaud's complaint; it reveals the nature of "the total physiological sensation" of the spiritual automaton that enters in to violate the subject even before birth.

In response to this new situation of thought, our question then becomes: How can we distinguish between all the images that compose the subject's conscious existence, or extract thought from all these clichés in order to set it up against them? How does thinking become truly "critical" of its own image? According to Deleuze, Artaud experienced this problematic concerning the image of thought, which can be summarized as follows: the impossibility of not thinking, the impossibility of thinking, and the impossibility of thinking differently. The first part of this triad, "the impossibility of not thinking," in relation to the subject of cinema, concerns the automatic character of thought which it shares with the movement-image, since even my refusal to think only signals that place where another thinks in my place. Not thinking, therefore, appears to Artaud as impossible *a priori*. Likewise, the second and third parts concern thinking as a special power or quality that belongs to the subject, which is also found to be impossible in the sense that thought (or "what is called thinking," whether this activity is represented as a common notion, a special class of opinions, or by a dominant historical image—e.g., "Hegelianism") must ultimately be determined as a transcendental cliché (or *Ur-doxa*).

Was it only because the automatic character of thought already found a resemblance with the automatic character of the movement-image that cinema discovered the dynamic principle by means of which it could appear as the force that causes the subject to think? The dominant image of thought appears within in this resemblance as a power in accordance with the power of Nature, or with the order of technology by which knowledge intervenes to "work over," to fundamentally transform the interval Nature-Culture. According to this dynamic representation, thinking is a Power that has as its beginning a point of projection (a subject) and as its end a transformed nature or a fabricated object (a world); between these two points there is a certain directionality or orientation by which thought is translated spatially from subject to object, from culture to nature, and from the idea of Whole to the Whole transfigured. Therefore, because of this mere resemblance the movement-image acquires a certain power to determine the Whole, and the appearance of this power is then consolidated as a specialized technical knowledge, and finally, the whole problem of the resemblance between the movement-image in cinema and the images deployed by the apparatus of the ideology ensues. Only on the basis of this understanding is Virilio's earlier thesis correct: that there has been no diversion of the movement-image to ideological ends, but rather the "movement-image was from the beginning linked to the organization of war, state propaganda, ordinary fascism, historically and essentially."[12] However, this resemblance in fact only implies that the problem of ideology was already latent in the subject and was simply awaiting its final birth. The monster that emerges is the automatic character of thought as a power that could internalize the Whole within a subject, and then externalize the collective subject as a Whole (a national conscience, a state, a world-order).

Should the failure of a classical cinema founded upon the movement-image, such as its goals and aspirations were formulated early on by Eisenstein, not be inferred from an image of thought that was still attached to this problematic resemblance? Did this resemblance not condition Eisenstein's belief that cinema will eventually achieve, by perfecting its knowledge of the movement-image, the means to repair the broken interval that appears as the cause of the subject's collective fragmentation? To unify the subject by crossing in both directions the gap between instinct and intelligence, and between thinking and action—both would amount to absorbing the interval into the synthesis of the movement-image. Because this perfection was understood primarily in terms of the action-image, conceived as the solution to neurosis of bourgeois art forms and to collective fragmentation effected by the ideological apparatus of mass culture, it is finally ironic to see that precisely the action-image itself was the cause of this neurosis in the first place. Thus, the "action-image" was itself a cliché of a very special type; to evoke the "revolutionary" potential of the new cinema seems contradictory. It was, in fact, a false solution that only furthered the break between the human being and the world, even realizing this impasse as an absolute and giving it an objectified form of purely optical and sound situations in which the subject appears to be trapped. Deleuze argues that this is an impasse upon which the new postwar cinema is founded—nihilism is not a spirit that is restricted to philosophy alone. At the same time, as he suggests, there may still be hope.

Beginning from this situation, and even affirming it as the fundamental condition of a new image of thought, is the solution Deleuze presents as the major thesis of *Cinema 2*: not to attach thought to a motor image that would extinguish it in action, or absorb it in knowledge, but to attach it directly to the interval itself so that thought would find its cause no longer in the image, but in what in the image refuses to be thought. In other words, if the whole problem of thought was that it was attached to an image that represented it, then postwar cinema turns this problem around to reveal its true experience of thinking for the subject.

"The spiritual automaton is in the psychic situation of a seer, a true visionary who sees better and further than he can react, that is, think."[13] What this experience reveals is precisely the automatic, habitual, and instinctual character of the thought that thinks within me, interpellating me with its image, and determining me as a subject. One might still define this experience under the principle of "nooshock" as in the classical cinema of the movement-image; however, the nature of this experience of thinking has undergone a radical transformation. Under its previous image, shock, the neuronal messenger, simply travels along the same path that was opened by a more fundamental power that appears as the goal of both modern cinema and ideology. But this implies that the cause of thinking remains unconscious in principle, because it can never really emerge as a motive of conscious understanding or become the condition of deliberative action. Instead, thought leaps over the interval to become in principle the conditions of an action that remains fundamentally unthought, like an involuntary reaction, habitual response, or nerve impulse. Under its new image, this dynamic representation of thinking as a force is no longer "the goal," and the problem is no longer in attaining an "image of thought" that would be equal to the force of the Whole (i.e., the perfection of "the action-image"), but rather that this image of thought itself, defined as a force or a power, is suddenly revealed as an "Other." It reveals precisely the shock that "I am not yet thinking" or that "what is called thinking" is a power that belongs to a subject whom *I am not* ("I is an Other"). The effect of this awareness, moreover, bears a certain "dissociative force" that pries thought from its image, at the same time as it cuts the image off from the world, and exposes it to what Deleuze calls its "reverse proof," the fact that we are not yet thinking.[14]

Because cinema and ideology are equally expressions of the same broken interval between the human and the world, an interval that has reduced the link to only what the subject hears and sees, this has precipitated in the transformation of the world as an object of belief, even if this belief should prove illusory. Precisely because everything I see and hear is capable of being false, only my belief is capable of reconnecting me with what I see and hear. "It was already a great turning-point in philosophy, from Pascal to Nietzsche: to replace the model of knowledge with belief."[15] This is what Deleuze calls the "reverse proof of thinking," which bears a resemblance to the Cartesian proof, except that the powers of the false do not lead to the certainty of the *modern cogito,* but only to the creative discovery of the false as a higher power that belongs to thought itself. (In some ways, this also recalls a statement made earlier in *Difference and Repetition:* "It is repetition that has made us ill; therefore, it is only repetition that will heal us."[16]) If there is a resemblance to the Cartesian solution, therefore, it represents a solution without any recourse to the principle of God who provides the subject with any certainty with regard to the true source of its perceptions, feelings, and desires. Likewise, the subject of modern cinema, after reducing the world to the conditions of the image, can only intervene into the fold that runs between the brain and the world in order to effect a transformation in the signs of perception and consciousness. After all, all thought is full of clichés, all memory is not to be trusted, and all perception is made-to-order. It is ironic then, that the only means we have of restoring a connection that has been broken or damaged is by the very means that has caused our separation, by means of perception-images, memory-images, sounds and statements. This is why postwar cinema, according to Deleuze, will be concerned with rendering an experience or connection between the brain and the world, creating new visual and sound images that might "give back" the brain's relationship to the world, which has been lost in a chaos of clichés. Even though cinema has lost the belief in its own "action-image," and cannot intervene directly into the world or cause this world to be transformed into another, cinema might be one of the only means we have of restoring our belief in the world as it is. Deleuze's optimism here is a strange optimism: to continue to believe in cinema, despite everything, despite even the repeated "failures" of cinema itself, is also to restore our belief in the world.

To summarize our brief historical trajectory from the dominance of the movement-image to a moment of crisis that reveals the conditions of the time-image, if Deleuze shares with Eisenstein a certain guarded optimism for intellectual cinema, he descends to discover its true principle, freedom, and its true subject, the brain. Freedom of what, or rather, freedom from what? Here Deleuze's response is quite simple: freedom from the motor-unity coordination of the movement-image and from the teleological unity of action-image. All of the different solutions to the problem of the image that cinema invents are real paths leading to the brain, in the sense that all paths lead to the brain, although the images that these paths actualize never resemble the brain. Therefore, the brain is not an image, even though every image actualizes a certain aspect (or lobe) of the brain. Thus, in a 1986 interview, "The Brain Is the Screen," Deleuze directly addresses the relationship between cinema and thought in terms of the brain:

> The brain is the unity. The brain is the screen. Around this point, I don't think that linguistics or psychoanalysis will offer much assistance, but rather the biology of the brain, or even molecular biology. Thought is molecular and is made up of molecular speeds that come together to compose the slower bodies we are. This is what Michaux said: "The human is a slow being, which is only possible thanks to the most fantastic speeds." The circuits and cerebral connections do not precede stimuli, nor the corpuscles and grains that trace them. Cinema is not theater, it composes bodies with grains. These connections are often paradoxical, and exceed in every sense the simple association of images. But precisely because it places the image in movement, or moreover makes of it an auto-movement, cinema never ceases to trace and retrace the cerebral circuits. Here, again, this could be for better or worse. The screen, that is we ourselves, can become a deficient brain of an idiot just as easily as a creative brain.[17]

In other words, the brain is the "goal." Of course, it was the goal all along, as we have seen in Eisenstein's remarks on the Kabuki. However, instead of conceiving of the brain as an organ, where thought is essentially a muscular contraction between stimulus and response, we might instead conceive it as the sensible screen (a membrane), an interval that is interposed between the human and the world (the chaos of clichés), as the quality of a creative emotion that is capable of revitalizing the link between the human and the world. That is to say, with the discovery of the time-image, cinema achieves a freedom from the sensory-motor schema, the spatial coordinates of the action-image and the movement-image. Eisenstein had already raised this possibility in 1929, concerning what he calls the "fourth dimension" of the cinematic image:

> For the musical overtone (a throb) it is not strictly fitting to say: "I hear."
> Nor for the visual overtone: "I see."
> For both a new uniform formula must enter our vocabulary: "I feel."[18]

In this sense, a third kind of image appears in the interval between perception and reaction—"emotion," understood as the "I FEEL" of the cinematographic subject, which occupies the interval without "filling it up." Thus, it shares a certain attribute with the image of the brain, which is simultaneously outside movement, before movement, and the cause of movement. "The interval is set free, the interstice becomes irreducible and stands on its own."[19]

Deleuze returned many times to what he described as "our new relationship to the brain." How does Deleuze define this relationship? In *Cinema 2,* Deleuze replies that because we now understand that "the brain is no more a reasonable system than the world is rationally constructed," now "the brain becomes our illness, our passion, rather than our mastery, our solution or decision."[20] What is crucial to observe in this description of the brain as a "symptom" is Deleuze's assertion that the interval between brain and world, between stimulus and response, is now governed by the irrational cut, marking the gaps *(écarts)* or the points of uncertainty between inside and outside (perception or hallucination, associative memory or representation of the past); hence, the relation between brain and world becomes a topological point between inside and outside in an uncertain, probabilistic, and a-centered system. In other words, this describes precisely our current relationship to the brain, to the world, one that psychoanalysis has also proposed by consciousness within an a-centered system of unconscious processes, and by asking the question whether it is "I" who thinks, perceives, wills, desires, or rather an "Other" that thinks in my place. At the same time, Deleuze argues that psychoanalysis is still based on a rational cerebral model (or system) of structure or language; consequently, the relation-ship between brain and world still appears "rational," "ordered," according to certain laws or principles that can be mapped onto Euclidean space. A psychoanalytic image of the brain, in other words, is still deterministic and based on the idea of an absolute causality even when this is assigned to an unconscious level of the psychic apparatus. Freud was absolutely certain that everything happens by necessity and that there are no accidents in the Unconscious, for without this certainty, the logic of the lapse, of the slips of the tongue, of wit or humor, would remain meaningless. Even with Lacan, the relationship between signifier and signified is open to definite metonymic displacements that appear irrational until they are "interpreted" by the law of the algorithm (that is, the bar that both separates and unifies both series, and allows for infinite substitutability in the signifying series), or what Deleuze and Guattari refer to as "The Law of the Signifier."

We might understand the algorithmic bar that separates signifier and signified as an image of the interval *(écart)* between inside and outside, which still functions according to a certain model whereby irrational significations refer to an underlying grid of semiotic determinations (hence, the image of the dream work). This is because pure associations are still determined as unconscious semiotic acts that can be reconstructed by analysis and shown to belong to a language, since "the Unconscious is structured like a language." By contrast, following Guattari's earlier rejection of the linguistic model, Deleuze refers to another cerebral model that is evolving in new studies of the Brain by modern sciences, no longer based on semiotic model, or structural paradigm, which itself is derived from an earlier metaphysical image of Reason. "The discovery of the synapse was enough in itself to shatter the idea of a continuous cerebral system (i.e., the Brain as a whole, or as a unified system), since it laid down irreducible points or cuts. . . . in the case of chemical synapses, the point is 'irrational,' the cut is important in itself and belongs to neither of the two sets it separates. . . . Hence the greater importance of a factor of uncertainty, or half uncertainty, in the neuronal transmission."[21] Here we see the image of an algorithmic function different from that of the bar that separates the two signifying series but that in a certain sense belongs to both series as their implicit relation.

Instead, we have the image of an "irrational cut" that operates according a principle of uncertainty, which implies an entirely different cerebral model, one no longer based on the idea of a Deep Structure.

How can we imagine this new model for representing the brain? In *What Is Philosophy?* Deleuze and Guattari argue that the brain is, very simply, a "Form in Itself" admitting no Gestalt image or exterior point of view from which it could be objectified.[22] They constantly employ the term *survole* (meaning "survey," or, in its verbal form, "to fly over") as a description of the plane occupied by the Brain, defining the movement across or over this plane as one of infinite speed without delay or distance. Thus, the nature of this movement is defined by its speed, which is instantaneous, in which there is no gap, interval, or hiatus. Consequently, *there is no "in-between" between the brain and the world*; the subject-object relation is merely a secondary, a posteriori addition to the plane of immanence constituted by Brain-World. The question then becomes: Why does this a posteriori divide emerge repeatedly in representational systems? And here is the real question Deleuze is attempting to answer by returning to the problem of the Brain, which he regards as the primary subject of philosophy even though modern philosophy shares *(partage)* this subject with both science and art: Given our relationship to the brain has changed, why does Representation remain a dominant principle that continues to structure this relationship?

Perhaps this might explain Deleuze's own interest in modern cinema, in particular, which he argues also opens to a different manner of depicting thought (or the cerebral interval), one that is no longer isomorphically modeled on the semiotic system of language, as in the statement from the conclusion of *Cinema 2* quoted at the beginning of this chapter; rather, "it consists of movements and thought processes (prelinguistic images), and of points of view on these movements and processes (presignifying signs)." Of course, cinema has always been conceived as a supplemental perception-consciousness apparatus that is built upon the scaffolding of the faculties of perception and the imagination—and let's not forget desire!—but how would we revise this secondary or supplemental function when viewed from the perspective of the Brain itself? This is the importance of Eisenstein for Deleuze, who constantly challenged the growing dominance of linguistic formalism for understanding the purely visual logic of cinema. Deleuze takes up Eisenstein's classic cause against the "talking cinema" and attempts to develop a new model for understanding the assemblage of optical and sonorous signs (but also "lectosigns," "chronosigns," "noosigns," and so forth) in film language, creating a new logic of montage itself. It is here that Kubrick and Resnais become important modern figures (or auteurs) in the period of the time-image, in some ways complementary to Eisenstein's role in the period of classical cinema, because the cinema of both directors functions as a mise-en-scène of the brain.

For example, in Kubrick's films the depiction of this mise-en-scène can be understood, on one level, as the depiction of the brain-world that is organized according to a rational model of the brain. Deleuze recounts many examples in the discussion of Kubrick: the alignment of the trenches in *Paths of Glory,* the apparatus of SAC and the military machine or chain of command in *Dr. Strangelove,* the regimented barracks or prison in *A Clockwork Orange* and *Full Metal Jacket,* the instrument panels and architecture of the *Discovery* in *2001: A Space Odyssey,* and the symmetrical patterns of carpeting in the hallways of the Overlook Hotel in *The Shining.* These form the background of all of Kubrick's sets, providing a "feeling" of an organization of all elements that is highly structured according to the image of the rational model of the brain. At the same time, there is always another image of the brain introduced around the point of an "irrational cut," representing a lapsus, an error, a moment of dementia that gradually enters into combat with this other image of the brain and threatens to overturn it entirely, producing disturbances of association, hallucination, memory, even wild disturbances that are interpreted through the conventions of psychosis and paranoia. For example, in *Dr. Strangelove* we have the demented mind of General Jack D. Ripper, who functions as the expression of an irreducible cerebral crash in the military brain (or the chain of command of SAC), but whose dementia cannot be accounted for according to a rational model. Here, Kubrick presents us precisely with the improbable synapse or connection (communist conspiracy = attack of precious bodily fluids, producing the signifiers O.P.E. and P.O.E.), which functions as the "irrational cut" that suddenly causes the whole system to crash. It is interesting to note that in a rare interview Kubrick himself commented on the question of the potential that the irrational cut poses in the military brain and its complete lack of any defense against its organic counterpart.

> It's improbable, but not impossible, that we could someday have a psychopathic president, or a president who suffers a nervous breakdown, or an alcoholic president who, in the course of some stupefying binge, starts a war. . . . Less farfetched, and even more terrifying is the possibility that a psychopathic individual could work his way into the lower echelons of the White House staff. Can you imagine what might have happened at the heights of the Cuban Missile Crisis if some deranged waiter had slipped LSD into Kennedy's coffee—or, on the other side of the fence, into Khrushchev's vodka? The possibilities are chilling.[23]

Of course, the most commonly discussed example is the simple computational error that eventually leads to "paranoid break" of the HAL 9000 in *2001: A Space Odyssey,* producing an uncertain and unfathomable point of view concerning HAL's actions or perception of the astronauts. (To view this as paranoia, however, is only a purely psychoanalytic interpretation of the HAL's mechanical decision to erase the astronauts as anomalous elements in his own program.) In *The Shining,* the primary topical location of the irrational lapse of memory and hallucination is the demented mind of the caretaker in the Overlook Hotel; it is also reflected in the hallucinatory visions of the gifted child, Danny (whose gift, moreover, is the result of physical abuse by the father, producing a consequent clairvoyant state, the production of a double as a form of defense against death), and in the Overlook Hotel itself, which represents the mise-en-scène of an overly traumatized brain producing the "feeling" (and the horror) of a psychotic interiority populated by the events of violence and perversion that have composed its past.

Building on many of these examples, Deleuze employs Kubrick's films to illustrate our new relationship to the Brain—our relationship to the world (the topological relationship between consciousness-thought and perception-reality) is governed by an uncertain and irrational principle that is represented by the Brain, producing an outside that extends much farther than external perception and an inside that is deeper than any subjective interiority of the subject. Thus, in place of the linguistic model of the Unconscious, whose origins are actually owed to Lévi-Strauss, who first proposed that the Unconscious is not reservoir for contents any more than the stomach has any relation to the food it digests. Following the work of Gilbert Simondon, Deleuze proposes a new model that is both nonlinguistic (nonstructuralist) and "a-centered": "a relative distribution of organic internal and external environments (milieus) on a plane that represents an absolute interiority and exteriority, that is, a topological structure of the brain that cannot be adequately represented in a Euclidean way."[24] As also demonstrated by the above examples from the cinema of Kubrick, the existence of an a-centered cerebral system, governed by uncertainty, is what actually determines our relationship between different levels of reality. In other words, the relationship between Brain and World is determined by an irrational cut, which cannot be re-centered in an image of a rationale structure, but opens to multiple levels where the *de-cision* between reality and hallucination, present and past, cannot be topologically determined. In other words, what is *real* in this a-centered system no longer refers to the position of external reality, because the real may also be located at another point of interiority, or deep in the past. It is precisely for this reason that the system is a-centered and the interval between stimulus and response, perception and hallucination, cannot be mapped on the coordinates of external space or interior subjectivity, for these were simply the earlier coordinates or vectors used to orient perception-consciousness in representation systems.

Once again, the relationship to psychoanalysis and its positive discovery of the Unconscious is relevant here, although Kubrick might owe more to Kafka than to Freud in his depiction of the reality of the Unconscious. For example, *The Shining* is perhaps the most perfect depiction of this new topology; the Overlook Hotel is the main point of view (or brain-image), the name itself meaning both "a state of survey," "a mistake," and "trance" (or hallucination). Of course, it could be understood to represent Jack's psychotic interiority, but this is quickly dismissed by Kubrick as we understand that the reality of certain scenes and events depicted are not "projections" of Jack's demented mind. In this sense, Kubrick uses Danny's visions (as well as those of the chef, played by Scatman Crothers) as counterproof, thereby producing an a-centered cerebral image in which the position of reality cannot be resolved, topo-logically speaking, by referring either to some external point of view that would be determining or to the place of the subject determined by the principle of internal projection. Jack's perceptions are, at once, imaginary and real, virtual and actual. They are the internal associa-tions of memory belonging to the hotel and, at the same time, external perceptions of actual events and characters from Jack's point of view. What is most important about this uncertainty is that it actually pre-sents a discontinuous image of the brain—what is real external percep-tion for Jack is identified as psychotic hallucination from the point of view of Mrs. Torrance, but is perceived in a trance or vision from Dan-ny's perspective, and is a memory association from the point of view occupied by the Overlook itself, in which every event happens internal in a timeless present. What is important, for our purposes, is that Ku-brick uses this topology to map all the coordinates that belong to the current position of "reality" in order to depict a new—and troubling—relationship between brain and world.

At the same time, we might ask what has happened that has made the brain appear as the object of the new cinema, something that De-leuze finds explicitly in the films of Resnais, where characters become the shadows of the living reality of mental theatre, and where feelings become "the true figures in a 'cerebral game'" that is nonetheless con-crete.[25] Perhaps this is because to a great degree modern memory is al-ready cinematographic, and the brain of the world (the past) is already produced from cinema, or fashioned after the manner of cinema. Ac-cording to Deleuze, this is what happens when the image becomes time-image: "The world has become memory, brain, superimposition of ages or lobes, but the brain itself has become consciousness, continuation of ages, growth of ever new lobes, re-creation of matter."[26] The matter of cinema thus shares a material aspect of memory by which it descends into the interval to create memory and to actualize the past; whether this past is one of a people or a culture (monumental past) or of a person (private associations) is simply owed to the quantitative volume of im-ages. This recalls a passage from *Bergsonism* where Deleuze first posits a fictive and fabulous faculty, or "storytelling function," which appears in the interval between intelligence and society.

> Virtual instinct, creator of Gods, inventor of religions, that is, of
> fictitious representations which will stand up to the representation of
> the real and which will succeed, by the intermediary of intelligence
> itself, in thwarting intellectual work.[27]

At the same time, as Bergson had earlier argued, it is also within the very
same interval that something appears without "filling it up" or causing it
to contract into the form of an instinct. This "something that appears,"
according to Deleuze, is emotion, because "only emotion differs in nature from both intelligence and instinct, from both intelligent individual
egoism and instinctive social pressures."[28] It is around the nature of this
emotion that Deleuze resorts to the solution that Bergson used to characterize the interval between perception and response as the "gap" that
allows the human being to become open to a duration that remains "outside" its own plane, to transform the limited and "closed" present of
habit or instinctive reaction into the openness of creative intuition.

Finally, we must ask why emotion is here described as primarily an
expression of the brain rather than the body. Does this alternative even
make sense? First of all, is there any body without a brain? In other words,
is the body not merely an image first produced by the brain and invested
with a degree of conviction, almost certainty? In response we must recall the situation we earlier described in which belief was the only thing
capable of restoring our connection to the world. Thus, in the statement
"I FEEL," we have, not an image, but rather a mode that expresses a degree of openness that only then is filled by an image (joy, sadness, pain,
conflict, and so on). Here we must understand belief (or disbelief) as a
fundamental expression of creative emotion; therefore, if the human
being finds itself in the situation where its only connection to the world
is by what she sees or hears, then the belief in what she sees or hears
determines the strength or weakness of this connection, as well as characterizes the creation or invention of the qualitative intensity that
defines these connections. We could say the same of disbelief. For example, in the statements we often hear ourselves and others pronounce
these days—"I can't believe what I'm seeing," or "I can't believe what I'm
hearing"—there is a certain quality that characterizes the connection to
our perception or understanding. At what level do we separate thought

from this emotional quality? Is not thinking itself a manner of developing perceptions and statements under the signs of belief or disbelief, in such a way that what we describe as real or true are simply the objective signs of belief that thinking has created? In other words, reality itself is composed of signs that produce a lesser or greater degree of belief, and these signs in turn are qualities that one finds in the world and are bound up with the qualities of conscious-perception or subjective memory, or with the qualities of objects themselves.

For this reason Bergson characterized thought or creative memory as in principle an emotional being, because thinking operates on the objective signs and traces of belief and disbelief, which compose the material connections that make up a world. Thinking operates on these signs either by giving them fresh new perceptions and reestablishing their connection, or by destroying them and working them over in favor of new connections. As Deleuze writes very early on concerning the creative principle by which thinking operates:

> The principle that works in this way does so through a notion of "detonating the past": a virtual or fabulous instinct in the human is super-added to the animal instinct, producing the capability of "destroying" previous relations between perception-images and recollection-images, thereby creating the path toward new linkages and associations.[29]

This could be called the primal work of intelligence. We can find this principle in "dream-work," where the brain is constantly "working over" and preparing matter by destroying previous relations (the residual traces of the day's experiences) and creating a complex assemblage of new linkages. However, when the form of the dream itself is mistaken for this principle, as it was in the solution offered by Surrealism, making the form of the dream represent the power of this principle, then we lose the principle by enclosing it within the image of the dream—that is, by subordinating the principle under its image, or representation. A similar state of affairs was already discussed concerning the relationship of cinema and thought, which was enclosed in the form of the movement-image and its resemblance to the automatic character of thought. As a result, thought was enclosed in this resemblance and lost touch with the principle of thinking. This is the principle of memory that plunges into the interval between perception and consciousness, that expands or scrambles the residues of perception and prepares them for new combinations and rearrangements by conscious recollection. Here, the "past itself" cannot be determined outside this possibility of being scrambled and entering into new combinations with the present, with any present whatsoever: thus, memory conditions the principle of freedom whereby life frees itself from determination from the past and its "it was." In other words, as Deleuze says, "freedom has precisely this physical sense: 'to detonate' an explosive, to use it for more and more powerful movements."[30]

How does this come about? Following Bergson's earlier intuition in *Matter and Memory*, it is possible only because the brain constitutes a special type of matter that is more supple and less "closed." Therefore, "nothing here goes beyond the physico-chemical properties of a particularly complicated type of matter."[31] Contrary to a kind of matter that is "determined," the matter of the brain is capable of becoming "determining determination" (a *naturing nature*). This is why, in *What Is Philosophy?*, Deleuze and Guattari will later identify the brain *(le cerveau)* as nothing less than spirit itself *(l'esprit)*, or the "spiritualization of matter." Deleuze's *Bergsonism* already contains this insight as well, and Bergson's concept of *élan vital* represents the positive "discovery" of the privilege of the brain, by which Life "makes use" of the matter of the brain (that is, the matter of memory) in order to "get through the closed nature of Man," to leap from the closed circle of an already determined and "closed" nature. This would appear to be a problematic moment, because Deleuze is here affirming that the form of Man "is the purpose of the entire process of evolution";[32] in other words, he would appear to be saying that the nature of human beings is of the highest duration, and occupies the pinnacle, of the teleology of all of Nature, as if all of nature not only is determined by the nature of the human, but even has as its only goal to become human. However, this would not be an accurate conclusion, which is why Deleuze and Guattari return to the very same argument in *What Is Philosophy?* to propose it again, since it was badly understood the first time around. If the nature of human beings is *(quid facti?)* the *naturing nature* of the brain, then the question becomes, What is human? With this question, the priority is reversed and the duration occupied by the human is thus opened again to the principle creation of memory (of the brain). "Nature" does not find its end with the form of Man, because this form is closed, is alienated from itself, and must be overcome, and the brain is the machine that is capable of making this happen.

Concluding with these observations from *Bergsonism* and on the importance of the brain in Bergsonian philosophy, this may help to clarify why Bergson returns later on as a central figure in the cinema studies. Using Bergson's distinction, there is only a quantitative difference in degree between the human brain (as "spiritual automaton," or determined determination) and the cinematographic automaton, although there is equally for both a qualitative difference, or difference in kind, when we speak of the brain in principle. That is, when we speak of cinema as a process (as both Eisenstein and Deleuze speak of it), the quantitative differences between the two brains are dissolved into a single dynamic principle of creation and order, similar to Whitehead's understanding of a "subject superject." This might also clarify why, for Deleuze, the "cinematographic subject" (I THINK) can sometimes provide an image of "a people who are missing," according to the famously misunderstood refrain, as in the examples of the American Westerns of John Ford and the Soviet cinema that Eisenstein dreamed of creating but never fully realized. The subject of such a cinema would necessarily have to be outside language and national culture (or story); that is, it would have to be a "people" that was created by cinema itself, and could not depend upon politics for its creation, because politics actually "creates" nothing but only makes use of the creations of philosophy, art, and science.

In an original manner, in some ways similar to the writing machines invented by early modernist writers (Proust, Joyce, Kafka, Durrell), Eisenstein discovered in the "machine" of cinema a means of transcending the mechanisms of perception, opinion (common ideas, or views), and cliché in order to invent newer and finer articulations of the linkages between the human and the world (linkages that Deleuze would later call the creation "percepts and affects"). Modern cinema does this precisely by making use of stock conventions and habitual determinations "to pass through the net of determinations that have spread out" into a world (determinations of perception, opinion, character, etc.); however, it fashions its own conventions, which become *doxa* as well—and there is always a danger that these forms will become too rigid and dominant. There is also the danger of cinema in the service of an already existing national character, a kind of monumental cinema, which represents both the propagandistic function of Soviet cinema, but also of American popular cinema. Applying the above statements to the brain constructed by cinema, we might recognize in the "goal" of intellectual cinema the desire to build a better brain, "to leap from the circle of closed societies"; cinema "makes use" of the matter of the brain (that is, the matter of memory) in order to "get through," to leap from the closed circle of na-tured nature, "to make a machine to triumph over mechanism," "to use the determination of nature to pass through the meshes of the net which this very determination has spread."[33] Finally, does this not imply a dou-bling of an earlier solution Bergson found in the *élan vital?* That is, if the brain was invented to surpass a closed plane of nature, does the human in turn invent cinema in order to surpass the closed duration of Man? Here, it seems, the entire question of the relationship between cinema and thought becomes: What kind of brain do we want, the deficient brain of an idiot or the creative brain of a thinker?

CONCLUSION
"WE WILL SPEAK OF THE BRAIN . . ."

- Gestalt Principles of Reason
- Between Current and Vital Ideas
- "Theory" as a Normal Science
- The Future of the "Brain-Image"

Let us return finally to 1991. The new image of thought proposed in Deleuze and Guattari's last work together is at once extremely beautiful and incredibly violent, depicting a process of thinking marked by explosions and incredible speeds, but also by moments of unsupportable slow motion, both of which outstrip conscious perception. Here, we are confronted with an image of the brain determined as an a-centered and probabilistic system that is always *subject* to a confrontation with chaos, unable to support the unconscious leaps of memory and association belonging to what they define as a "Non-Objectified Brain." In fact, there are multiple leaps and just as many levels; each level or chain of associations representing what they define, following the thought of Michel Serres, as "successive filters placed over chaos."[1]

In the Conclusion I will focus on just one level of association—the leap between philosophy and cognitive psychology, Gestalt theory in particular, as one language of possibility space they employ to explore the plan of immanence that is defined by the modern brain *(cerveau)*. In fact, many of the terms they propose, such as productive thinking (i.e., creation) vs. reproductive thinking (i.e., opinion), also have their corollaries in Gestalt theory. Here, I underline three major principles of productive thinking:

1. A relative increase of speed in mental processes
2. The relative quantity of short-circuiting that occurs in normal reasoning
3. Finally, an unconscious leap in thought

I will take these up in order, because the third principle, the unconscious leap in thinking, is perhaps the most difficult to achieve and the first two themes might be understood as its conditions.

But first we need to have a better idea what Deleuze and Guattari mean by thinking as a creative process. Just as a painter does not paint on a blank canvas, or a writer on a blank page, the philosopher does not think from the beginning. Thought, the act of thinking, is predetermined from the outside and from within by a model of recognition (what Deleuze identifies with the functions of *doxa*, or opinion) that already gives what can be thought, what can be identified as thinking, and what remains to be thought (or, according to a term often employed by Heidegger, "what gives food for thought" [*Denkanstoß*]).[2] Yet, to paraphrase a statement by Michaux, what often suffices as a meal for "current ideas" does not suffice for "vital ideas," and the latter must be created rather than merely recognized.[3] Our problem, therefore, is to determine a process that would necessarily result in the creation of vital ideas— thus, to produce an image of a cerebral interval during which the genesis of thinking occurs.

Taking up the first principle, Deleuze and Guattari offer an initial description of this process in the following manner: to arrive at a concept, one must go beyond mere abstractions and arrive *as quickly as possible (le plus vite possible)* at "mental objects determinable as real beings"; one must make use of ideas and abstractions to get to the plane "where we leap from real being to real being."[4] Later on, I will return to the phrase "as quickly as possible" *(le plus vite possible),* which designates the act of leaping from ideas and abstractions to arrive at "mental objects determined as real beings." This represents only the first leap in Deleuze and Guattari's description; it does not stop there, because once the plane of real being is attained, then one must leap from real being and advance through the construction of concepts. To think quickly, to think on one's feet, entails a movement of leaping away from ideas and abstractions. Ideas and abstractions are merely the springboard for the philosophical diver to achieve the plane occupied by concepts ("mental objects determinable as real beings"), as if crashing through its surface and touching its depths. According to this analogy, any philosopher (or "theorist," for that matter) who spends too much time on the preexisting plane of ideas and abstractions is like the diver who never enters the pool.

As an example of this, let us take the "current idea" of the virtual. This idea still remains an abstraction. Is this the fault of the concept, of Deleuze who first introduces it in *Bergsonism* (1966) and then returns to take it up many times throughout his works? Or rather is it the responsibility of the kind of thinking that never takes a leap and advances from the idea itself to the virtual as a real being? Many recent commentaries dwell on the idea of the virtual, trying to define it as if it belonged to an ontology (e.g., the virtual *is* this, the virtual *is not* that), but Deleuze himself already left these questions behind long ago by taking a veritable leap with the following intuition: The virtual *is* the brain itself (or rather, it is the "turning point" where the brain becomes a subject). But at this point the question immediately becomes, What is a brain? Here the task is to create an image of the brain that is capable of supporting the leap of association in the construction of the concept of the virtual.

The organic brain, the one we have as an image, is not yet capable of such a leap, and it is only for this reason that the brain-image remains abstract or is immediately lost in a chaos of associations. Chaos is not simply a disorganized whole, but rather the infinite speed by which ideas disappear, half formed, "already eroded by forgetfulness and precipitated into others we no longer master."[5] Thus, chaos is the constant pressure of formlessness, and here we might understand the deep image of Gestalt as the expression of the organic brain that is trying to maintain all of its integral connections in the face of a constant pressure to dissipate its intensities and excitations into an immobile block of purely chemical energy. It is into the interval opened by the specific tension that the function of "opinion" (intelligent instinct, or instinctual intelligence) emerges as a representative of the brain in its struggle with chaos, since "we require just a little order to protect us from chaos."[6]

But who is the "we" here? It is not the "subject" (neither man, the *cogito*, a transcendental Subject, nor an original and pre-ontological intentionality) that issues this demand for a little order as protection against chaos. In other words, as Deleuze and Guattari write, *"there would not be a little order in ideas if there was not also a little order in things or states of affairs, like an objective anti-chaos."*[7] In fact, it is the brain itself that becomes the true locus of this order, or rather, the idea of order itself appears as a certain "cerebral crystallization" of a *Non-Objectified Brain,* which might very well have assumed the image of Reason, as in the case of Kant's transcendental synthesis, or of God as the principle of *Harmonia Prestabilitia,* as in the system of Leibniz, or the mystery of parallelism that belongs to Nature itself according to Spinoza. In each case, the brain becomes the subject, or rather *"superject,"* as Deleuze says following the thought of Whitehead.

> The concept becomes object as created, as event or creation itself . . .
> and philosophy becomes the plane of immanence that supports the
> concepts that the brain lays out.[8]

It is here perhaps that we find Deleuze and Guattari's greatest insight, which is to link the Gestalt principle of psychophysical isomorphism to Spinoza's earlier doctrine of parallelism in order to update, and at the same time introduce, the brain as the true representative of *Natura naturans.* The classic example of a plane of immanence that could be offered by Gestalt theory is that of a soap bubble, whose spherical shape is not defined by a rigid template, a Structure, or a mathematical formula; rather, its plane emerges spontaneously by the parallel action of surface tension acting at all points in the surface simultaneously. Thus, a correlation exists between actual things and cerebral activity, but this correlation (or parallelism) must now be understood as the relationship between two random variables that exist within a Non-Objectified Brain. In turn, this corresponds to a further parallelism in social organization that is the subject of one of Deleuze's earliest texts, *Instincts and Institutions* (1953), and is also the basis of *Bergsonism* (1966), specifically concerning the concept of *élan vital* and what Deleuze calls at that point "the virtual instinct."[9]

According to this early text, the "we" of opinion constitutes the "pressure of society" that determines order in the form of closure and thus reduces that quantity of variability that can take place on the plane *(plan)* of nature. Deleuze writes in this earlier text, "The societies that the human forms are no less closed than animal species; they form part of a plane *(plan)* of nature; and man goes round in circles in his society just as much as species do in theirs or ants in their domain."[10] In fact, the only difference between these two societies in reaction to their specific environment *(Umwelt)* is not found in the order of Nature, but is owed to the fact that the human order of society is founded upon a kind of "virtual instinct," which is composed partly of intelligence and partly of purely instinctual life, such that instinct produces an ersatz of intelligence, and intelligence becomes an equivalent of instinct.[11] We must regard this statement in some ways as pure speculation on Deleuze's part, because we have no way of knowing, for example, if ants also have something comparable to a metaphysical explanation for their domain. In any case, in the closed society of the human species, the virtual instinct would descend into this interval *(écart)* between the mere requirement for order (forming the basis for institutions and disciplinary orders that shape and enforce the forms of opinion and habit) and the discernment of an agreement between instinct and intelligence: a common sense, a special faculty whose function is to create reasons to believe in "the necessity of Order" and thus to cause it to be obeyed. According to Deleuze, however, because the brain is no more founded on a rationale system than the world is reasonable, the absolute requirement for order is itself partly instinctual; "it is not grounded in reason, but in a requirement of nature, in a kind of 'virtual instinct,' that is, on the counterpart that nature produces in the reasonable being in order to compensate for the partiality of his intelligence."[12]

In many commentaries, including the later writings of Deleuze and Guattari themselves, this "virtual instinct" is often provided with an emancipatory value (whether this is expressed in moral and political terms as "freedom," or aesthetically in terms of "creative openness"). This is an apparent contradiction in the theory of the virtual, because initially it serves an essentially conservative (or reactive) function of supra-intelligent instinct that reinforces the force of opinion *(doxa)*. For

example, in *Bergsonism,* the power of the virtual instinct is first identified as a "storytelling function": "it is the creator of gods, inventor of religions," and of all fictitious representations "which will stand up to the
representation of the real and which will succeed, by the intermediary of
intelligence itself, in thwarting intelligence itself."[13] How can we account
for or explain this apparent contradiction? For example, it cannot be
resolved by creating a moral division in instinct, as if there were two
creative and semi-autonomous forces of nature, one of which serves a
positive or liberating function, the other of which only serves to enslave
and repress, or to mystify. (This is the moral image of the virtual, for
example, that is offered by most traditional conceptions of ideology.)
Therefore, it is a form of contradiction that can be resolved, not by means
of dualism, but as Deleuze writes, by recognizing "a circular play" between instinct and intelligence, and making use of the play of circles "in
order to break the circle, *just as memory uses the circular play of excita-
tion and reaction to embody recollections in images.*"[14]

The concept of the virtual that Deleuze gives us in 1966 is primarily
indebted to his reading of Bergson, which remains somewhat unsatis-
factory because it fails to resolve the contradiction stated above without
resorting to some degree of mystification. How can the same instinctual
intelligence be, at once, the condition of closure by which society causes
its specific order to be obeyed (by the invention of new storytelling functions, or ideology, *tout court*) and, at the same time, the condition of
openness by which the human species accedes "to another cerebral interval" between instinct and intelligence in man, thereby "going beyond
his plane *(plan)* and his condition"?[15] I would even risk saying that Deleuze's earliest conception of the virtual is uncannily Heideggerian, particularly in the reference to "man's circular play in order to break the
circle of closed society." For example, it is precisely this solution, or at
least a variation thereof, that Deleuze and Guattari will later take up in
Anti-Oedipus in their theory of unconscious desire that makes use of the
circular play of instinct and intelligence that exists in schizophrenia in
order to break through the closed society produced by an essentially
Oedipalized and neurotic form of individuation.

Furthermore, I would argue that Deleuze's earlier conception of this
virtual instinct runs the risk of mythologizing the concept of creation

itself by turning it into the expression of cosmic memory communicated across time and space by "great souls": "This liberation, this embodiment of cosmic memory in creative emotions, only takes place in privileged souls. It leaps from one soul to another, only every now and then, crossing closed deserts."[16] In other words, the solution of leaping from a closed society, bounded by the circular play of instinct and intelligence, to an open society, "a society of creators," appears a bit too aristocratic and Nietzschean at this stage; like Bergson before him, Deleuze must have recourse to a notion of a cosmic and transpersonal memory that leaps from one closed society to the next, "but undoubtedly only takes place in privileged souls."[17] Here Deleuze evokes the original idea of reminiscence, partly Platonic and partly derived from Bergson's notion of the *élan vitale,* as "mystical intuition," in order to resolve the problem of scarcity, or rather, the temporal intervals between vital ideas that can serve to "liberate man from the plane *(plan)* that is proper to him, in order to make him a creator and adequate to the whole movement of creation."[18] But is this not also the return of one of the most autochthonous myths of philosophy itself? An original myth that is equally embodied in a quasi-mystical form of community: a society of individuals liberated from the conditions of time and place, from history and territory (language); a form of communication that transcends these local conditions and passes between one genius and another *"through the intermediary of disciples or spectators or hearers"*—in short, a transmigration of souls, a metempsychosis of transhistorical faculties, an "open society" of philosophers?[19]

These judgments might appear a bit harsh to some readers, but they only serve to correct a common misperception that Deleuze's solution to the problem was there from the beginning and all we need is a little hermeneutic investigation to make it more explicit and less abstract. As Deleuze says also in *Bergsonism,* in this case concerning the evolution of the brain, each problem has more than one solution-state; accordingly, all we can say each time is that it is the best solution possible "given the way the problems were stated."[20] Therefore, we must conceive of the state of problems and solutions in terms of "creative evolution" (Bergson) and not from the Hegelian, quasi-eternal conception of Absolute Knowledge. According to this former viewpoint, if the concept of the virtual was there from the beginning, it was only in the form of an intuition and concerned a problematic that is stated clearly throughout the final chapter of *Bergsonism:* How is it possible to leap from a closed society to an open society by achieving another intercerebral interval between "instinct" and "intelligence"?

The second answer Deleuze provides to this question in 1966 is "creative emotion," or the composite of emotion and representation that appears in the interval "between the pressure of society and the resistance of intelligence," producing the conditions of a variability that allows emotion to become embodied in a "pure element" that is personal, though not individual—*this is the specific emotion of thinking itself.* "It is like the God in us."[21] Here the genesis of creation is likened more to mystical intuition than to a philosophical concept, and it still remains for Deleuze to construct a concept of what still remains "virtual" and "indeterminate," as if to extend the lines of probability to a point where it transmutes into certainty, becomes actualized as a purely philosophical concept of creation, as opposed to a mystical or spiritualist notion of absolute knowledge.

Now, let us return to the conclusion of *What is Philosophy?,* written with Guattari twenty years later, to see if a concept of creation (and the virtual) is achieved there. Of course, we immediately discover the concept of "creation" emphasized again, although here it is identified with the activity of the philosopher ("the creator of concepts") in contrast to the disciplines of science and art—these are no less creative in their own domains, but it is in philosophy that the art of creating concepts achieves its specialized faculty. This thesis has become well known. As Deleuze clarifies in a seminar on the concept of creation:

> Philosophy is a discipline that is just as creative and inventive as any other discipline. It is only that philosophy is a discipline that involves creating or inventing concepts, and concepts do not exist in a kind of heaven where they would expect a philosopher to understand them. Of course, it does not work that way. You do not say one day: "Hey, I'll make such and such a concept," or "I'll invent that concept." No more does a painter say, "Hey, I'll make a picture like that!" There must be a necessity . . . otherwise, nothing happens.[22]

With regard to the concept of the virtual, moreover, what is most striking is Deleuze and Guattari's optimistic assertion that philosophy, science, and art cannot be reduced to being merely the representatives of the "storytelling function" of society. They "are not like religions that invoke the dynasties of the gods, or the epiphany of a single god, in order to paint a firmament on the umbrella, like the figures of an *Ur-doxa* from which opinion stems."[23] In other words, they cannot be reduced to becoming purely ideological functions as in most "anti-Enlightenment," Marxist, and postmodernist interpretations of philosophy, science, and art. On the contrary, Deleuze and Guattari argue that while "we [i.e., the subjects of opinion, of habit, members of a closed society] want a little order to protect us from chaos, they [i.e., the planes composed by philosophy, science, art] *want more*," that is, a little bit of chaos released back into our idea of Order.[24] What was earlier defined in *Bergsonism* as "the little interval . . . that defines a variability appropriate to human societies," in this later argument becomes embodied within these three disciplines (or rather, these faculties). According to the well-known and frequently quoted refrain, in their respective encounters with Chaos philosophy brings back variations, science introduces variables, art returns with varieties.

In response to the above statement, "they want more," this claim should immediately strike us as being somewhat contradictory to the dominant tenants of critical theory over the last fifty years or so, particularly with regard to our normal opinions concerning science, following the influence of the Frankfurt School. In *What Is Philosophy?* this assertion even assumes a characteristic of certainty extending along a line of probability that determines the specific form of "variability" belonging to science, philosophy, and the arts. What form does this variability take? According to the descriptions offered in the passages following this claim, variability occurs when chaos is reintroduced into an interval between thinking and intelligence. Initially it takes the form of "a leap in thought," which might actually appear as a form of error at first. In art (more specifically, in painting), for example, it might assume the event of a catastrophe that leaves its trace on the canvas in a splotch or spill that destroys the work—representing a failure and loss of form, at first, but then suddenly transforming into the force of a creative leap that causes the painter to break with conventions of form and technique. In science, Deleuze and Guattari suggest, it might occur when the mathematician, in the example offered, "skips over calculations" by introducing the hastened desire to arrive at the truth, which disturbs the tranquility of calculation until finally a "eureka moment" appears. Finally, in philosophy, the event of error occurs when the philosopher attempts to bring all of his concepts into a final accord (within a system supposedly ruled by consensus and friendship), only to find this "image of thought" suddenly traversed by a spirit of hatred that threatens to return everything to "coexisting chaos." By this, I understand Deleuze and Guattari to be referring to those moments when philosophy is dispersed by polemic and disagreement at the very point where it had succeeded in expressing a state of "absolute knowledge," as in the case of the Hegelian image of thought, which quickly dispersed into the last century of "anti-Hegelian" philosophies.[25]

However, it is essential to point out that this expression of variability does not refer to an active intelligence, but rather to what Deleuze also calls a "pure contemplation without knowledge," following the philosophy of Leibniz. In other words, the event of "creation" could be said to be virtual when something happens that, in different ways, resembles haste and miscalculation, crisis and shock, forgetfulness or a lapse of memory, exhaustion and weariness, catastrophe and failure. (As an aside, this understanding of the event of creation might immediately lead us to reconsider the notion of "vitalism" that is so often ascribed to Deleuze's philosophy.) What is an *event* of creation when this does not seem to occur by means of an active intelligence or will, but appears to be detached from both conscious action and movement (as also in the case of the "crystalline-image" in *Cinema 2*, which I will return to below)? If the concept of creation that Deleuze and Guattari invoke occurs without the intervention of an active intellect or will, "a pure contemplation without knowledge," then the event can in some ways be likened to the particular duration that follows a "brutal accident," or even to the duration when nothing happens.

> Events always involve periods when nothing happens . . . they're part
> of the event itself: you can't, for example, extract the instant of some

terribly brutal accident from the vast empty time in which you see it coming, staring at what hasn't yet happened, waiting for ages for it to happen.[26]

In fact, the image of the brain that Deleuze and Guattari give to philosophy is not young and vital, but can be compared to a tired and aging brain that is unable to maintain its connections and integrations of memory. Instead of falling back on opinion, however, the brain of contemporary philosophy is divided by the relative speeds at which it moves from one point to the next, or from one idea to the next, or from one "current idea" to the next. For example, there is the speed of discourse and moving quickly from one topic to the next one with a mental agility and quickness that is often ascribed to younger philosophers; or there are slow-motion and stagnant discussions that take place in the emptiness of an aging philosopher's head, as if he were sitting alone like one of Beckett's characters going back over all of his earlier opinions only to find that they are unfounded once again. If the brain of philosophy is divided between these relative speeds, as if divided against itself both externally and internally, then it is not capable of making a vital leap that would arrive in a moment of certainty and decision.

How would we then introduce vitality back into the philosophical brain, or "image of thought"? Returning now to the first Gestalt principle listed above, "an increased speed in mental processes," how would the imperative of "more speed" become part of the solution? As stated above, one of philosophy's relative speeds is that of discourse, which moves from one associated idea to the next, constituting a signifying chain of associations, but is unable to reconstitute these associations into the form of a concept. The concept gets lost in the dizzying array of significations; it remains abstract, referring to the specific quality of emotion that is attached to the appearance of the idea. An abstract notion evokes the "I FEEL" of the given idea or concept, like in the case of an image in cinema; it represents an image of thought that has failed to "section and distribute the reality of the given domains," causing the zones of indetermination to converge in the form of intuition. This is because its method was insufficient and "the virtual" (idea) fails to become actualized in relation to perception and cognition. I think what I am describing here happens frequently in the discourse of what is commonly called "theory" today, which exhibits many of the features of the Gestalt diagram of a possibility space called a "Klondike Wilderness," or a "clueless plateau" where many parts of conceptual space, being similar, give no clues as to the direction in which answers may lie. For example, this might describe the kind of discussions that have taken place most recently around the ideas of "bio-power," "the event," "immanence," and as I noted in the beginning, the idea of "the virtual" itself. This is not intended as a criticism, necessarily, and I am offering these only as examples of ideas associated with an enormous amount of discussion that has attempted to give them reality but as of yet has yielded little more than a number of conflicting definitions that resemble different opinions, or in the language of possibility space, "a large region of neighboring possible states where the measure of promise does not vary much, or varies erratically from state to state around the average for the whole plateau, so there is no trend."[27]

As Deleuze and Guattari write, "ideas can only be associated as images and can only be ordered as abstractions"; once again, "the point is to go beyond both of these and arrive as quickly as possible at mental objects determinable as real beings."[28] In this description, the specific speed referred to, "as quickly as possible," is the leap from ideas to "mental objects determinable as real beings." One might immediately object that these "mental objects" are no less abstract than the aforementioned ideas. What are, after all, "mental objects determinable as real beings"? Are we—that is, am I—not just speaking in circles? Actually—no. Very simply, "mental objects determinable as real beings" are what Deleuze and Guattari call "concepts," which must be distinguished from ideas. Ideas may very well be mental objects, but they are not necessarily determinable as real beings. "A concept," however, is defined as "a set of inseparable variations that is produced or constructed on a plane of immanence insofar as the latter crosscuts the chaotic variability and gives it consistency (reality)."[29] In other words, concepts are ideas rendered consistent (real), and "vital"; all concepts are vital, and this is the quality that distinguishes them from "current ideas." Consequently, Deleuze and Guattari will often speak of the "mental objects" of philosophy, science, and art as "vital ideas" that emerge only "in the deepest synaptic fissures, hiatuses, intervals, and meantimes of a nonobjectified brain."[30]

Turning now to the second Gestalt principle, "the amount of short-circuiting that occurs in processes of normal reasoning," the problem of scarcity can also be explained by the organization of instinctual thought into institutions that are governed by habit and opinion. (This is Foucault's great thesis of disciplinary orders.) Institutions are the habitual and disciplinary orders that shape closed societies, which is why institutions are composed partly from instinct and partly from intelligence. Here I am not speaking simply of the grand institutions, but also of the little institutions erected in our heads that already make our brains function as "subjects." In other words, if variability occurs only through the introduction of a little chaos into the order of opinions and already associated ideas, which is said to happen quite rarely due to the instinctual dominance of opinion and habit, then the chances for vital ideas are *necessarily scarce*. For example, this is why Deleuze and Guattari argue that in the institutions of philosophy and politics, the Western democratic ideal of the conversation between friends has never created any new concepts ("vital ideas"); it is the same old conversation, only the number of conversational partners has increased exponentially, which is not to say that the concept of friendship has radically changed either in the concept or in its diversity of forms. This is highlighted at the very beginning of *What Is Philosophy?* where Deleuze and Guattari argue that the democratic idea of friendship has remained an abstraction, despite centuries of philosophical discussion, and today might no longer even designate "a transcendental-lived category" *(une catégorie vivante, un vécu transcendental).*[31] This is to say, if it was once created as a concept, as a living category of the societies that took it up and infused it with new variables, today the concept of democracy has been demoted to the level of an idea; moreover, it is an idea that has become jaundiced, having lost much of its former vitality, and thus fails any longer to "make new friends," much less to create new forms of society. "To create concepts is, at the very least, to make something."[32] An idea without a concept, on the other hand, is like a conversation that fails to actualize the very thing it takes up as its very subject matter.

Today, another form of conversing without concepts is what Deleuze and Guattari refer to by the term "communication." But what is this? Have we not been told, at least since we were children, that communication is a good thing, particularly in democratic societies? For example, that it is necessary to learn to communicate effectively (and for this we were given little notebooks and introduced to techniques of forming our thoughts and our subjective identities in written exercises, and then later on, in communicating all our desires and fantasies in the various forms of writing)? We are never informed of those occasions when lying and keeping silent may be more effective than communicating openly; we gain this practical knowledge only through the trials of experience. This is because the categorical obligation to communicate is not itself founded on a rational principle, even in democratic societies where this principle assumes the form of an essential gregariousness, or the demand to speak out in the public sector. In this sense, the demand to communicate can be compared to what Deleuze also says in *Bergsonism* concerning morality, or the "obligation to have obligations," which is that "it has no rational ground."[33] Similarly, we might say the same thing concerning the democratic imperative of communication: the only thing that is grounded in communication is the fact of having to communicate, "the whole of communication," and often without regard to having anything to say. As a result of this obligation, each particular form of communication may be conventional and can border on a kind of "speech for speaking's sake"—as in the case of fiction, or today, in most digital communications like e-mails and Twitter.

Aside from the fact that most communication is grounded upon an irrational principle, one that is determined by convention and by the institutions of opinion and habit (particularly the habits of saying "I" in the statements "I think," "I feel," and "I believe," which have no necessary or determinable relationship to the real subjects of thinking, emotion, and belief), what else can Deleuze and Guattari possibly have against communication? If communication is the quasi-organic socialization of the idea, is there another sociality of the idea that they privilege? As Deleuze remarks in a 1990 interview with Antonio Negri, today the problem is that communication is already permeated by money. Thus, anything communicated is already invested with value, which is to say that capitalism has invested the idea of communication *to the point of completely saturating it,* in order to turn it about so that it appears that every social form of communication is already an expression of value that is consistent with capitalist society. Consequently, if certain forms of communication are in the process becoming less effective, or have already become outmoded forms (such as the novel), it is because they have been less efficient in reproducing social values and new collective subjectivities than newer technological media. Negri remarks in the same interview:

> In the Marxist utopia of the *Grundrisse,* communism takes precisely the form of a transversal organization of free individuals built on a technology that makes that possible. . . . Maybe in a communication society it's less utopian than it used to be.[34]

What happens to the original idea of philosophy when, according to a major argument put forward in the conclusion of *What Is Philosophy?,* the emergent capitalist disciplines of communication (computer science, marketing, design, advertising) lay claim to the actuality of the concept as their specific domain, or area of concern?

From philosophy, Deleuze and Guattari suggest, marketing has preserved a certain relationship between the concept and the event; the event has become the exhibition or display of the concept's actuality, which must be distinguished from its reality. The earlier relationship can be discerned the history of philosophy when the act of introducing of a concept is also identified with the object of its own self-positing, which has a form of actuality (if not always reality) from that moment onward. This could be called the Hegelianism of the concept, or "the concept of the Concept." As Deleuze and Guattari write, it is the "post-Kantians, and notably Schelling and Hegel, who . . . paid most attention to the concept as a philosophical reality in this sense."[35] For example, Hegel traced all the moments in which the concept of "Mind" *(Geist)* was figured in this activity of self-positing; therefore, each moment in the history of the Spirit was grasped as the event of the concept's own self-positing reality. However, it is this very relationship between the reality of the concept and its event of self-positing that marketing today has grasped as an essential mode of realization. The concept has become a set of creative product displays *(Darstellungen),* and the event has become an exhibition that sets up various displays for product promotion.[36] Here, the inner unity between concept and event is the power of the concept's productivity (i.e., creativity) in setting up various displays that exhibit the concept's passage from virtual to actual; however, the true objective of the exhibition of the concept is always to present the virtual as being in excess of the actual so that the most essential portion of the concept's reality is its pure potentiality. It is still a bit like Hegelian *Geist,* in the sense that its myriad forms *(Gestalten)* do not grasp the concept's essential reality, but instead reveal-conceal a surplus of virtuality, which is excessive and purely potential *(en potentia),* and becomes the source of future forms. Apple is perhaps the best contemporary example of pure potentiality communicated by a marketing concept; all of its product displays exhibit this same excessive sense of virtual over actual, the sense of constant innovation, or *élan vital.*

As Deleuze and Guattari have also observed, this new relationship between event and concept, between exhibiting power and the actuality of the idea, has also returned to determine the manner in which contemporary philosophy communicates, and philosophers and theorists today are no longer immune to promoting their own products (or theories) through exhibitions and displays, or to communicate the actuality of their own brand of philosophy according to contemporary marketing strategies. In a very real and demonstrable sense, of which there are many contemporary examples, *every new theory dreams today of being Apple.* Consequently, the most powerful theories are those that lay claim to the concept's self-positing actuality and express ideas that appear suddenly (as if sprung from the head of Zeus himself) to dominate an entire field or discipline. It is not purely accidental that academic conferences and auto shows have essentially the same manner of exhibiting their "mental object's" mode of self-positing actuality, including the ideas of innovation and progress, but also the active forgetting of last year's products and stale models. Some would limit this resemblance to a merely superficial analogy, or "mere resemblance," that does not touch upon the essence of both activities; others, more inclined to cynicism, have grasped this resemblance as an opportunity to fulfill the desire of essential egoism, and have fashioned a philosophy that is perfectly fitted to the marketing and promotion of a new product brand, along with all the promises that their philosophical line has surpassed all others and is best positioned to seize the reality of the "truth-event." In *Bergsonism*, Deleuze already remarks that the greatest leaps of thought often occur in the name of an essential egoism; however, this already limits the possibility of leaping outside the closed circle of human societies, since the ego is only a cog in the wheel of a vast machinery, and the philosopher today would have to be a saint to resist the temptations offered by this form of communication—and, most of all, recognition and fame—even when these qualities are barely measurable in larger market standards. In *What Is Philosophy?* Deleuze and Guattari caution us against these grosser virtues, but here they are speaking more like old men who can resist this temptation only because they have grown too weary of their own worldly desires and, thus, have been surpassed by a younger and impudent breed of commercialized philosophers. Nevertheless, they argue, "this is an absolute disaster for thought whatever its benefits might be, especially when these benefits can only be extolled from the viewpoint of universal capitalism."[37] But why is this so surprising? After all, would it not be natural to expect that philosophy, as a social form of communication, would presuppose an "image of thought" that is more or less consistent with the society in which it finds itself located, or would employ the same models of recognition and subjectivity that reflect the dominant values of communication and communicability?

In what sense can what is called philosophy today, that is, a certain tradition of institutionalized thinking ("theory"), lay claim to *another idea of communication* and another manner of socializing thought? In other words, how can "theory" accede to a point of view other than that of universal capitalism? Many philosophies today make this claim, but recalling the argument made in the Introduction concerning a new form of dogmatism, how can this major *presupposition* that belongs to contemporary critical philosophy be grounded upon anything more than a form of transcendental opinion *(Ur-doxa)*? How can we be assured that this is not merely a foundational myth of philosophy itself—the belief in metempsychosis of great souls communicating across closed deserts of time? Even the promise of a leap from a closed to an open society has become a clichéd form that can be found in many major philosophies and theories today. Again, these potential criticisms may seem a bit harsh, even somewhat contradictory, since we have already detected the presence of the same myth—perhaps even the same cliché!—circulating in Deleuze's early philosophy, or even in the major presuppositions of Deleuze and Guattari's *Capitalism and Schizophrenia*. Nevertheless, how can thinking become critical of the actual image it presupposes and, at the same time, completely fail to become critical of the aspect of the virtual image that serves as our own particular "storytelling function"— that is, an image created to compensate for the partiality of our own intelligence?

Here, I will illustrate how several current theories perform a storytelling function, that is, referring to the quasi-mythic (even unconscious) leap in thought that presupposes an open society beyond the current closed societies of late capitalism. For example, Hardt and Negri essentially create the image of an open society from the perspective where the very form of Empire completely turns about in its own circle and discovers that it is no longer able to include, as moments internal to its own sovereignty, the new societies created by "the Multitude," which is why they constantly say that the societies created by the Multitude disperse themselves across the surface of Empire as purely exterior and autonomous social forms—"the movements of the multitude designate new spaces, and its journeys establish new residences."[38] As a second example, Giorgio Agamben's entire theory of sovereignty attempts to trace the trajectory of "the fundamental bio-political paradigm of the West" to the "very threshold of modernity," at which point every subsequent division upon which closed societies are based (nation, territory, race, and/or ethnicity) empties out into bare political life.[39] At this very threshold, however, Agamben continues to speak of the pure potentiality of an "opening," no longer determined by this earlier division, and "the constitution and institution of a form of life that is exhausted in bare political life and a bios that is only its own *Zoē*," even though he also fails to grasp the concept form of life and vaguely refers his intuition of this threshold "to the analogies between politics and the epochal situation of metaphysics."[40] In his later works, Derrida will continually speak of a "politics of deconstruction" from the perspective o an *aporia* between the determinations of the concept of Democracy, that is, beyond the limit of this closure demarcated by the concept's current reality, and of a "democracy to come."[41] In turn, Jean-Luc Nancy, after the manner of Derrida, has more recently defined what he calls "the (auto)deconstruction of Christianity" as precisely the horizon of an opening "beyond" the Christian enclosure of Being. As he writes, "The Open (or 'the free' as Hölderlin also called it) is essentially ambiguous. . . . In its absoluteness it opens onto itself and opens only onto itself, infinitely."[42] In all these examples, the question to ask concerning this image, as Nancy also immediately observes, is this: "What would be an opening that would not sink into its own openness?"[43] In other words, if theoretical discourse often speaks of an opening, or posits its subject beyond the leap from closed society, we might recall that the essential part of what is called an "event" refers to a duration in which "nothing happens," since the exact instant of the leap either remains unconscious, or has not yet become a definite moment of experience. Here, I believe we have returned precisely to the same place that Deleuze earlier articulated as the relationship between philosophical method and mystical intuition, which can be viewed only from "the outside."

According to the last Gestalt principle, what is called "an unconscious leap in thought" can now be characterized in two different manners. First, according to the more critical understanding already noted above, it is unconscious because it is mythical, that is to say, it is conditioned by the possibility of genre and language that allows us to "speak of things beyond the boundaries of the lived and the livable." (This is one of the original definitions of mythic speech, *mythos*, in Plato.) It is because of the possibility of language that "an unconscious leap in thought" can too easily be mistaken for a series of forms *(Gestalten)* that attempt to signify its "taking place," its "immanent arrival," or to provide an "intuition of openness" as in the examples above, and these forms of signification and discourse can often be mistaken for the sense that can only belong to the event itself. This would be one way of understanding what Nancy calls "an opening that sinks back into its own openness." For example, when Derrida writes of a "democracy to come," Agamben of "the coming community," or Hardt and Negri of the arrival of "the Multitude," we may already have an abstract signification of what this means, and it is this sense that belongs to the order of myth that makes this sense possible; however, does the specific sense of the "event" designated by the above statements actually refer back to the possibility of statements and propositions themselves, that is, to a specific kind of "openness" that belongs to language? In this regard, it is especially important to note that Deleuze was more interested in other kinds of statements like "there's a concert this evening," or "there's going to be a naval battle tomorrow"; moreover, he would not have determined the sense of the events that these statements express to be fundamentally different from the statements concerning the arrival of the Multitude, the coming community, or "Absolute Democracy." Both kinds of statements express a similar, if not the same, incorporeal sense of the event, which is perhaps one reason Deleuze also did not privilege statements concerning "the end of Metaphysics." As he said, in fact, "the most ordinary events cast us as visionaries."[44]

Perhaps another way of understanding the manner in which "an opening (an event, an intuition of a real determinable being) sinks back into its own openness" occurs most often in the function of commentary and "secondary representation." In other words, why so much commentary? In reply, commentators can be understood as the reproductive instances or, as Bataille might say, the sexual organs of opinion. To avoid being misunderstood, I am not rejecting either the function of commentary or secondary works, but rather see these functions as quite necessary and corresponding to the requirements of an organically coordinated brain, made up by its connections and secondary integrations.[45] Therefore, commentary serves the necessary function of connection and integration. According to the allegory of the umbrella that appears in the conclusion of *What Is Philosophy?*, for example, artists and writers tear a little slit in the umbrella of common perception and opinion to allow a little chaos in; "then come the crowd of imitators who repair the umbrella with something vaguely resembling the vision, and the crowd of commentators who patch over the rent with opinion: communication."[46] Hence, the function of commentary and imitation (for example, of copying in art and music) must be understood as the deindividualized process of an organically based brain trying to remain integrated and ordered in its confrontation with the little bit of chaos that seeps in through the rent. The product–moment correlation of reproduction is the very manner in which these connections and secondary integrations are introduced into a social assemblage that includes all of the following: ideas, thoughts, statements, descriptions, institutions ("schools," "movements"), and lastly, individuals. For this process of integration to occur on the plane of ideas, for example, first a relative degree of similarity is required for a corresponding degree of connection and fusion as the condition of reproduction. This similarity occurs, first of all, on a literal level in citation, but it also occurs in the creation of a Gestalt image (i.e., a deep image) that the secondary work participates in creating (e.g., in philosophy: neo-Kantianism, Hegelianism, Marxism; the phenomenological image, the image of deconstructionism, and the Deleuzian image). This Gestalt image may or may not be presented by the so-called primary work, and something interesting occurs when this Gestalt takes on a life of its own and begins to become instituted in all kinds of manners to determine the work's meaning in the form of a "theory." However, rather than referring to the specific meaning that belongs to a discrete body of written works, this determination actually refers to the "vitality" of an idea as a force that causes us to think and reproduce the same idea as a distinctive social assemblage. In other words, according to the standard definition, the virtual is not opposed to the real, but rather to the actual; the virtual is real and is capable of producing real effects. These effects are not restricted to being merely discursive events (or ideas), but also take place in forming new opinions and habits in social institutions, in creating new epistemological subjects of study, if not new subjective forms of desire and identification that have real social existence. (As I have discussed elsewhere, Fredric Jameson perhaps best understood this productive sense of commentary—communication and opinion—in the opening pages of *The Political Unconscious*.)[47]

As long as we continue to understand what is called "theory" as simply a chain of discourse or associated ideas, without regard to what social and institutional assemblages it produces, but more importantly what kind of desires it invents as its conditions of possibility, then its particular image of thought will always remain abstract. All of the examples I have offered above can be understood as different collective assemblages of "theory," or what I have called *the different living languages of possibility space*. In fact, it would be an interesting exercise to create a cognitive map of all the current solutions offered by contemporary theories that, upon first glance, would be seemingly remote from one another in terms of their stated objectives and theoretical problems. If my suspicion is correct, such a map would quickly resemble the diagrams of a "Klondike Wilderness" and the solutions themselves could be compared to the various different "Klondike traps" in possibility space: "clueless plateaus," "narrow canyons of exploration," and the inevitable "oasis of false promise." As an example, I will simply list the four problems of possibility space and their corresponding solutions:

1. *The Problem of Rarity*: Valuable solutions are sparsely distributed in a large area of possibilities, because of the virtually infinite recombinations or configurations of past elements, many of which are not viable as solutions. (Solution: Employ quick conceptual sketches to identify a range of possible solutions.)

2. *The Problem of Isolation*: The places in the conceptual space where valuable solutions are to be found can be widely separated and unconnected. (Solution: Cultivate "chance leaps" around the space, rather than following a path of logic toward a deterministic solution.)

3. *The Problem of Oasis of False Promise*: When solutions have been found in one place, it is hard to leave them to try elsewhere. (Solution: Deliberate a move to other parts of the space to achieve a different perspective.)

4. *The Problem of Clueless Plateaus*: Many parts of conceptual space, being similar, give no clues as to the direction in which fruitful or fruitless explorations may lie. (Solution: Jump around or "trawl" using systematized chance.)[48]

Concerning the last problem, which has been the subtext of my entire argument, it is apparent that most theories today express some version of the leap from closed society to open society (whether the former is defined nationally, sexually, ethnically, or in terms of the "open society" that lies outside universal capitalism). In other words, although the actual terms and stated problems may vary, the different manners in which the virtual is actually conceived do not vary much from one expression (or theory) to the next. The above examples I have provided all demonstrate characteristics of the same basic Gestalt image of how an "open society" might appear *between the positing of the concept of the self-positing (or arrival) of the event.*

I return to Deleuze and Guattari's complaint concerning the current relationship between the event and the concept's self-positing reality, which is expressed most powerfully by the languages of contemporary advertising and marketing. Some will say I have simplified things and have moved too quickly from one level of the problem to the next. "Certainly," my philosophical friends will say, "you are not suggesting we abandon the more sophisticated and theoretical concepts of philosophy for those of cognitive psychology and Gestalt theory! After all, they are just metaphors!" But in response, in what sense can philosophy prove that its own concepts are founded upon anything more than belief, and are simply another language of possibility? I cannot say. Nevertheless, I have found it to be an interesting "thought experiment," if only to raise the possibility, that is, to bring one language into proximity with another, to draw a different map in order to survey the current state of "what is called theory"; moreover, to ask questions like "What have we been doing?" and "What are we looking for?" rather than "What is the next Big Theory?" Too often, I feel, students of "theory" are all scrambling around this plateau looking for hints and clues that will lead them to the next theoretical trend, somewhat like the joke told by Nietzsche in *The Gay Science* that after Kant discovered the categories of reason, all the seminarians at Tübingen were out in the bushes looking for new categories. Discussions in "theory" seem particularly prone to this kind of trend-setting thought, which is why I employed it as an example, since the idea of an unconscious leap in thought already presupposes a kind of "turning" *(Die Kehre).*

How many times in the past twenty or thirty years have we been witness to some version of the idea of "the turning" *(Die Kehre)*—the phenomenological turn, linguistic (or structuralist) turn, the post-structuralist, the cultural turn, the visual turn, the affective turn, the turn to religion? Of course, it is not merely coincidental that these mark institutional trends in production and reproduction, particularly in academic publishing and conference proceedings, but what is most surprising is that this parallelism has been remarked upon by almost every major theorist, and yet this has never led to any real questioning regarding the adequacy of this form in representing the true nature of progress in thinking. I might even suggest that the form has become so rampant that any major thinker, either living or dead, is now required to have one; if such a turning is not evident, then one will be provided by secondary readers, and the body of their work will be interpreted accordingly. Although our understanding of this event was first derived from Thomas Kuhn's *Structure of Scientific Revolutions,* in which normal science is portrayed as operating through the suppression of new paradigms, what is crucial to observe is that what Kuhn called a "paradigm shift" has become the run-of-the-mill business, or the normal science called "theory," and might even explain why there have been just as many claims concerning the "end of theory" as there have been announcements of the "next Big Theory." However, *if the Form (Gestalt) of a "paradigm shift" has become the epistemological business of "theory" as a normal science, and the function of normal science is to suppress all new paradigms, then the actual event of a "turning" will not resemble the Form (Gestalt) of the "paradigm shift" that "theory" produces as the condition of perpetuating its institutions and its authorities.* This is our particular circle, today, and its perpetual revolution constitutes the closed society of "theory" itself. All the various turnings recounted above—including the next one yet to be named—can be understood as figures that express the different regions of the clueless plateau we occupy today.

Finally, let us return more specifically to the image of "the turn" that belongs to the last work of Deleuze and Guattari. It is given in the proposition with which we began: The virtual *is* the brain itself (or rather, it is the "turning point" where the brain becomes a subject). "It is the brain that says I, but I is an other."[49] How is this image of turning any different from those I have recounted above? If I stated in the beginning that the image of the brain now shared by philosophy, science, and art is both beautiful and violent, it is because here we have a description of a process of real thinking that is full of explosions and detonations that first take place in the brain, "an uncertain system," defined by probabilistic, aleatory, quantum mechanisms.[50] In understanding this statement, I would like to call attention to something quite remarkable, which becomes visible only when we compare the conclusion of *Bergsonism* (where the concept of the virtual is first introduced) to the conclusion of *What Is Philosophy?* where it returns as a major theme. A passage from the 1966 text:

> Servant of an open and finite God (such are the characteristics of the *Élan Vital*), the mystical soul actively plays the whole of the universe, and reproduces the opening of a Whole in which there is nothing to see or to contemplate. Already motivated by emotion, the philosopher extracted the lines that divided up the composites given in experience. He prolonged the outline to beyond the "turn": he showed in the distance the virtual point where they all met.[51]

In this early passage we see the passage of the virtual "beyond the turn of experience," which is figured as the probability lines that the philosopher extracts from the composites of experience in order to achieve a point of view, albeit always from the Outside, comparable to that of the mystical soul, except that the philosopher's viewpoint lacks certainty. By contrast, the point of view of the mystical soul is that of creation itself; "it plays with the whole of creation [and] invents an expression of it whose adequacy increases with its dynamism."[52]

In 1991, however, the faculty of creation becomes in *What Is Philosophy?* the "signature" of the philosopher's activity, "or the art of creating concepts." Moreover, what is called a concept can also be defined precisely as "an expression whose adequacy increases with its dynamism" (a vital idea); however, what is more important to notice is that the figure of the mystical soul is replaced in the latter text by the brain, and here it is not only the philosopher who extracts the lines of experience and extends them beyond the turn of experience (formed by opinion and habit), but science and art as well. And yet the brain is not a perspective in this latter text, but rather what must be subtracted from all perspectives, given that it is immanent to all perspectives, and in a certain way it could also be said to be a "Whole in which there is nothing to see or to contemplate"—in other words, here we have precisely the image of a Non-Objectified Brain! Has the brain simply become a metaphor of the mystical soul, or was the mystical soul already a certain cerebral crystalization of the brain? The visionary, the seer, or the mystical soul of the thinker—all figures of "the one who sees in the crystal, and what he sees is the gushing of time as dividing in two, as splitting."[53]

According to the above thesis, what now appears in the interval (*écart*) between intelligence and instinct is an image of thought that is now associated with the brain, but that for this reason must also be distinguished from both the perception-image and the memory-image. The nature of the image is affection, or self-affection, which is identified with thinking, because thinking is also defined as what happens in the interval (*écart*) between stimulus and response; therefore, intuition may very well be an image of what appears in this interval, but this primarily refers to a quality of affection that is different from perception-image, the action-image, or the memory-image. In other words, the idea of "mystical intuition" is no longer even necessary, because we have no more certainty regarding the source of our most common intuitions than we have regarding the specific functioning of the brain (which modern neurology is still only in the process of discovering). As Deleuze exclaims in a 1987 seminar on the movement-image, in part rejecting the common view of spiritualism ascribed to Bergson's concept of intuition: "What is an écart? The brain is an écart! There can be no more materialist a solution."[54] Although the material reality of both forms of intuition and knowledge continues to elude our perspective and thus remains purely virtual, we *can* say with more or less certainty that the brain is real, no less than the universe, as the distant point where all the lines extracted from given experience meet, *beyond the turn of experience*. To arrive at this distant point, a point that is farther than the external world composed of objects, and nearer than the subjective form of intuitions, requires a leap, as well as a method of leaping.

Again, in *Bergsonism,* Deleuze first compared this method to "mystical intuition" following Bergson—"as though the properly philosophical 'possibility' extended itself into mystical certainty"—but then immediately qualified this by saying that "philosophy can only consider the mystical soul from the outside," that is, "from the point of its own lines of probability."[55] In 1988 Deleuze clarifies this method:

> The means used by intuition are, on the one hand, sectioning and distributing reality in a given domain according to lines of different natures, and on the other hand, intersecting lines taken from various domains that converge together.[56]

In other words, philosophical intuition is achieved by means of constructing a method of combining the aspects of perception, emotion, imagination, and thought into one form that represents the virtual point where all these aspects meet; mystical intuition, by contrast, appears as a form of thinking without method and, thus, represents the kind of "leap in thought" that philosophy always seeks to achieve but fails to actualize because it lacks the power of pure intuition. Perhaps this is another way of explaining why many of its concepts remain abstract, or fail to leap beyond abstraction to express the condition of vital ideas ("mental objects determinable as real beings"). However, in this later text the true subject of the leap is not man as a subject who thinks, invents, or creates; it is the brain that thinks, not man. A brain is not in your head, any more than it is in the next thought, or the next perception, association, or memory; it is all of these at once and more. What is more is the plane on which all of these take place at once, as if simultaneously, even though this plane never appears as an object of representation, that is to say, does not refer to any external point of view. Thus, the brain is not opposed to the world, but rather the world is composed of a special type of brain-matter. Therefore, when Deleuze and Guattari talk about a "survey" *(survol)* of a plane of immanence, they are referring to the "absolute speed" by which a concept composes a reality.

In the last text, "The Virtual and the Actual," supposedly written by Deleuze shortly before his death and later published in 1996 as an appendix to *Dialogues II,* Deleuze returns once more to meditate on a key passage from Bergson's *Matter and Memory* that forms the basis of *Bergsonism,* and which we also find in *Cinema 2* concerning "the crystals of time." Eric Alliez is purported to conjecture that the telegraphic style of this small piece, which is almost completely "styleless," should be understood as notes on an incomplete or unfinished project.[57] Instead, I would argue, it addresses the most essential problem of Deleuze's entire philosophical project begun in 1966 with *Bergsonism* and returned to at several points, including in the works by Guattari: the problem of the genesis of intuition as a method of philosophy, or the creation of the concept of the virtual. If this remains in a state of being incomplete or unfinished at the end of Deleuze's philosophical career, this is because this already refers to a duration of philosophy recounted above in which the actual number of concepts ("vital ideas") are relatively few and the interval between new concepts must be viewed from the perspective we have likened to the evolutionary brain, which is to say, from the perspective of *Natura naturans* ("nature doing what nature does," which can even be phrased as "nature doing the best it can," given what it has been given to work with, namely, the organic composition of the human brain).

It is important to note, moreover, that in this last text all the above themes come together around a tightly contracted point or "peak" of the actual present: mystical intuition, brain-image, the image of thought, a method of extending the lines of probability beyond the turn of experience. Recalling the Bergsonian diagram of the cone, here the brain can be said to occupy both poles, above and below, the peak of intuition and the unconscious ground (even the "*sans fond*," the filter or sieve placed over chaos), except, as in Bergson's original scheme, the cone is inverted to show the position of the ground occupied by the actual, and not by memory or unconscious intuition. According to Bergson's original definition, however, the actual does not encompass perception only, but the most intensive point or peak where the body-image is concentrated on a plane that both receives and emanates every other image of which this plane is composed: "it represents each moment of my present incessantly advancing, and also incessantly in contact with the mobile plane (*plan P*) composing my actual representation of the universe."[58] This scheme will become the basis for Deleuze's "transcendental empirical method": the image of the actual object is the ground, but the image is already divided into virtual and actual, producing a crevice that is located between the brain and the world. On one end, therefore, the brain-image would be the narrowest circuit, at that point where the two aspects of the image are so close that they become indistinguishable, or split apart into virtual image and actual object. The other pole is defined by degrees of dilation and envelopment, which at its furthest point becomes a world, a universe. Thus, brain-image and brain-world are related to one another within a single duration.

But the point is far more radical for Bergson, which is why Deleuze will refer to his philosophy as the "Theory of Multiplicities." At each pole, or extreme limit, this splitting between virtual image and actual object "never goes right to the end," but also exchanges or leaps from interval to interval, never arriving at a point of completion that would be represented by pure intuition of the Whole.[59] Thus, in *Cinema 2*, Deleuze describes the virtual and the actual as "the little crystalline seed and the vast crystallizable universe . . . memories, dreams, even worlds are only the relative circuits that depend on variations of this Whole."[60]

This also seems to echo an intuition that we find in Proust as well: true subjectivity assumes the form of nonchronological time that is grasped in its foundation.

> Subjectivity is never ours, it is time, that is, the soul or the spirit, the virtual. The actual is always objective, but the virtual is subjective: it was initially the affect, that which we experience in time; then time itself, pure virtuality which divides itself in two as affector and affected, "the affection of self by self" as definition of time.[61]

In the above passage, the virtual is defined as the subjectivity of time itself, or a subjectivity that is never ours, but within which we dwell nevertheless. Therefore, the virtual is defined as the spiritual self-affection of the present, "the affection of self-by-self," from which the actual subject is always excluded as *an other*. As Deleuze explains, although it is commonplace to assert that Bergsonian duration is only the equation of the most general form of subjectivity and the form of time (i.e., duration is subjective, and constitutes our internal life), in fact what Bergson actually understood was far more radical: "The only subjectivity is time, non-chronological time, grasped in its foundation."[62] What is this foundation, as we have seen, but that point that represents time in its most contracted state, as in the brain? Here, the brain is the subject. If the brain is the foundation of subjectivity, then it is only at this point that we might now understand the phrase from Cezanne: *man absent from the landscape, but completely within the brain!*

What does all this mean? In other words, what does contemporary philosophy (according to a Deleuzian image of thought) now "presuppose" as its pre-philosophical image? The brain? But as we have seen earlier, the brain is not an image but rather a line of probability beyond the turn of experience where all the divergent lines must meet in order for there to exist human and world, subject and object. I only point out that in contrast to the earlier solution, rather than resorting to the Platonic myth of reminiscence, or to "cosmic Memory," the search for another cerebral interval between instinct and intelligence ends here in the brain itself, the most contracted circuit where virtual and actual split apart, in a constant gushing forth of both time and space. What happened? Simply put, at the end of his career Deleuze simply changed his "plan of immanence," drawing new coordinates and causing a variation in what it means to think and "how to orient oneself in thought." Except that this time, rather than resorting to myth, he refers for his pre-philosophical image (upon which philosophy depends as the condition for the creation of its concepts) only to our current knowledge of the brain. This would seem a less than triumphant ending, the final discovery of a lofty philosophy career: only the brain and the limited knowledge of it that neurobiology has thus far discovered. According to these new coordinates, philosophy still remains "outside" and has no more certainty with regard to the brain that it did concerning mystical intuition. There is no certainty in our knowledge of the brain either, or whether this will lead to the "right" construction of the plan(e) of immanence. "We've got no model for dealing with this question, no guide even, but there is something that we can constantly refer and relate it to: what we know about the brain."[63]

If it is true, as Deleuze and Guattari write, that every great philosopher lays out a new plan(e) of immanence, introduces a new substance of being and draws up a new image of thought, so that we could not imagine a philosopher of whom it could not be said that he has changed what it means to think, or has "thought differently," then this last claim appears somewhat anachronistic to Deleuze's final image of thought. What does philosophy now presuppose? The brain. But what is the brain? In response to this new presupposition, Deleuze explains, "It's not that thinking starts from what we know about the brain but any new thought traces uncharted channels directly though its matter, twisting folding, fissuring it. . . . New connections, new pathways, new synapses, that's what philosophy calls into play as it creates concepts" on a plane of immanence, which now means both *in* and *with* the brain.[64] Thus, each time new images are created, like new circuits in the brain, they also first become possible in a world, enlarging our sense of reality.

The crystal of time gave me for the first time a direct image of time in the form of the unfolding of the present. Here, we have for the first time a direct figure of the thought, in the form of the complementarity of the levels of thought. What I am calling levels of thought, as Bergson also knew, is that each time I am obliged to make a new circuit. These are not metaphors, each time an increasingly major aspect of reality will emerge. . . . There is an infinity of cuts that do not preexist; they must be fabricated. All this is very moving. It is necessary to place everything in movement. Just like the circuits, this mobile plan does not preexist movement.[65]

The description of the brain-image as a circuit already determines the infinite speed of this very special kind of circuit as well as its various avatars: computer circuits, chemical signals, light waves. Although they might give a more approximate image of the nature of the perception and intuition that take place in the brain, these new images are themselves too slow to capture the precise point of the splitting of every perception into actual object and its virtual image. The fact that human consciousness can only be located in the middle of the scale, bordered in one direction by memory that expands into the longest duration imaginable, limited only by unconsciousness and death, and in the other direction, by actual perceptions that enter into tighter and more contracted circuits that, at their assignable limit, are equated with a period of time that is smaller than the smallest period of continuous time imaginable. It is only in this sense that thinking is creative, because actualized perception is equivalent with the creation of the object of thought; in other words, thinking is actual—that is, *real*—being. Or, as Deleuze says earlier, it is only in this sense, and according to this image of thought, that we can now understand why "philosophy merges with ontology," as in the famous proposition (one that has been so famously misunderstood by Badiou!) "Being cannot be said without also occurring"—that is, if we now understand this image of simultaneity (i.e., nonchronological duration) to refer to what happens in the brain, and not to a philosophical image of temporality, such as the one most recently offered by phenomenology.[66] (After all, where is the foundation of time itself if not already in the brain?) According to this new image, thought can still be defined as soul or force (using the old language), and can still take on the form of "pure contemplation," but it now assumes the image of a crystalline event. It is only once we perceive this image, as founded also in reality, that we might also come to understand why it is "the brain that thinks, not man—the latter being only a cerebral crystallization."[67]

NOTES

Preface and Acknowledgments

1. Gilles Deleuze, *Différence et répétition* (Paris: Presses Universersitaire de France, 1968), 4 (my translation).

2. Gilles Deleuze, *Difference and Repetition*, trans. Paul Patton (New York: Columbia University Press, 1994), xvii.

3. Raymond Bellour, "The Image of Thought: Art or Philosophy, or Beyond?," in *Afterimages of Gilles Deleuze's Film Philosophy*, ed. D. N. Rodowick (Minneapolis: University of Minnesota Press, 2010), 3–4.

4. Gregg Lambert, *The Non-Philosophy of Gilles Deleuze* (New York: Continuum, 2002).

5. Gilles Deleuze and Claire Parnet, *Dialogues* (Paris: Flammarion, 1996), 115.

Introduction

1. Gilles Deleuze, *Desert Islands and Other Texts: 1953–1974*, ed. David Lapoujade, trans. Michael Taormina (Cambridge, Mass.: MIT Press, 2004), 139.

2. Ibid., 140.

3. Michel Foucault, *The Order of Things: An Archaeology of the Human Sciences* (New York: Vintage Books, 1994), 324.

4. Ibid., 325.

5. Deleuze, *Difference and Repetition*, 129.

6. Deleuze, *Desert Islands*, 137–38.

7. Ibid.

8. Ibid.

9. Ibid., 142.

10. Ibid., 137.

11. "Das Bedenkliche, das, was uns zu denken gibt, ist demnach keinesweg durch uns festgesetzt, nich durch uns auf gestestellt, nich durch uns nur vorgestellt." Martin Heidegger, *Was Heist Denkin?* (Tübingen: Max Niemayer Verlag, 1984), 3; *What Is Called Thinking?*, trans. J. Glenn Gray (New York: Harper and Row, 1968).

12. See especially the passages concerning the new "conceptual personae" introduced into contemporary philosophy by writers like Blanchot; these personae refer to ideas born from living, "face-to-face" relationships that are given "new a priori characteristics" (e.g., the "friend" expresses the idea of friendship as a face-to-face experience that also bears a priori characteristics that change over time). It is in this sense one can speak of madness, in relation to Artaud's experience, or to amnesia and aphasia, in relation to the figures of Blanchot, Celan, Chestov, and Michaux. Deleuze and Guattari, *What Is Philosophy?*, trans. Hugh Tomlinson and Graham Burchell (New York: Columbia University Press, 1994), 4–5.

13. See especially the collection published in 1959 and translated as Martin Heidegger, *On the Way to Language*, trans. Peter Hertz (San Francisco: Harper and Row, 1971).

14. Deleuze, *Difference and Repetition*, 178.

15. From the French *survol*, which Deleuze and Guattari frequently employ to signal a manner of "flying over" the problematic field of a concept, "at infinite speed," but in a manner also compared to the movement of a slow-motion shot that traces the contours of the problem and the finite number of conceptual components in what they call a "fragmentary whole."

16. Foucault, *The Order of Things*, 327.

17. Deleuze and Guattari, *What Is Philosophy?*, 55.

18. Ibid., 37.

19. To my knowledge, Deleuze publicly claimed to have "signed" only three concepts: "the ritornello," which is actually a concept first invented by Guattari; "the other person" *(autrui)*, a concept that goes back to Leibniz but Deleuze recasts given that "Leibniz did not believe that possibles exist in the real world"; and finally, the "crystal of time," which is derived from Bergson's concept of duration, in which Deleuze claims to have discovered a "direct presentation of the image of thought" (see the Conclusion, n. 59).

20. Deleuze and Guattari, *What Is Philosophy?*, 23.

21. Ibid., 51.

22. Alan D. Schrift, *Twentieth-Century French Philosophy: Key Themes and Thinkers* (London: Blackwell, 2006), 300.

23. Ibid., 93.

24. Ibid., 299–300.

25. Of course, the contradiction to this thesis is Bergson (not Spinoza!), whom Deleuze chooses to champion very early in his career, for reasons I will discuss in the Conclusion.

26. Deleuze, *Desert Islands*, 142.

27. This contradiction is perhaps best summarized by Constantine Boundas in the following passage: *"Philosopher, stutterer, thinker of an outside*—but never marginal or parasitic. His philosophical apprenticeship and, later on, his career as a 'public philosopher' have been in accordance with France's best and time honored ways: *La Sorbonne, Professeur de Lycée, Professeur de l'Université en Province*, researcher at the *Centre national des researches scientifiques, Professeur de l'Université de Paris VIII*, first Vincennes, and later on, St. Denis. But this rather orthodox French academic career—this molar, segmented line, as he would call it—never managed to conceal a certain taste for the outside, a desire for nomadic displacements, an openness to encounters which could cause the molar line to deviate and the rhizome to grow in the middle, or a kind of humor with which to displace the philosopher's old irony." Constantine V. Boundas, ed., *A Deleuze Reader* (New York: Columbia University Press, 1993), 3.

28. Deleuze, *Desert Islands*, 142.

29. Ibid.

30. Ibid.

31. Ibid., 41.

32. Ibid., 40.

33. Ibid., 42.

34. Ibid., viii.

35. Epigraph appearing on the back cover of Gilles Deleuze, *Two Regimes of Madness: Texts and Interviews, 1975–1995*, ed. David Lapoujade, trans. Ames Hodge and Mike Taormina (Cambridge, Mass.: MIT Press, 2006).

36. On this point, see my "French Theory: The Movie," *Symploke* 18, nos. 1–2 (2010): 293–303. See also the concluding chapter of Gregory Flaxman, *Gilles Deleuze and the Fabulation of Philosophy*, vol. 1 (Minneapolis: University of Minnesota Press, 2012).

37. Deleuze, *Desert Islands*, 56.

38. *Machine* is a term first employed by Guattari to designate a concrete multiplicity, or later an assemblage *(agencement)*, integrated into any Structure and thus causing it to function, or to produce, the primary example being the Lacanian notion of *"l'objet petit a."* It becomes the modal point of Deleuze and Guattari's analysis of historical structures, because each contingent structure is dominated by a system of machines; therefore, in approaching any structure one must first identify its actual machines and determine how they work. Félix Guattari, *Molecular Revolution: Psychiatry and Politics*, trans. Rosemary Sheed (New York: Penguin Books, 1984), 111–19.

39. Deleuze, *Desert Islands,* 93.

40. Deleuze, *Difference and Repetition,* 138.

41. Ibid.

42. Deleuze and Guattari, *Anti-Oedipus: Capitalism and Schizophrenia,* vol. 1, trans. Robert Hurley (Minneapolis: University of Minnesota Press, 1986), 42 (emphasis added).

43. We might see why Badiou later misunderstood the metaphysical claim of Deleuze's entire system of philosophy, or preferred to see it as a return to Scholasticism, because he failed to understand the relationship between the metaphysical problem of the One and the Many in terms of its relations to the real social problem of desiring production (i.e., the whole and the parts). For example, Deleuze does not understand multiplicity as the singularly differentiated One that is infinitely distributed in its parts; neither is multiplicity the predicative distribution of the One in the multiple, or the Set of all sets. See Alain Badiou, *The Clamor of Being,* trans. Louise Burchill (Minneapolis: University of Minnesota Press, 2000), 20.

44. Deleuze and Guattari, *Anti-Oedipus,* 42.

45. Ibid. With regard to the above statement, or provocation, the case of Bergson is more complicated; Deleuze defines Bergson's philosophy as a "Theory of Multiplicity" (see Conclusion, n. 58). Nevertheless, I will return in the Conclusion to show how, even in the case of Bergson, there is a strange amalgamation with Proust concerning the new image of thought that corresponds to real multiplicity, or what Deleuze defines as the "crystal image of Time."

1. The Image of Thought in Proust

1. Gilles Deleuze, *Proust and Signs: The Complete Text,* trans. Richard Howard (London: The Athlone Press, 2000), 145. Because the chronology of the French editions and thus the probable dates of composition are crucial for my argument in this chapter, I will refer to dates of French publication in the text; however, all English citations are taken from this edition, which is based on the second edition of *Proust et les signes (1970).* See note 6 below.

2. As Gregory Flaxman and I have discussed elsewhere, this "sensory-motor training" is vividly and ironically portrayed in several of Kubrick's films, particularly *A Clockwork Orange* (1971) and *Full Metal Jacket* (1987). See Gregg Lambert and Gregory Flaxman, "Ten Propositions on Cinema and the Brain," *Pli: Warwick Journal of Philosophy* 16 (2005): 114–28.

3. Deleuze, *Difference and Repetition,* 139.

4. Heidegger, *What Is Called Thinking?,* 184–85.

5. "Words" is also the title of a late meditation by Heidegger on the poetic saying of Stefan Georg, which gives the embryonic sense of language in the images of a buried, yet undead, child and a stranger, or one "who wanders beyond the limits."

6. The history of publication and translation of *Proust and Signs* is complicated. The first edition appeared in 1964, under the title *Marcel Proust et les signes.*
The augmented second edition, which ends with a new, lengthy chapter titled "Antilogos ou la machine littéraire," was first published in 1970. The third and final
edition was published in 1976. As the preface to the third edition indicates, the
"Antilogos" chapter from the second edition was broken into chapters for the third
edition, and the third edition's closing section, titled "Conclusion: Présence et
fonction de la folie l'Araignée," originally appeared in an Italian volume in 1973
(which Deleuze reworked for the 1976 edition), and was the basis of the 1975
"Roundtable on Proust." The 1976 edition includes a preface to the third edition,
but the preface to the second edition is not reprinted in the third. (The French
prefaces are merely labeled "Avant-propos de la deuxième édition" and "Avant-
propos de la troisième edition.") The first English translation of the 1970 French
edition appeared as *Proust and Signs,* trans. Richard Howard (New York: George
Braziller, 1972).

7. Guattari, *Molecular Revolution,* 111–19.

8. Deleuze, *Proust and Signs,* 102.

9. Ibid., 142.

10. Ibid., 147.

11. Ibid., 148. "An involuntary machine of interpretation" is another name for
the literary machine, or certain kinds of writing devices in general. It is involuntary because writers do not know beforehand what kinds of signs the machines
they invent will produce; in fact, they don't even know how the machine they have
created will actually work—if it will work at all! The art of writing is also a process
of interpreting the machine in determining the conditions of its production, in
addition to interpreting the signs and effects that these created machines produce.
Thus, all writers interpret according to both senses and aspects of the literary machines they create, but not all writers can be said to be good interpreters of their
own machines. (In some respects, Proust and Kafka are exceptions to this general
rule.)

12. Quoted in ibid., 187n.

13. Ibid.

14. Deleuze, *Two Regimes of Madness,* 30–31.

15. Deleuze and Guattari, *A Thousand Plateaus: Capitalism and Schizophrenia,*
vol. 2, trans. Brian Massumi (Minneapolis: University of Minnesota Press, 1987), 10.

16. Franz Kafka, "The Metamorphosis," in *The Metamorphosis and Other Stories,* trans. Joyce Crick (Oxford: Oxford University Press, 2009), 30.

17. Deleuze, *Proust and Signs,* 94.

18. Deleuze, *Difference and Repetition,* 131.

19. "I waited until I had attained an age so mature as to leave me no hope that at
any stage of life more advanced I should be better able to execute my design. On

this account, I have delayed so long that I should henceforth consider I was doing wrong were I still to consume in deliberation any of the time that now remains for action. To-day, then, since I have opportunely freed my mind from all cares and am happily disturbed by no passions and since I am in the secure possession of leisure in a peaceable retirement, I will at length apply myself earnestly and freely to the general overthrow of all my former opinions." René Descartes, *Meditations on First Philosophy*, trans. John Cottingham (Cambridge: Cambridge University Press, 1996), 10.

20. Ibid., 24.

21. Deleuze, *Proust and Signs*, 97.

22. Descartes, *Meditations*, 23.

23. Deleuze, *Difference and Repetition*, 130.

24. Quoted in Deleuze, *Proust and Signs*, 95–97.

25. Marcel Proust, *Du Cote de chez Swann*, vol. 1, 67–69, quoted in Walter Benjamin, *The Arcades Project*, trans. Howard Eiland and Kevin McLaughlin (Cambridge, Mass.: Harvard University Press, 1999), 408; emphasis in original.

26. Deleuze, *Proust and Signs*, 174.

2. Notes from a Thought Experiment

1. Gilles Deleuze and Félix Guattari, *Rhizome: Introduction* (Paris: Éditions de Minuit, 1976), reprinted in revised form in *Capitalisme et schizophrenie*, vol. 2: *Mille plateaux* (1980). English translation: Deleuze and Guattari, *On the Line*, trans. John Johnston (New York: Semiotext(e), 1983).

2. Deleuze and Guattari, *What Is Philosophy?*, 36.

3. Deleuze and Guattari, *A Thousand Plateaus*: Capitalism and Schizophrenia, vol. 2, trans. Brian Massumi (Minneapolis: University of Minnesota Press, 1987), 3.

4. Badiou's dismissal of Guattari's contribution is well known and appears in statements at the beginning of *The Clamour of Being* (2000). In a seminar on *Difference and Repetition* at The University of California at Irvine in 1993, when asked about Deleuze's collaboration with Guattari, Derrida replied: "Deleuze est un philosophe vrai. Mais, quoi penser à l'autre type. L'affaire est très bizarre" (communication with the author).

5. See also my preface, "The Art of Commentary," in *The Non-Philosophy of Gilles Deleuze*. Of course, some readers thought I was rejecting the function of commentary in my argument, or exhibited some form of "bad faith" in appearing to dismiss commentary *in the very act of doing commentary*. Rather, I was simply bringing into focus, as the very condition of my own discourse, what Foucault called the author's—the commentator's, in this case—"Will to Truth." This critique has two edges, certainly, one of which would fall back on my own production of yet another "interpretation of Deleuze." As I have already discussed and return

555

again to address in the Conclusion, many commentaries in philosophy appear as if they are all written by Saints, as if the stain of what Deleuze calls "an essential Egoism" must be erased from the conditions of enunciation.

6. Deleuze and Guattari, *A Thousand Plateaus*, 3.
7. Ibid.
8. Ibid.
9. Félix Guattari, *The Anti-Oedipus Papers,* ed. Stéphane Nadaud, trans. Kélina Gotman (New York: Semiotext(e), 2006), 401.
10. Deleuze and Guattari, *A Thousand Plateaus*, 6. The following passages are found in the French edition of *Mille Plateaux* (Paris: Les Éditions de minuit, 1980), 11–12.
11. Guattari, *Anti-Oedipus Papers*, 6; Deleuze and Guattari, *Mille Plateaux*, 12.
12. Ibid., 8.
13. Ibid., 19.
14. Ibid., 7.
15. Ibid.
16. "Machine et structure" is the title of the paper first sent to Deleuze by Guattari in 1969. In return, Deleuze makes copious notes and comments, and this exchange becomes the first occasion of their collaboration. See Françoise Dosse, *Gilles Deleuze and Félix Guattari* (Paris: Éditions de découverte, 2007), 233.
17. Quoted in ibid., 233.
18. Deleuze and Guattari, *A Thousand Plateaus*, 19.
19. Ibid., 12.
20. Ibid., 13.
21. Ibid., 15.
22. Ibid.
23. Ibid., 22.
24. François Zourabichvili, *A Philosophy of the Event,* ed. Gregg Lambert and Daniel W. Smith, trans. Kieran Aarons (Edinburgh: University of Edinburgh Press, 2012), 205–9.

3. The Image of Thought in Kafka

1. Gilles Deleuze and Félix Guattari, *Kafka: Toward a Minor Literature,* trans. Dana Polan (Minneapolis: University of Minnesota Press, 1986), 16.
2. Zourabichvili, *A Philosophy of the Event*, 208.
3. This formulation is owed to Nick Nesbitt's interpretation of the four hypotheses in "Before the Law: Deleuze, Kafka & the Clinic of Right," in *Franz Kafka: A Minority Report,* ed. Petr Kouba and Tomas Pivoda (Prague: Litteraria Pragensia Books, 2011), 87.
4. Deleuze, *Proust and Signs,* 97.

5. Deleuze and Guattari, *Kafka*, 3.

6. "Rhizome," Wikipedia, http://www.wikipedia.org (emphasis added). I'm certain that there are more authoritative definitions available, but this one was ready to hand and I liked the arrangement of description and species.

7. Deleuze, *Proust and Signs*, 174.

8. Ibid., 163.

9. Deleuze and Guattari, *Kafka*, 4.

10. Ibid., 5.

11. Ibid.

12. Ibid., 4.

13. Ibid., 26.

14. Ibid., 28.

15. Ibid., 41.

16. Deleuze, *Proust and Signs*, 142.

17. These two positions, the paranoid-schizoid and the depressive, are derived from Mélanie Klein's theory of infantile development, particularly in relation to the partial object and around the theme of guilt. Deleuze and Guattari consistently pose these terms in their reading of both Proust and Kafka; thus, Proust is defined from a schizoid-paranoid position, which is distributed across the characters of Charlus, Albertine, and the narrator; Kafka is often described in terms of a depressive position in relation to the Law (i.e., infinite debt and guilt, which amounts to the same thing in the German *Schuld*). And yet, in combining the literary machines of Proust and Kafka, Deleuze and Guattari attempt to incorporate both positions in their theory of desire and the unconscious. See Mélanie Klein, "Some Theoretical Conclusions Regarding the Emotional Life of the Infant," in *Envy and Gratitude and Other Works: 1946–1963* (New York: Free Press, 1984), 61–93.

18. Deleuze, *Proust and Signs*, 132.

19. Deleuze and Guattari, *Anti-Oedipus*, 43. On the advice of Ronald Bogue, I have altered the translation of "attitude," in the second instance, to correspond to the original French: "En termes kleiniens, on dirait que la position dépressive n'est qu'une couverture pour une position schizoïde plus profonde" (Deleuze and Guattari, *L'Anti-Oedipe* [Paris: Éditions de Minuit, 1972], 51). This can also be confirmed by Deleuze's constant reference in *Proust and Signs* to the status of the law and the contract in terms of the modern world that is fragmented and not ruled by *Logos*. Consequently, the problem of the law appears as a formidable unity or as a primary power that controls the world of untotalizable and untotalized fragments. "The law no longer says what is good, but good is what the law says (i.e., it is good because I say it is), revealing an order that is absolutely empty, uniquely formal, because it causes us to know no distinct object, no Good of reference, no referring *Logos*" (Deleuze, *Proust and Signs*, 131).

20. Deleuze and Guattari, *Anti-Oedipus*, 43.

21. Ibid., 212.

22. Deleuze and Guattari, *Kafka,* 73.

23. In other words, throughout Deleuze and Guattari's writings we find that there is always this tendency of the writer to begin or to affirm the position of the bachelor, or the thinker to begin from a depressed position of solitude, just as the masochist must begin from a perverse position at least with regard to the Oedipal organization of sexuality and "human desire." (Kafka only offers us the most unique example of all three positions: depressive, schizophrenic, and the masochist.) But is this any different from those who begin or seek to begin again on the plane composed by their own sexuality, to become thinkers and artists, just as often as they become strangers and refugees (if not confessed perverts or criminals, as in the cases of Proust and Genet). And yet, on the basis of the above dialectic, the path via sexuality is never the final answer and more often than not leads to sadness and failure because the sexual pair always obstructs the more primary couple and sooner or later becomes an image or simulacra that blocks any access to this couple, since it is only a superficial path on the way to the primary social division: between the species and "a people who are missing." On this question of the primary couple, or social division, also see my "The Non-Human Sex," in *Deleuze and Sex,* ed. Frida Beckman (Edinburgh: University of Edinburgh Press, 2011), 135–52.

24. Deleuze and Guattari, *Kafka,* 49.

25. Deleuze, *Proust and Signs,* 145.

26. Ibid., 115.

4. A Minor Question of Literature

1. Guattari, *Molecular Revolution,* 111.

2. Deleuze and Guattari, *Kafka,* 71.

3. Ibid., 19.

4. Gilles Deleuze, *Critique et Clinique* (Paris: Les Éditions de Minuit, 1993), 11 (translation mine). All following citations are from Gilles Deleuze, *Essays Critical and Clinical,* trans. Daniel W. Smith and Michael A. Greco (Minneapolis: University of Minnesota Press, 1997).

5. Ibid., 15.

6. Jean-Paul Sartre, *Search for a Method,* trans. Hazel E. Barnes (New York: Vintage Books, 1963), 96–98.

7. Guattari, *Molecular Revolution,* 118.

8. Sartre, *Search for a Method,* 96.

9. Ibid., 147.

10. Fredric Jameson, *Singular Modernity: Essay on the Ontology of the Present* (London: Verso, 2002), 199–200.

11. Deleuze, *Essays Critical and Clinical,* 7.

12. Ibid.

13. Peter Hallward, *Absolutely Postcolonial* (Manchester: Manchester University Press, 2001), 333.

14. Deleuze and Guattari, *Kafka*, 16.

15. See *Franz Kafka: The Office Writings*, ed. Stanley Corngold (Princeton: Princeton University Press, 2009). It is quite striking to see that Kafka's style was not restricted to literary works, letters, and the diaries, but can also be found in letters and briefs in his occupation as a lawyer and insurance investigator. In particular, there is a series of letters to the company concerning a lack of salary increase over a period of several years with clear insinuations of anti-Semitism as the true cause. Almost term for term, the arguments and method of "free indirect discourse" employed can also be found in the stories and especially in the later novels.

16. Deleuze and Guattari, *Kafka*, 83.

17. Ibid.; emphasis added.

18. Ibid.

19. Ibid., 140.

20. Ibid., 55.

21. On the definition of "order words," see my *Who's Afraid of Deleuze and Guattari?* (London: Continuum Books, 2008), 13–66. See also "Expression," in *Gilles Deleuze: Key Concepts,* 2nd ed., ed. Charles J. Stivale (London: Acumen, 2011), 33–42.

22. Elias Canetti, *Kafka's Other Trial* (New York: Schocken Books, 1974).

23. Franz Kafka, *Letters to Felice*, ed. Erich Heller and Jurgen Born, trans. James Stern and Elizabeth Duckworth (New York: Vintage Books, 1999), 253.

24. Ibid., 70–71.

25. Deleuze and Guattari, *Kafka*, 70.

26. Ibid.

27. Ibid., 70–71.

28. Ibid., 70.

29. Ibid., 71.

30. This will be the basis for Hallward's critical appraisal of Deleuze's philosophy of "creative univocity," as well as the conceptual personae of the postcolonial writer as an "absolute bachelor" (i.e., the subjective determination of a globalized literature), as two of the most powerful expressions of a singularizing form of individuation shared between two dominant traditions of philosophy and literature today. Consequently, when Hallward agrees with Badiou's assessment that Deleuze is "the philosopher of our century," this should be understood, not necessarily as praise, but rather as a bit like Marx's assessment of the philosophy of Max Stirner in the first part of *The German Ideology* (i.e., the form of acknowledgment is ironic, given that Stirner is criticized as a pure ideologist). In this sense, "bachelor desire" would be the name for the framework of the corporate desires of the late-modernist writer and philosopher to become "singular," "autonomous," and

finally, "impersonal"—as in Mallarmé's famous dictum, "liberated from all servitude to any [socially] marked order of language." See Hallward, *Absolutely Postcolonial,* 13–17.

31. Deleuze and Guattari, *Kafka,* 84.

32. Gilles Deleuze, *The Fold: Leibniz and the Baroque,* trans. Tom Conley (Minneapolis: University of Minnesota Press, 1993), 93.

33. Ibid., 95.

34. Deleuze, *Critical and Clinical,* 3.

35. Ibid., 4.

36. Ibid., 3.

5. A Question of Style in the Philosophy of Difference

1. A more accurate concept would be that of the "transitional object," following Winnicott, since literary texts sometimes function as partial objects; however, for Deleuze and Guattari, partial objects are fundamentally machinic terms belonging to social assemblages, so the question would be how to "connect" the literary work to a collective assemblage of enunciation in order to account for the effects of individual identification they sometimes produce (for example, Mark David Chapman's reading of Salinger's *Catcher in the Rye,* or the number of suicides that occurred around the reading of Goethe's *The Sorrows of Young Werther*). On the theory of literature and the question of transference, see especially Gabriele M. Schwab, *Subjects without Selves: Transitional Texts in Modern Fiction* (Cambridge, Mass.: Harvard University Press, 1994).

2. Of course, not all contemporary philosophers have engaged in this kind of reflection, which is particularly true of most academic philosophy today. In a late interview, Derrida remarked on this avoidance (without naming any particular movement or school of philosophy), saying: "Those who protest against all these questions [concerning writing in general] mean to protect a certain institutional authority of philosophy against these questions and the transformations that these questions call for and presuppose. What they are actually protecting the institution against is philosophy." Jacques Derrida, *Points: Interviews 1974–1994,* trans. Peggy Kamuf (Stanford: Stanford University Press, 1995), 218.

3. Deleuze, *Difference and Repetition,* xxi.

4. Derrida, *Of Grammatology,* corrected edition, trans. Gayatri Chakravorty Spivak (Baltimore: Johns Hopkins University Press, 1998), 4.

5. See Introduction, 11.

6. Jacques Derrida, "Passions: An Oblique Offering," in *Derrida: A Critical Reader,* ed. David Wood (Oxford: Blackwell, 1992), 5; Deleuze, *Essays Critical and Clinical,* 3.

7. Jacques Derrida, *Writing and Difference,* trans. Alan Bass (Chicago: University of Chicago Press, 1978), 171.

8. For example, in 1959 Blanchot publishes *Le Livre à venir,* which contains a discussion of both figures around the themes of writing and madness, and Jean Laplanche publishes his influential *Hölderlin et la question du père* in 1961.

9. Derrida, *Writing and Difference,* 171.

10. Ibid.

11. Ibid., 175.

12. Ibid., 171.

13. Gilles Deleuze, *Logic of Sense,* trans. Mark Lester with Charles Stivalle (New York: Columbia University Press, 1990), 92.

14. Gilles Deleuze, *Présentation de Sacher-Masoch* (Paris: Éditions de Minuit, 1967), 10; translation mine.

15. Derrida, *Writing and Difference,* 173.

16. Deleuze, *Difference and Repetition,* 148.

17. Derrida, *Writing and Difference,* 170.

18. Ibid.

19. Deleuze, *Difference and Repetition,* 105; emphasis in original.

20. Derrida, *Writing and Difference,* 175.

21. Deleuze, *Essays Critical and Clinical,* 7.

22. Ibid., 194.

23. Deleuze and Guattari, *Anti-Oedipus,* 311.

24. Gilles Deleuze, *Cinema 2: The Time-Image,* trans. Hugh Tomlinson and Robert Galeta (London: Athlone Press, 1989), 172.

25. Deleuze, *Essays Critical and Clinical,* 7–20. Elsewhere he will call this phenomenon of madness a "black hole," referring to a nature that traps all light within itself and never emits anything but an absence of the work (Deleuze and Parnet, *Dialogues,* 46).

26. Derrida, *Writing and Difference,* 175.

27. Deleuze, *Essays Critical and Clinical,* 11.

28. Derrida, *L'écriture et la différence* (Paris: Éditions de Seuil, 1967), 253; translation mine.

29. Derrida, *Writing and Difference,* 174.

30. Deleuze, *Difference and Repetition,* 155.

31. Derrida, *Writing and Difference,* 194.

32. Ibid.

33. Deleuze, *Difference and Repetition,* 148.

34. Ibid., 150.

35. Derrida, *Writing and Difference,* 195.

36. Deleuze, *Essays Critical and Clinical,* 76.

37. Ibid., 69.

38. Jacques Derrida, *The Gift of Death,* trans. David Wills (Chicago: University of Chicago Press, 1995), 75.

39. Derrida, "Passions," 17–18.

40. Deleuze, *Essays Critical and Clinical,* 73.

41. Ibid., 33n.

42. Portions of this seminar are reproduced in the article I have been quoting from, Derrida's "Passions: An Oblique Offering," although the direct commentary on Deleuze's reading has been erased and only the references to Melville's character remain (from author's notes).

43. Deleuze, *Essays Critical and Clinical,* 75.

44. Jacques Derrida, *Margins of Philosophy,* trans. Allan Bass (Chicago: University of Chicago Press, 1985), 17.

45. Deleuze, *Essays Critical and Clinical,* 68.

46. Notes from seminar, "Questions of Responsibility," University of California at Irvine, spring 1996.

47. Quoted in Deleuze, *Essays Critical and Clinical,* 75.

48. Derrida, "Passions," 23.

49. Ibid.

50. Gilles Deleuze, *Negotiations: 1972–1990,* trans. Martin Joughin (New York: Columbia University Press, 1995), 143.

51. Derrida, *Margins of Philosophy,* 15.

52. Ibid., 10.

53. Ibid., 11.

54. Ibid., 3.

55. Derrida, *Of Grammatology,* 4.

56. Ibid., 7.

57. Deleuze, *Difference and Repetition,* xxi.

58. Derrida, *Of Grammatology,* 7.

59. Derrida, *Points,* 218.

60. Ibid., 219.

61. Ibid.

62. Ibid.

63. Deleuze, *Difference and Repetition,* xxi.

64. Deleuze, *Proust and Signs,* 161.

65. Ibid., 162.

66. Ibid.

67. Ibid., 168.

68. Deleuze, *Essays Critical and Clinical,* 113.

69. Ibid., 168–69.

70. Derrida, *Points,* 354.

71. Ibid., 354–55.

72. Deleuze, *Essays Critical and Clinical,* 113.

73. Ibid.

74. Ibid., 109.

75. Derrida, *Points,* 347.

76. Derrida, *Of Grammatology*, 5.

77. Derrida, *Writing and Difference*, 5.

78. Ibid., 6.

79. Thus it is significant to note that Derrida never completely renounces the word "critique," whereas Deleuze never really makes it central to his own philosophical project. The difference is that Derrida understands his project in the tradition of a certain style of "Enlightenment" [*Aufklärung*] and Deleuze certainly does not; however, for Derrida the problem with the earlier philosophical works in this tradition (certainly those of Kant, but also of Hegel, Husserl, and Heidegger) is that their understanding of critique was not critical enough. (Is this not Derrida's constant criticism of Kant's heliocentricity, Leibniz's and Hegel's Eurocentricity, Husserl's logocentricity, of Heidegger's spiritual nationalism?) The point, therefore, to push the possibilities of the critique further, to make it "hyperbolique," to become "hypercritical," and finally, to constantly refuse the point where the labor of negativity congeals into simple negation, or turns to reveal the resemblance of a properly metaphysical entity. As Derrida remarks, "This thinking perhaps transforms the space and, through *aporias*, allows the (non-positive) affirmation to appear, the one that is presupposed by every critique and every negativity" (Derrida, *Positions*, trans. Alan Bass [Chicago: University of Chicago Press, 1982], 357).

80. See Jacques Derrida, "I'll Have to Wander Alone," trans. David Kammerman, *Tympanum* 1 (1998), http://www.usc.edu/dept/comp-lit/tympanum/1/.

81. Samuel Beckett, *The Unnamable*, in *Complete Works*, vol. 1 (New York: Grove Press, 2006), 331.

6. The Image of Thought in Modern Cinema

1. Deleuze, *Cinema 2*, 262.

2. Sergei Eisenstein, "The Filmic Fourth Dimension," in *Film Form*, trans. Jay Leyda (New York: Harcourt Brace Jovanovich, 1949), 64–71. The principle that Eisenstein witnessed in the Kabuki is the function of a pure montage in which each element is viewed from the perspective of the total effect produced by the complete theater: "In the Kabuki . . . the Japanese regards each theatrical element, not as an incommensurable unit among various categories of affect (on the various sense organs), but as a single unit of theater. . . . Directing himself to the various organs of sensation, he builds his summation [of individual "pieces"] to a grand total provocation of the human brain, without taking any notice which of these several paths he is following" (Eisenstein, *Film Form*, 64). The emphasis upon a free indeterminate accord of the elements of expression, with no one determining the significance of the others, recalls a fundamental principle that belongs to Deleuze's theory of the faculties under the arrangement of a new image of thought. See also Deleuze, *Difference and Repetition*, esp. chap. 5, "Asymmetrical Synthesis of the Sensible," 236ff.

3. Eisenstein, *Film Form*, 64.

4. Ibid., 65.
5. Ibid., 69.
6. Deleuze, *Cinema 2*, 156.
7. Ibid.
8. Ibid., 158.
9. Ibid.
10. Eisenstein, quoted in ibid., 211.
11. Deleuze, *Cinema 2*, 167.
12. Ibid., 165.
13. Ibid., 170.
14. Ibid., 167.
15. Ibid., 172.
16. Deleuze, *Difference and Repetition*, x.
17. Deleuze, *Two Regimes of Madness*, 283–84; translation modified.
18. Eisenstein, *Film Form*, 71.
19. Deleuze, *Cinema 2*, 277.
20. Ibid., 212.
21. Ibid., 318n.
22. Deleuze and Guattari, *What Is Philosophy?*, 198.
23. Stanley Kubrick, *Interviews*, ed. Gene D. Philips (Jackson: University Press of Mississippi, 2001), 69.
24. Deleuze, *Cinema 2*, 318n.
25. Ibid., 125.
26. Ibid.
27. Deleuze, *Bergsonism*, trans. Hugh Tomlinson and Barbara Habberjam (New York: Zone Books, 1988), 108.
28. Ibid., 110.
29. Ibid., 105.
30. Ibid., 108.
31. Ibid., 107.
32. Ibid., 106.
33. Ibid., 107.

Conclusion

1. Deleuze and Guattari, *What Is Philosophy?*, 206. The image of contrary ideas as "successive filters over chaos" is derived from Michel Serres's reading of this principle in the philosophy of Leibniz. See Michel Serres, *Le Système de Leibniz et ses modèles mathématiques* (Paris: Presses universitaires de France, 1968), 122–24.

2. "Das Bedenkliche, das, was uns zu denken gibt, ist demnach keinesweg durch uns festgesetzt, nich durch uns auf gestestellt, nich durch uns nur vor-gestellt." Heidegger, *Was Heist Denkin?*, 3.

3. Ibid., 207.

4. Ibid.

5. Ibid., 202.

6. Ibid., 201.

7. Ibid., 202.

8. Ibid., 211.

9. For the above, see the introduction to Gilles Deleuze, ed., *Instincts et institutions* (Paris: Hachette, 1953), viii–xi; Deleuze, *Bergsonism*.

10. Deleuze, *Bergsonism*, 109.

11. Ibid., 108.

12. Ibid.

13. Ibid.

14. Ibid., 111.

15. Ibid., 108.

16. Ibid.

17. Ibid., 112.

18. Ibid., 108.

19. Ibid.; emphasis added. I would simply point out to the reader that it is difficult to discern in the above passages whether Deleuze, at this point, is merely citing Bergson or actually "channeling" the dead philosopher.

20. Ibid., 106.

21. Ibid., 107.

22. *Qu'est-ce que l'acte de création? Conférence donnée dans le cadre des mardis de la fondation Femis* (May 17, 1987), accessed on www.deleuzeweb.com.

23. Deleuze and Guattari, *What Is Philosophy?*, 202.

24. Ibid.

25. On this point, see my "Deleuze and the Political Ontology of the Friend *(philos)*," in *Deleuze and Politics*, ed. Ian Buchanan and Nick Thoburn (Edinburgh: University of Edinburgh Press, 2008), 35–53.

26. Deleuze, *Negotiations*, 160.

27. David Perkins, *The Eureka Effect: The Art and Logic of Breakthrough Thinking* (New York: W. W. Norton, 2000), 83.

28. Deleuze and Guattari, *What Is Philosophy?*, 207.

29. Ibid., 210.

30. Ibid., 209.

31. Deleuze and Guattari, *Qu'est-ce que la philosophie?* (Paris: Éditions de Minuit, 1991), 9.

32. Ibid., 7.

33. Deleuze, *Bergsonism*, 108.

34. Antonio Negri, quoted in Deleuze, *Negotiations*, 174.

35. Deleuze and Guattari, *What Is Philosophy?*, 11.

36. Ibid., 10.

37. Ibid., 12.

38. Michael Hardt and Antonio Negri, *Empire* (Cambridge, Mass.: Harvard University Press, 2000), 397.

39. Giorgio Agamben, *Homo Sacer: Sovereign Power and Bare Life,* trans. Daniel Heller-Roazen (Palo Alto: Stanford University Press, 1998), 181.

40. Ibid., 188.

41. On this point see my video lecture "Derrida and Violence" for the *Histories of Violence* web-based project created by Brad Evans, University of Leeds, United Kingdom, at http://www.historiesofviolence.com/theory/derrida/.

42. Jean-Luc Nancy, *Dis-Enclosure: The Deconstruction of Christianity,* trans. Bettina Bergo et al. (New York: Fordham University Press, 2008), 157.

43. Ibid.

44. Deleuze, *Negotiations,* 160. For this reason I might suggest that the contemporary analytic tradition of "possible world theory" may be more correct in taking up the most ordinary statements and events, such as "John is arriving at 9 a.m.," rather than the partly mythic and historically spectacular events in order to determine the sense of events, or the existence of possible worlds.

45. See my preface on "The Art of Commentary," in *The Non-Philosophy of Gilles Deleuze,* x–xiv.

46. Deleuze and Guattari, *What Is Philosophy?,* 204.

47. See my *Who's Afraid of Deleuze and Guattari?,* esp. the chapter "The Right to Desire," 129–38.

48. Simon Bell, *Landscape: Pattern, Perception, and Process* (London: Taylor and Francis, 1999), 107–10. Also see p. 109 for a diagram of Klondike Space based on Perkins.

49. Ibid., 211.

50. Ibid., 149.

51. Deleuze, *Bergsonism,* 112.

52. Ibid.

53. Ibid.

54. Seminar on "L'image movement, l'image-temps" (June 7, 1987), accessed on www.deleuzeweb.com.

55. Deleuze, *Bergsonism,* 112.

56. Gilles Deleuze, "Postscript to the American Edition: *A Return to Bergson,*" in *Two Regimes of Madness,* 335.

57. Gilles Deleuze and Claire Parnet, *Dialogues II,* trans. Hugh Tomlinson and Barbara Habberjam (London: Continuum Books, 2006), 120n.

58. Henri Bergson, *Matière et mémoire* (Paris: Presses universitaires de France, 1939), 169; translation mine. For our purposes, let plan P = plan(e) of immanence.

59. Deleuze, *Cinema 2,* 79. In the 1988 postscript quoted above, concerning Bergson's philosophy as a general theory of multiplicity, Deleuze writes: "In *Time and Free Will,* Bergson defines duration as a multiplicity, a type of multiplicity.

This is a unique word since he changes multiple from a mere adjective to a veritable noun. By doing so, he condemns as a false problem the traditional theme of the one and the multiple" (Deleuze, *Two Regimes of Madness,* 336–37).

60. Deleuze, *Cinema 2,* 78. In this regard it is quite significant that this "crystalline image of time" can also be ascribed to Walter Benjamin's observation in the following passage that appears in *The Arcades Project*: "Indeed, to discover in the analysis of the small individual moment the crystal of the total event. And, therefore, to break with vulgar historical naturalism" (Walter Benjamin, *The Arcades Project,* trans. Howard Eiland and Kevin McLaughlin [Cambridge, Mass.: Harvard University Press, 1999], 461). What is even more remarkable, however, is the fact that the observations of both Deleuze and Benjamin are derived from the same passage in Proust's *Recherche.*

61. Deleuze, *Cinema 2,* 80.

62. Ibid.

63. Deleuze, *Negotiations,* 149.

64. Ibid.

65. Seminar on "L'image movement, l'image-temps."

66. Deleuze, *Logic of Sense,* 180. See also Badiou, *The Clamor of Being,* 20.

67. Deleuze and Guattari, *What Is Philosophy?,* 210.

INDEX

abstract, 59, 64; conceptual and, 4
abstractions, ideas and, 181
a-centered model, 167, 172–73
action-image, 163, 164, 165, 166, 204
actual, 194; cerebral activity and, 182;
  virtual and, 173, 206, 207, 208
Agamben, Giorgio, 196, 197
agencement, 87, 88, 96, 99, 111
À la recherche du temps perdu (Proust),
  31, 34, 35, 40, 81, 84, 87
algorithm, law of, 168
Alliez, Eric, 205
alterity, 100; anthropological expression
  of, 11
Althusser, Louis, ideology and, 135
Amerika (Kafka), 69, 102
amnesia, 8, 88, 212n12
animal-*logos,* 46, 78, 84, 87, 104
anthropology, true, 123
anthropomorphism, 37, 153
anti-interpretation, 63, 64, 66, 82
anti-Kafka, creating, 106
anti-method, 60, 63, 99
Anti-Oedipus (Deleuze and Guattari), 21,
  31, 32, 43, 45, 49, 50, 56, 80–81, 83, 85,
  122, 126, 184; schizophrenia and, 125;
  writing machine of, 143
anti-philosophy, 15, 24, 31

aphasia, 8, 212n12
aporia, 197, 224n79
Arcades Project, The (Benjamin),
  228n60
Aristotle, philosophy and, 53
art, 5, 202; bourgeois, 163; communication by, 145–46; conceptual, 8;
  goals of, 157; heteronomy of, 6;
  as machine, 25; mental objects
  of, 190–91; philosophy of, 177;
  postmodernist interpretation of,
  187
Artaud, Antonin, 8, 29, 30, 50, 121, 137,
  160, 212n12; critical/clinical exegesis
  and, 120; Deleuze and, 161; Derrida
  and, 125–26, 128; image of thought
  and, 161; influence of, 13; life/law and,
  118; metaphysics and, 126; minor
  writers and, 75; not thinking and, 162;
  protests and, 120; schizophrenia and,
  122–23, 124; style and, 119; on
  thought/metaphysics, 128; writing
  and, 118–19
assemblage, 99, 175; collective, 199–200;
  social, 55, 103, 108, 199, 221n1
associations, 170, 175; chain of, 146, 189
author, as discursive function, 141
author-God, 47

automaton: cinematographic, 177; spiritual, 156, 159–60, 164, 177

bachelor, 88, 96–97, 100, 102, 103, 105, 107, 137; absolute, 220n30; becoming, 108; minority, 109; political/sexual/ social, 109; virtual community and, 111
bachelor desire, 96–97, 100, 109, 220n30
Badiou, Alain, 48, 209, 214n43, 216n4, 220n30
Balzac, Honoré de, 102
Barthes, Roland, 52, 151
"Bartleby, the Scrivener" (Melville), 89, 123, 128; attorney and, 129, 135; Deleuze and, 129, 130, 133, 134, 137, 138; Derrida and, 14, 131, 132, 133, 134, 135; enunciation and, 136; formula of, 130, 131, 133; identification of, 129–30; life/law and, 118; sign of, 131, 133; social relationships and, 132; subjacent identifications and, 130; as zone of indetermination, 133
Bataille, Georges, 198
Bauer, Felice, 103
Beckett, Samuel, 5, 50, 68, 85; characters of, 189; influence of, 13; singularity and, 92
becoming, state of, 108, 115
becoming-a-bachelor, 103, 109
becoming a writer, 92–93, 108, 111
becoming-revolutionary, 82, 91
Becoming-Woman, 68, 91, 94, 102, 103, 109
being, 13; solicitude/solicitation of, 152; understanding of, 16
being of beings, 54
Benjamin, Walter, 13, 157, 228n60
Bergson, Henri, 17, 23, 205, 206, 209, 213n25; creative evolution and, 185; Deleuze and, 174, 214n45, 226n19; duration and, 212n19; élan vital and, 176, 178, 185; fabulation and, 113; human brain and, 177; intuition and, 176; multiplicity and, 227n59; philosophy of, 16, 214n45; spiritualism

and, 204; thought/creative memory and, 175
Bergsonism (Deleuze), 173, 176, 177, 181, 182, 184, 185, 186, 187, 192, 195, 202–3, 204, 205, 207
Big Theory, 201, 202
Blanchot, Maurice, 8, 13, 119, 212n12
body, 55; Other and, 161
body-image, 51, 206
body without organs (BWO), 33, 34, 38, 43, 47, 64, 68
bondage, form of, 107
boom, crash and, 148, 149, 150
Boundas, Constantine, career of, 213n27
Bovary, Madame, 91
brain: cerebral crystallization of, 203; cinema and, 28, 155, 156, 161, 166, 171, 178; creation of, 177; identifying, 176; image of, 166, 170, 173; military, 171; model for, 169, 170; naturing nature of, 177; organically coordinated, 198; organic composition of, 206; Other and, 161; philosophy and, 189; provocation of, 157; spiritual automaton and, 160; subjects and, 191; thought and, 158; unity and, 166; virtual, 27, 181; world and, 167, 168, 169, 170, 172, 173, 206
brain-image, 51, 181, 206, 209
"Brain Is the Screen, The" (Deleuze), 166
Brod, Max, 83, 101
burrow, 78, 87, 99, 107, 112; rhizome and, 69, 70, 71, 72, 82, 84; spiders and, 71
bust, 149; boom and, 148
BWO. See body without organs

Canetti, Elias, 103
capitalism, 125, 193; open society and, 196; universal, 195, 200
Capitalism and Schizophrenia (Deleuze and Guattari), 45, 196
Carroll, Lewis, 29
cartography, principles of, 56
Castle, The (Kafka), 69, 71, 72, 84, 98
Catcher in the Rye (Salinger), 221n1
Cather, Willa, 89

error: multiple forms of, 11; in principle, 128

Essays Critical and Clinical (Deleuze), 113

essential Egoism, 217n5

ethnicity, 55, 100, 115

event, 26, 129, 190, 194, 197, 198; concept and, 193; self-positing reality and, 201

evolution, 26–27, 176, 185

exceptionalism, 102

experience, 36, 117, 165, 212n12; beyond the turn of, 204

experimentation, 5, 8, 18, 60, 66, 99, 152

expression, 1, 3, 6, 23, 49, 74, 97, 99, 110, 200; anthropological, 11; blocks of, 76; collective, 109; forms of, 76, 77, 78, 98, 101; materials for, 6, 75; method and, 63, 95; minority, 110; philosophical, 46; revolutionary, 47

fascicular root, 51, 53

fascism, 98, 99, 162

Faulkner, William, 89

feeling, 30, 140

Flaubert, Gustave, 91–92, 102; becoming a writer and, 92–93; Becoming-Woman and, 94; petty Bourgeois and, 91; theory of mediation and, 96

Flaxman, Gregory, 214n2

Fold, The (Deleuze), 111, 143

"Force and Signification" (Derrida), 150

Ford, John, 177

formlessness, 59, 161, 181

forms, 5, 77, 197

Foucault, Michel, 3, 11, 55; author and, 141; *cogito* and, 118; disciplinary orders and, 191; "Will to Truth" and, 216n4

Frankfurt School, 187

freedom, 18, 176

Freud, Sigmund, 152, 172

friendship, 188; democratic idea of, 191; as face-to-face experience, 212n12

Full Metal Jacket (film), 170, 214n2

Gardner, Chance, 31

Gay Science, The (Nietzsche), 201

Geist, 193, 194

Genet, Jean, 86, 219n23

Genette, Gérard, influence of, 13

Georg, Stefan, 79, 214n5

Gestalt image, 169, 181, 199

Gestalt principle, 182, 189, 190, 191, 194, 197

Gestalt theory, 179, 201, 202

Gift of Death, The (Derrida), 131

Glas (Derrida), 143

God, 13, 182; Self and, 20

Goethe, Johann Wolfgang von, 101, 221n1

good readers, 49, 58

"Great Wall of China, The," 79, 81, 84

Guattari, Félix, 7, 15, 18, 19, 23, 47, 48, 52, 78, 80, 93, 147; Badiou and, 216n4; Deleuze and, 48, 87, 125, 217n16; encounter with, 13; Kafka and, 64, 65, 66, 67, 74, 75, 76, 82–83, 91, 103; philosophy and, 16, 17, 19, 22, 24, 45, 49, 54, 67, 187, 188, 189, 191

guilt of the subject, 78–79

habit, 2, 203

hallucination, 112, 170, 171; literary production and, 113; psychotic, 173; reality and, 172; writer, 111

Hallward, Peter, 220n30

Hardt, Michael, Multitude and, 197–98

Harmonia Prestabilitia, 182

Hawthorne, Nathaniel, 89

Hegel, Georg Wilhelm Friedrich, 116, 144; concept and, 193; Eurocentricity and, 224n79; *Geist* and, 194; image of thought and, 2; Mind and, 193; phenomenology of, 46; philosophical *Bildungsroman* and, 142; philosophy and, 160; unthought and, 8

Hegelianism, 162, 193, 199

Heidegger, Martin, 2, 3, 8–9, 41, 54, 118, 160, 214n5, 224n79; Being and, 16; food for thought and, 180; image of thought and, 9; philosophy and, 30–31, 57; thinking and, 30, 31; unthought and, 8

hermeneutic theory, 49, 65, 66

narrator: as in-human, 43; presuppositions and, 34
naturalism, 157, 159, 228n60
natura naturans, 182, 206
nature, 182, 183; naturing, 176, 177;
power of, 162; semi-autonomous
forces of, 184
Nature-Culture, 162
Negri, Antonio, 192, 193, 197–98
Nesbitt, Nick, 217n3
neurobiology, 208
neurology, 56, 164, 168, 204
Nietzsche, Friedrich, 50, 116, 142, 148,
164, 201; Deleuze and, 14
Nietzsche and Philosophy (Deleuze), 14
nihilism, philosophy and, 163
nonlinguistic model, 172
Non-Objectified Brain, 179, 182, 203
nonorganic life, 138
nonphilosophy, 6; philosophy and, 9, 16,
19–20, 23, 25
nonresponse, 132, 134, 136, 137
non-sense, forms of, 124
nonstyle, 15, 147–48, 150
nooshock, 157, 159, 164
noosigns, 170
not thinking, impossibility of, 161, 162

object: desire and, 85; subject and, 207
objective conditions, 9, 36, 100
objective determination, 87, 108, 111
object-world, 10
Oedipus, 123, 126
Of Grammatology (Derrida), 15, 117, 139,
151
One, 13, 63–64, 66, 80, 85; identifying,
64; Many and, 22
One-All, power of, 16, 17
"On Nietzsche and the Image of
Thought" (Deleuze), 4
On the Genealogy of Morals (Nietzsche),
14
"On the Two Regimes of Madness"
(Guattari), 18
ontology, 11, 181, 209
openness, 174, 198

open society, 185, 196, 200
opinion, 2, 179, 180, 181, 199, 203;
determination of, 178
Order of Things, The (Foucault), 3
order words, 78, 102, 220n21
original thinker, model of, 13
Other, 126, 131, 161, 164, 167

pain, physical experiences of, 36
painting, 5; cinema and, 27
parallelism, 182, 201
paranoia, 170, 171
paranoid law, schizo-law and, 81
paranoid-schizoid position, 79, 80, 82,
218n17
Pascal, Blaise, 164
Paths of Glory (film), 170
perception, 20, 21, 34, 113, 140, 165, 174,
175, 205; actualized, 209; cognition
and, 189; conscious/empirical, 111;
consciousness and, 112, 169, 171, 172,
176; determination of, 178; external,
173; memory and, 1; microscopic, 111;
natural, 28, 29; reaction and, 167;
thought and, 160; unconscious, 112;
writing and, 35
perception-images, 165, 175, 204
phenomenology, 7, 10, 11, 199, 209
philosophers, 14, 131, 142, 149, 150, 181;
activity of, 152, 186; contemporary,
221n2; open society of, 185; signature
of/activity, 203
philosophy, 6, 17, 30, 53–55, 58, 94, 141,
147, 169, 185–87, 196, 202, 208;
academic, 7; anti-Hegelian, 188;
bankruptcy of, 18; book of, 143–44;
brain and, 189; cinema and, 160;
classical, 37–38; cognitive psychology
and, 179; contemporary, 13, 16, 21,
45–46, 56; creation of, 152, 177;
delirium and, 116–17; duration of,
205–6; future of, 15; history of, 16, 144,
164; intuition and, 16, 205; literature
and, 142; machines and, 20, 24, 45, 46;
marketing and, 194; mental objects
of, 190–91; modern, 18, 20, 24, 155;

GREGG LAMBERT is Dean's Professor of Humanities and founding director of the Humanities Center at Syracuse University.